MW01284448

Case Studies in Deaf Education

Case Studies in Deaf Education

Inquiry, Application, and Resources

Caroline Guardino, Jennifer S. Beal, Joanna E. Cannon, Jenna Voss, and Jessica P. Bergeron

Gallaudet University Press
Washington, DC

Gallaudet University Press
Washington, DC 20002
http://gupress.gallaudet.edu

Library of Congress Cataloging-in-Publication Data

Names: Guardino, Caroline, author.
Title: Case studies in deaf education : inquiry, application, and resources /
 Caroline Guardino [and four others].
Description: Washington, DC : Gallaudet University Press, [2018] | Includes
 bibliographical references and index.
Identifiers: LCCN 2017059591| ISBN 9781944838188 (hard cover : alk. paper) |
 ISBN 9781944838195 (e-book)
Subjects: LCSH: Deaf--Education--Case studies.
Classification: LCC HV2430 .G83 2018 | DDC 371.91/2--dc23
LC record available at https://lccn.loc.gov/2017059591

∞ This paper meets the requirements of ANSI/NISO Z39.48-1992 (Permanence of Paper).

Contents

Foreword

John Luckner

This is what we have been waiting for! A resource that helps us understand the challenges as well as develop the knowledge and skills to use a collaborative, problem-solving process that leads to the provision of quality, effective services for children and youth who are d/Deaf or hard of hearing (d/Dhh).

Providing quality, effective services for d/Dhh students is complex and often difficult because of the heterogeneity of the population. Students who are d/Dhh vary across a wide array of factors. Similar to their hearing peers, aspects such as genetics, family support, socio-economic status of the family, home language and culture, composition of the family, and community resources can affect their development and achievement. However, additional circumstances that may influence how d/Dhh individuals progress include: age of identification and initiation of services, quality and quantity of early intervention services provided, degree of hearing levels, primary mode of communication used, and amplification use and benefits. Also, many individuals who are d/Dhh have multiple learning challenges (i.e., learning disabilities, attention deficit disorder, autism) with medical origins as a result of the etiologies of their hearing loss (e.g., preterm birth, meningitis, cytomegalovirus, measles, encephalitis, ototoxicity, Usher syndrome, Waardenburg syndrome).

In addition to the challenges of addressing the vast individual differences among d/Dhh students, educators and families are faced with a shortage of evidence-based practices (EBPs) that have been tested and demonstrated as effective with d/Dhh students (e.g., Beal-Alvarez & Cannon, 2014; Cannon, Guardino, Antia, & Luckner, 2016; Easterbrooks, & Stephenson, 2006). The lack of EBPs results from multiple reasons including the low-incidence of the d/Dhh population and the wide geographic dispersion of students. However, the problem is exacerbated by a historical overreliance on sources such as experience, tradition, expert opinion, and personal beliefs rather than demonstrated efficacy to determine how and what to teach (Luckner, 2006). This point is encapsulated by Spencer and Marschark (2010), who wrote, "For too long, practice in education of deaf and hard-of-hearing students has been based more closely on beliefs and attitudes than on documented evidence from research or the outcomes of interventions" (p. 25).

In order to offset the tendency to rely on intuition and tradition, as well as one-size-fits-all approaches to providing services for d/Dhh students, there is a need for careful and objective assessments and ongoing evaluation of services and placement. It is essential to keep in mind that there is not one way to provide educational services for d/Dhh students successfully. As noted by Knoors and Marschark (2014), "There are no 'silver bullets' that are going to work for all deaf children in all situations" (p. 160). There is no panacea that can address the needs of all d/Dhh students, whether focusing on mode of communication, placement, service delivery model, or curriculum. Rather, determinations about what to teach, how to teach, and where to teach each student should be based on assessment and collaborative problem solving undertaken by a team of professionals that includes a person or persons knowledgeable about the educational impact of a hearing loss, family members, and when appropriate, students themselves, using assessment data as the stimuli for discussion and decision making. Also, it is important to use multiple sources of information and never make decisions about a student based on a single assessment (e.g., Luckner, 2016). This recommendation is especially important for d/Dhh students who have a disability or disabilities because their performance and behavior across settings and situations can be highly variable.

This text will be a valuable resource for multiple reasons. First, case studies are an excellent supplement to traditional in-class instruction, structured field experiences that include hands-on practice, as well as in-service professional development. Case studies are beneficial because they encourage detailed analyses, critical reflection, and consideration of multiple perspectives. Second, case studies provide an avenue for improving collaborative problem-solving and decision-making skills in a nonthreatening environment for the benefit of students. Third, and equally important, case studies provide an opportunity for individuals to anticipate issues they may encounter and need to resolve while providing services to students.

The case studies included in this text are truly representative of the types of students and scenarios that professionals encounter regularly. The text invites you to meet some of the unique d/Dhh children and youth, their families, and the professionals who are privileged to serve them. Furthermore, the text provides real-life examples to encourage inquiry-based learning, which involves asking questions, critical thinking, and shared decision-making.

In contrast to their hearing peers, d/Dhh individuals exhibit diversity in the linguistic, social, experiential, and educational backgrounds. Therefore, these children and youth and their families need caring, knowledgeable, and skilled professionals who can provide accessible instruction, collaborate and consult with educational professionals and families, and advocate for students' individual needs so that each and every child and youth can develop the appropriate attitudes, knowledge, and skills needed to successfully meet the demands of adult living. If we want d/Dhh students to succeed throughout school and in their adult lives, rather than failing to achieve their potential, we need to address students' individual differences and work collaboratively to provide quality educational services.

In closing, I want to congratulate the authors for the hard work they have put into developing this practical, quality resource that will be useful for both pre-and in-service professional development, where members of professional learning communities can learn from one another using the case studies as stimuli for discussion. I am certain that the professionals who use this text as well as the students, families, and fellow educators they serve will benefit.

REFERENCES

Beal-Alvarez, J., & Cannon, J. (2014). Technology research with deaf and hard of hearing learners: Levels of evidence. *American Annals of the Deaf, 158*(5), 486–505. doi: 10.1353/aad.2014.0002

Cannon, J., Guardino, C., Antia, S., & Luckner, J. L. (2016). Single-case design research: Building the evidence-base within the field of education of deaf/hard of hearing students. *American Annals of the Deaf, 160*(5), 440–452.

Easterbrooks, S. R., & Stephenson, B. (2006). An examination of twenty literacy, science, and mathematics practices used to educate students who are deaf or hard of hearing. *American Annals of the Deaf, 151*(4), 385–397.

Knoors, H., & Marschark, M. (2014). *Teaching deaf learners: Psychological and developmental foundations.* New York, NY: Oxford University Press.

Luckner, J. L. (2006). Evidence-based practices and students who are deaf. *Communication Disorders Quarterly, 28*(1), 49–52.

Luckner, J. L. (2016). Educational assessment measures. In G. Gertz and P. Boudreault (Eds.), *The SAGE deaf studies encyclopedia.* (pp. 379–382). Thousand Oaks, CA: Sage Publishing Co.

Spencer, P. E., & Marschark, M. (2010). *Evidence-based practice in educating deaf and hard-of-hearing students.* New York: Oxford University Press, Inc.

Acknowledgments

This road has been a long but incredibly special learning experience. We began this journey in 2012 at an Association for College Educators of the Deaf and Hard of Hearing Conference in Atlantic Beach, Florida. At the beginning of this journey was Dr. Sarah Ammerman, who greatly contributed to the first case studies that our team developed. We sincerely appreciate the work she did to launch us forward. We are also very grateful to several colleagues for their contributions to this book. Dr. John Luckner for reviewing our manuscript and writing an outstanding foreword that truly highlights the uniqueness of this book. Dr. Christy Borders for sharing her expertise in serving children who are deaf with autism. Dr. Harold Johnson for reminding us to always Observe, Understand, and Respond to our deaf and hard of hearing children, so they can be protected not neglected. Dr. Kim Zebehazy for her professional insight on children with deafblindness and their assessment needs. Mr. Michael Boyles for his artistic eye and imaginative mind that created the beautiful cover and helped select case study photos found in the instructor's manual. Ms. Sarah Rearick who masterfully mated the speech banana with the speech string bean to create what we now call the *bananabeangram*.

We were fortunate to work closely with two Deaf teachers of the deaf, Mrs. Jessica Stultz and Anonymous. They served as our fearless editors who scrupulously reviewed every case study through a cultural lens. In addition, because of their teaching expertise, they creatively added to select discussion questions and activities. We are also thankful to Dr. Cathy Schroy, who created the amazing audiograms for each case study. These professionals further assured that *Case Studies in Deaf Education: Inquiry, Application, and Resources*, has a balanced perspective and can be used among professionals in various preparation programs.

And finally, we want to acknowledge all of our former students, their families, and even our own children, who over the course of our 80 cumulative teaching years, inspired components of the case studies within this book. To you all, we are indebted and full of never-ending gratitude.

Introduction

The purpose of this book is to present an extensive collection of case studies that highlight the diversity within the d/Deaf and hard of hearing (d/Dhh) student population. Cumulatively, these case studies represent a snapshot of the overall population of school-age d/Dhh students as determined by the U.S. Department of Education (2015) and the Gallaudet Research Institute (2013). Within this population, between 5 and 10% are Deaf children of Deaf parents, 25% come from a home where the parents speak a language other than English, 50% have a disability, 50 to 60% are in inclusive settings, and 50% are using listening and spoken language (LSL) for instruction. Appendix A illustrates the expansive nature of the case studies presented in this text.

As a group of educators with multiple graduate degrees and over 80 years combined experience in the field of deaf education, we found a lack of comprehensive resources available that represent the unique and diverse learners with whom professionals will work in their careers. We realized that blending our individual teaching experiences with our varying areas of expertise (early intervention, listening and spoken language, ASL discourse analysis, reading, learners with disabilities, multilingual learners, etc.) offered an opportunity to present a rich and broad perspective of the diversity within our field. In addition, we incorporated the expertise of two Deaf teachers of the d/Dhh who have over 37 years of experience within the field to ensure that each case study was vetted through a Deaf cultural lens. In short, this textbook was derived from the need to supplement instruction with authentic case studies so professionals can better understand the complex and unique learners they will encounter in our diverse field.

These case studies illustrate the variable challenges professionals working with students who are d/Dhh address on a daily basis. In order to prepare professionals for these challenges, the case studies are framed to promote inquiry-based learning by including a multitude of characteristics that influence communication, psychosocial, and educational services. The uniqueness of hearing status and its impact on learning is exemplified by these characteristics and their interaction, which include a student's background experiences, language and communication mode (sign and/

Note: All name and case study scenarios in this text are fictitious. No identification with actual persons (living or deceased) or places is intended or should be inferred.

or listening and spoken language), language and academic proficiency levels, use of assistive listening devices (hearing aids, cochlear implants, FM/DM systems, etc.), family dynamics, and diversity related to culture and disabilities that may accompany deafness. These case studies include authentic supplemental materials and documents, including an audiogram for each case, supporting documents (e.g., Individual Education Program and Individual Family Services Plans, assessment results, transition plans, behavior intervention plans, etc.) to support readers in making data-based decisions related to individual case studies. Each case study is followed by a sequence of discussion questions and activities to engage the reader and classmates in rigorous thought-provoking debate, application, and critical thinking activities. Sample answers to the discussion questions and PowerPoint slides outlining the characteristics of each case study are provided in the instructor's manual (available online).

Additional resources are also provided to guide the reader to further information about topics of interest and can be utilized to assist the reader in completing the activities provided. These resources can be found in the appendices. Appendix B provides a comprehensive list of assessments; whereas Appendix C lists a collection of theories with related evidence-based practices. Appendix D is a combination of the traditional speech banana with the newer speech string bean (Madell, 2015). Appendix B offers readers the option of choosing various assessments that could be used to measure specific skills of their students. The list of assessments is categorized by language, literacy, motivation, auditory development, and so forth. Appendix C guides the reader to better understand learning and developmental theories as they relate to evidence-based instructional strategies. By understanding the relationship between theory and practice, readers can better determine why and how children learn, thus matching the theory to the skills their student is likely to benefit from. Appendix D, the *bananabeangram* is provided to help readers better understand the speech sounds a child is able to hear when aided, or unable to hear when they are unaided. Students can make a transparency of the *bananabeangram*, and overlay it with the case study audiograms, thus clearly demonstrating the child's hearing level and access to sound.

Inquiry-based learning allows the reader to solve student-centered challenges that teachers, parents, service providers, and administrators face on a daily basis. The authors incorporated the following student variables throughout the 35 case studies:

- communication factors, including mode(s) and language(s) (e.g., American Sign Language, spoken and written English, spoken Spanish, etc.), age of identification of hearing loss, age of language acquisition, useable auditory and visual access to communication, and consistent use of listening strategies;
- learning experiences, including the effects of language and literacy issues on students' academic success and learning across the curriculum;
- educational services, including access to mode(s) and language(s) of instruction, instructional materials (e.g., language and reading levels), assessments,

accommodations, modifications, amplification management, use of technology to support learning, evidence-based instructional practices, and incorporation of both mandated learning standards and individual learning goals and objectives;

- learning environments, including early intervention, preschool, primary and secondary school, day and residential schools for the deaf, signing and listening and spoken language environments, and placement options, such as inclusion, small group, and one-on-one settings; and
- social, emotional, and intellectual development.

In the current realm of data-based instruction (e.g., Council for the Accreditation of Educator Preparation [CAEP], State/Provincial Standards, Institute of Education Sciences [IES], etc.), all teachers should be able to justify why they do what they do. These 35 case studies present multifaceted data and supporting materials from which readers can make educated decisions and discuss topics in-depth regarding individual learners. Why does Ms. Cortez use visual organizers in her math lesson? Why does Mr. Foster use repeated viewings of American Sign Language narratives in his language arts class? Why does the speech-language pathologist use explicit instruction in categories of language? Why does the early interventionist use active learning at bath time? These case studies provide real-world scenario-based learning experiences and related activities applicable to any educator who works with d/Dhh students. This text offers a current perspective of the diverse learning environments prevalent in the field of deaf education across a variety of ages, settings, and learner characteristics.

Readers using these case studies can directly incorporate these instructional strategies within their scenario-based learning activities, integrating theory and research with application to practice. This text can be used to enrich courses that discuss topics relative to audiology, speech and language, curriculum and instruction, early intervention, literacy, introduction to deaf education, language development, as well as others (see Appendix A for an expanded list of topics). These case studies also can be utilized with online courses to generate discussion and provide activities for students to participate in virtually; this was taken into account when developing the activities and discussion questions within the cases.

Terminology

As professionals specializing in specific areas in deaf education, we chose to use collaborative terminology that respects one another's differences, including *hearing level* or *hearing status* in place of *hearing loss* (when applicable); *identification* in place of *diagnosis* (when applicable); *received a cochlear implant* in place of *implanted*; and DM where FM systems are noted to reflect the changes in this type of technology. This perspective aligns with the mission of The Radical Middle (http://radicalmiddledhh .org/), and we invite readers to join our collaborative perspective. Keeping this perspective in mind, we have also provided a glossary of essential terms in our field.

Summary

Case Studies in Deaf Education provides a practical and widely applicable resource for professionals in the field of deaf education, such as teachers of students who are d/ Dhh, speech-language pathologists, educational interpreters, audiologists, and general and special educators. Professionals working with children who are d/Dhh can use these real-world scenarios and cases to prepare them for the diversity they may encounter when serving a range of learners. Thus, we present a series of cases developed by teachers and researchers from a broad spectrum of backgrounds, creating a comprehensive resource for practitioners in the field of deaf education.

1
Anwar

Key Topics

Assistive Technology, Audiological Management, Early Intervention, IEP/IFSP/504, Language Development, Parent Involvement

Anwar is a 4-month-old boy, born full-term to married first-time parents. Anwar's mother is a physician and his father is a biomedical researcher with a PhD. The pregnancy was uncomplicated, as was the birth. On the day prior to Anwar's discharge home from the hospital, Anwar's mother noticed a yellow card was placed in his crib upon returning to her room from the well-baby nursery. The card indicated that Anwar had been *referred for follow-up* on his newborn *hearing screening*. When his parents inquired as to the somewhat surprising test results, the nurse suggested it was likely nothing to worry about stating, "It's probably just fluid." Though his parents were unsatisfied with this explanation, Anwar and his family were discharged the following day with instructions to follow-up with their pediatrician regarding further hearing evaluations. When Anwar's parents expressed their concern about his referral on the hearing screening to their pediatrician at the first well-baby visit, the pediatrician recommended they "wait and see" suggesting a re-screen at the 4-month checkup.

Unsatisfied with this "wait and see" approach, Anwar's parents contacted one of their colleagues, an *Ear, Nose, and Throat physician* (ENT), also known as an *otolaryngologist*, at a hospital system where they both work. The ENT acknowledged that there could be several reasons why children would not pass their newborn hearing screening but affirmed that it was important to receive additional audiological testing as soon as possible. Following this conversation, Anwar's parents scheduled follow-up testing for the first available appointment at the hospital where his mother works. The diagnostic evaluation, including a sleep *auditory brainstem response* (ABR) test at 6 weeks of age, revealed that Anwar had a *severe bilateral sensorineural hearing loss*. The cause of Anwar's *hearing level* was unknown. When the *audiologist* began to review the family history, Anwar's father recalled that he had an uncle and distant cousin in Pakistan who both had hearing loss. The family plans to seek genetic testing in the future.

Anwar began a *hearing aid trial* with loaner *hearing aids* at 7 weeks of age, and he received his personal *behind-the-ear hearing aids* when he was 3 months old. The parents were frustrated with the lack of clarity in the referral process between Anwar's hearing screening and diagnostic evaluation. While they were proactive and sought out expert guidance, in part because of their professional backgrounds, it was clear to them that other families might not have the same resources. They intend to seek an opportunity to address this at the systems level to ensure their state system is able to support families in meeting the *1-3-6 guidelines* outlined by the Joint Committee on Infant Hearing (JCIH, 2007; Muse et al., 2013). They visited the National Center for Hearing Assessment and Management (NCHAM) website to identify the point of contact for the newborn hearing screening program in their state. However, in the meantime, they are thankful they knew to follow-up and moved from a screening to a diagnostic evaluation in a timely manner.

As soon as the audiologist confirmed Anwar's diagnosis, she completed an online referral form to initiate enrollment in the statewide *early intervention* system, provided via *Part C program of the Individuals with Disabilities Improvement Act* (IDEIA). An *early intervention service coordinator* contacted the family within 48 hours. Within a short time, the service coordinator visited the family's home and explained how the early intervention system might assist the family in supporting Anwar's development. The family is in the process of enrolling in the early intervention system, but is generally unfamiliar about what to expect from *family-centered early intervention* systems as compared to the *medical model* systems with which they are generally more familiar. They were concerned about their ability to participate in sessions during daytime hours as they both work outside of the home. The service coordinator reassured them that the *early intervention provider*s (EIs) would work around their availability to best meet family needs. The service coordinator met with Anwar's parents on his mother's last week of her 12-week maternity leave. Anwar's parents are hopeful they can arrange for an EI to come to their home for evening visits. They also plan to include the maternal grandmother in these sessions, as she will provide care for Anwar when his mother returns to work.

This family's support system and network includes many members of the extended family who are highly supportive of Anwar's parents (both through emotional guidance and financial support) and are consulted regarding family decision-making, despite residing out of town. The family decided, after learning of Anwar's hearing status, the maternal grandmother who was in town for the birth will stay for an extended time period (at least several months) to help out in providing care.

The parents have expressed concerns about Anwar's ability to communicate with their family and friends in Arabic. Prior to learning of Anwar's hearing status, his parents intended to raise him bilingually with two spoken languages (English and Arabic). They are concerned about how his hearing level might impact his ability to communicate effectively in both languages, especially as his maternal grandmother does not speak fluent English. Discussion of these concerns related to bilingual language acquisition with their university colleagues, encouraged them to expose Anwar to both languages (Bowen, 2016; Pizzo, 2016). See Appendix C for instructional strategies related to language acquisition and development.

The family has an upcoming appointment with their service coordinator to develop the initial *Individual Family Service Plan* (IFSP) and complete a *Routines Based Interview* (RBI; McWilliam, Casey, Sims, 2009) to identify those daily routines that will become the focus of the intervention sessions. The family is continuing to monitor Anwar's hearing status. For now he is learning to use bilateral behind-the-ear hearing aids, though his extended family and parents are learning more about *cochlear implants* (CI).

While Anwar is currently being cared for in his home by his maternal grandmother, this arrangement is temporary. Anwar's parents are exploring childcare options for him and considering what environment will best support the development of his *listening and spoken language* (LSL) skills. They want to be sure to find a day care provider or nanny who will prioritize the use of Anwar's hearing technology and give him the opportunity to communicate in a positive listening environment.

The current challenges for this family include keeping hearing aids on as he becomes more mobile and grabs at his hearing aids; practicing/preparing for *visual reinforcement audiometry* (VRA) and *conditioned play audiometry* (CPA) to ensure high quality audiometric testing; and to better understand the process surrounding *cochlear implant evaluation* and candidacy determination.

Discussion Questions

1. What questions do you have about Anwar and his family's experience in the *Early Hearing Detection and Intervention* (EHDI) systems thus far? Why were Anwar's parents frustrated with the EHDI process? How did Anwar's experience match with the Joint Committee on Infant Hearing's (JCIH) 1-3-6 guidelines? What steps could have gone better to reduce their frustration?

2. To best serve children and families who have different lived experiences than our own, providers are called to examine their own *cultural humility*. How will you learn/ask about the cultural values that Anwar's family brings to their family-centered early intervention experience?

3. Consider the influence of extended family in your own decision-making process. Have you ever used the input from extended family or friends to help you make critical decisions? How might you capitalize upon and honor these influences in the family systems of the children you serve as a professional?

4. How would Anwar and his family's experience differ if the following variables were present?
    a. Anwar's parents were Deaf.
    b. Anwar had a physical disability.
    c. The birthing process was atypical and traumatic.
    d. They did not have the support of extended family.
    e. Anwar's parents lacked financial resources.

Activities

1. Explore family systems theory and the ecological approach to early development. List the key decision makers and influencers in Anwar's family system. Create a visual representation or diagram of the family relationships and influencers in Anwar's life. See an example at: firstyears.org/c1/u1/eco.htm

2. Using a template or rubric to plan a family-centered early intervention session (e.g., Brown 2005; Stredler-Brown, Moeller, Gallegos, Corwin, & Pittman, 2004), design a session to promote enriched caregiver talk. Be sure to consider both child and family goals. Identify the ways in which you might coach the caregivers to support Anwar's development.

3. Using the additional resources provided at the end of the activities and those references cited in the case study, explore the recommended practices to support children learning two languages. What supports will children who are *d/Deaf* or *hard of hearing* (d/Dhh) need to successfully learn two spoken languages and become fluent bilingual communicators? What, if anything, about the developmental patterns are different for dual spoken language learners? How might these patterns vary for d/Dhh dual spoken language learners?

4. Investigate the concept of *developmental synchrony* to understand how early intervention has the capacity to support synchronous learning, as opposed to *remediation*. Reflect on Anwar's experience. Would the timeline he experienced, relative to identification and enrollment in intervention, have led to developmental synchrony or remediation? How does supporting families and children in a developmental manner differ from a remedial approach? What is hopeful about the timeline and necessary resources and supports for children who are learning in a developmentally synchronous manner?

5. Investigate the *phonetic level inventories* comparing spoken English and any possible cognates in Arabic. How would this knowledge inform your expectations for Anwar's spoken language development? How might this information impact your service delivery, including planning and instruction when Anwar begins to use simple words and phrases?

Additional Resources

Advanced Bionics, Tools for Schools, Bilingual Family Interview (BIFI) by Amy McConkey Robbins, MS, CCC-SLP, LSLS Cert AVT https://www.advancedbionics .com/content/dam/advancedbionics/Documents/Regional/BR/3-01066-B-5_ Bilingual%20Family%20Interview%20(BIFI)-FNL.pdf

ASHA, Bilingual Service Delivery Practice Guide http://www.asha.org/PRPSpecific Topic.aspx?folderid=8589935225&section=Key_Issues

Bilinguistics https://bilinguistics.com/
International Children's Digital Library http://en.childrenslibrary.org/
The Ling Consortium http://www.ridbc.org.au/renwick/ling-consortium
Verbal Bilingualism http://verbalbilingualism.wixsite.com/deaf
World Wide Hearing http://www.wwhearing.org/member-association

SUPPORTING DOCUMENT

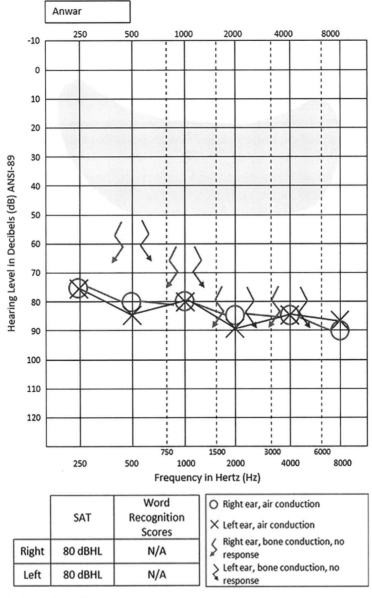

Figure 1.1. Anwar's audiogram.

2
Jackie

Key Topics

Assessment; Collaboration; Culture; Deaf of Deaf; Language Development; Literacy; Parent Involvement

Jackie is an outgoing little girl who is 1 year and 6 months old. She was identified as having a *profound bilateral sensorineural hearing level* via *Universal Newborn Hearing Screening* (UNHS) at the hospital when she was born. Both of her parents are *deaf*, meaning Jackie is a *deaf child of deaf parents*, and use *American Sign Language* (ASL) as their primary *mode of communication*. Both her parents attended *schools for the deaf*. Jackie's parents communicate easily with her using ASL. Jackie also has a 5-year-old sister who is deaf. Jackie's maternal grandparents are both deaf and use ASL; her paternal grandparents have typical hearing and use some *sign language* paired with spoken language. Jackie currently does not use *hearing aids*; however, her parents have discussed this possibility in the future if the hearing aids will provide Jackie with access to environmental sounds. *Deaf culture* is a natural part of Jackie's life. Jackie's parents are active in the local *Deaf community*, and they frequently attend local Deaf events and take Jackie and her sister with them. Her family cherishes their close ties with other Deaf community members and turns to these friends for play dates and babysitting for their daughters.

Jackie frequently requests that her parents read to her by bringing books to them in the evening at home. She has a few favorite books, such as *Ten Little Ladybugs* (Gerth & Huliska-Beith, 2006), which her parents read to her repeatedly. Jackie's parents engage in reading strategies that are common among deaf parents with deaf children, such as sitting across from Jackie during reading; using joint eye gaze and pointing to engage in shared attention; signing on both the book and Jackie's body as appropriate when they read; expanding the content on storybook pages; and sandwiching of signs in ASL with *fingerspelling* (Schleper, 1995; Swanwick & Watson, 2007). For example, when reading *Ten Little Ladybugs*, her parents often provide additional information on the animals in the story that is not presented in the text, such as the different environments in which the ladybugs are shown. They also pair fingerspelling with signs, such as spelling G-R-A-S-S-H-O-P-P-E-R in addition to signing GRASSHOPPER. They form this sign on the page and show it jumping around and sign it on Jackie's arm in a playful manner to engage her in the reading process. Because of these literacy strategies, Jackie is engaged and loves to read familiar and new books in the home and at school (see Appendix C for instructional strategies related to language and literacy acquisition and development).

Jackie's parents recently decided to enroll Jackie in a newly formed toddler playgroup at the nearby day *school for the deaf*, where her sister attends kindergarten, to continue her language development outside of the home. Teachers and students at the school for the deaf use ASL within a *bilingual/bicultural philosophy* of instruction (i.e., communication and instruction via ASL and access to English via print). Her parents contacted the lead teacher of the toddler program and established a meeting to acquire more information on the program. The lead teacher requested an assessment of Jackie's current language skills based on parental knowledge and explained that she would document Jackie's language development every few months to monitor her progress in the playgroup. She requested that Jackie's parents collaborate by completing the *MacArthur Communicative Development Inventory for American Sign Language* (ASL-CDI; Anderson & Reilly, 2002; see Appendix B), which is a parental checklist, to assess Jackie's current receptive ASL knowledge, and the *Visual Communication and Sign Language Checklist* (Simms, Baker, & Clark, 2013; see Supporting Documents; see Appendix B) from *Gallaudet University* to assess her expressive sign language skills. Jackie's parents were happy to do so and appreciated the lead teacher's view of them as experts on their daughter's language skills. Based on the assessment results, Jackie's language development is typical for her age.

After Jackie had been enrolled in the playgroup for a month, the lead teacher mentioned Jackie's love of reading books in the playgroup and chatted with her parents about their reading practices at home. After her parents explained how they engage in *shared reading* with Jackie's favorite books, the teacher requested that her parents visit the playgroup and model these literacy strategies for the other teachers and *educational assistants* who work with the toddler and preschool students. Once again, her parents were happy to collaborate with school professionals and modeled reading with the students weekly. The teacher's view of Jackie's parents as important stakeholders in their child's education resulted in consistent parent involvement in her education.

DISCUSSION QUESTIONS

1. What criteria might Jackie's parents use to determine the success of the toddler playgroup on Jackie's continued language development?
2. As an educator, how might you utilize the strengths of parents such as Jackie's in the classroom?

3. Suppose Jackie's language development progresses beyond that of her peers. What other options might her parents and teacher consider to enrich Jackie's education?
4. What might be some considerations for support services if Jackie's parents decide to enroll her in an *inclusion* setting at her local school in lieu of the school for the deaf?

ACTIVITIES

1. Contact deaf parents of a deaf child. Discuss the strengths and challenges the parents have experienced related to their child's educational experiences. Based on their experiences, what do they wish other parents and teachers of deaf children knew?
2. Using the results from the Visual Communication and Sign Language Checklist, create a list of Jackie's current strengths and needs and her future needs that you might address through instruction as a *teacher of the d/Deaf and hard of hearing* (TODHH).
3. Design an activity that meets the needs of a culturally diverse group of deaf children, like Jackie, in the early stages of developing ASL and English competencies.
4. Observe a deaf student during social interaction (i.e., extracurricular activities that take place during after school hours). Write a description of this student's interactions and her/his language use.

ADDITIONAL RESOURCES

Simms, L., Baker, S., & Clark, M. D. (2014). *Visual Communication and Sign Language Checklist*. Visual Language and Visual Learning (VL2). Retrieved from http://vl2 .gallaudet.edu/files/4814/2254/7807/VCSL_cklistnorms-final.docx-1_Page_1_ only.pdf

Supporting Documents

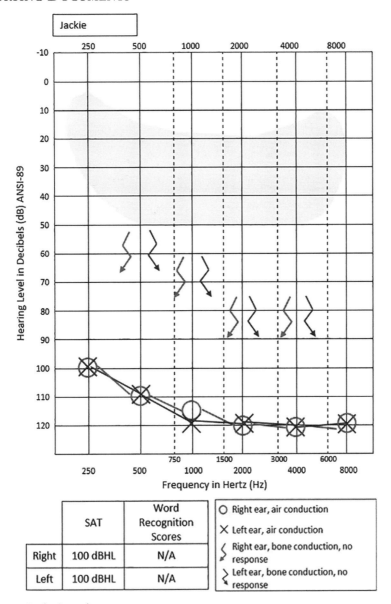

Figure 2.1. Jackie's audiogram.

VCSL

Visual Communication and Sign Language Checklist

Name of student: _Jackie_

D.O.B.: _____ Chronological Age: _1_ years _5_ months

Evaluator: _Jackie's parents_ Date of assessment: _____

Birth to 12 Months	Not Yet Emerging	Emerging	Inconsistent Use	Mastered
Looks in direction to which the signer is pointing				✓
Hand babbling emerges (ex: opens and closes hands, wiggles fingers, wrists twist)				✓
Waves bye-bye				✓
Copies physical movements involving the arms, hands, head, and face				✓
Enjoys finger-plays and finger-games				✓
Follows the eye gaze of the signer				✓
Attends to signed motherese (ex: Sign with slow tempo, repetitions, and exaggerated movements)				✓
Distinguishes facial expressions (ex: anger or friendliness)				✓
Joint reference (ex: parent and child look at same object)				✓
Participates in communicative play (ex: peek-a-boo)				✓
Enjoys holding and cuddling				✓
Enjoys hand play: Plays with hands and fingers				✓
Looks attentively at a person's face				✓
Looks at the visual environment with alertness				✓
Smiles when sees a familiar person			✓	
Laughs when seeing fingers approaching to tickle				✓
Turns head in response to attention getting behaviors (ex: hand waving, lights on and off, or foot stomping)				✓
Smiles, makes eye contact and laughs				✓
Expresses excitement and displeasure				✓
Eyes track/following movement with alertness				✓
Fixates on the face				✓
1 year to 2 years	Not Yet Emerging	Emerging	Inconsistent Use	Mastered
Recognizes own name sign			✓	
Recognizes names signs of family members (ex: siblings)			✓	
Finger babbles back to conversations or to self				✓
Points to self and objects in his/her environment				✓
Uses negative headshake alone or with sign			✓	
Responds to simple commands (ex: COME HERE; EAT DINNER)			✓	

© Simms, Baker, & Clark, 2013

Figure 2.2. Jackie's Visual Communication and Sign Language Checklist.

3
Liam

Key Topics

Assessments; Assistive Technology; Audiological Management; Collaboration; Early Intervention; Language Development

Liam just turned 2 years of age and was referred to an *Auditory-Verbal Therapist* (AVT) in a private clinic to receive support for development of his *listening and spoken language* (LSL) skills through his *cochlear implant* (CI). The AVT completed several assessments and spent some time reviewing his case history. His case history is as follows.

Liam was identified with a *moderate* to *profound bilateral sensorineural hearing level* at 3 months of age after being referred twice on the *hearing screening*. Liam received *hearing aids* at 5 months of age but appeared to receive no usable benefit from them and was referred to a *CI team*. At 12 months of age, he received a CI in his right ear and uses it presently. At home, his family primarily uses spoken English to communicate. Liam has three older brothers and sisters who are close in age and spend a great deal of time talking and playing with Liam. Liam and his family live about two hours from the hospital where the CI team and the AVT work.

From the time of identification, Liam received *early intervention* services to focus on language development from a state-funded program. His *Speech Language Pathologist* (SLP) was unfamiliar with working with children who are *d/Deaf* or *hard of hearing* (d/Dhh) and knew very little of the therapy and intervention needed for his *hearing level*. The SLP recommended the family learn to use *sign language* by using a free app accessible on a mobile device and told the family she would "keep an eye" on any developing language delays. Between diagnosis and Liam's first birthday, the SLP made several home visits to the family to support the development of language in the home setting, but there were several cancelled visits due to childhood illnesses with Liam's siblings. After Liam received his CI, the CI team referred the family to an LSL program so they could begin working with an AVT. The team also recommended that Liam's family have conversations with him all waking hours across his regular routines (e.g., bath time, dinnertime, etc.) to support development of the auditory pathways in the brain.

After activation of the CI, Liam's family planned to attend an LSL program to work with an AVT, but an unexpected death in the family delayed both the audiological follow-up visits and the visits with the AVT. Secretly, Liam's mom and dad really had hoped that the CI would allow Liam to hear like his siblings because the CI team and the AVT were over three hours away. It was challenging and expensive for the family to get to and from the appointments.

Liam's parents realized that Liam was not progressing like he should based on their prior experiences with his siblings. He is now 2 years of age and not talking or *babbling* like his siblings did at this age. He also does not always turn to sound as expected. Liam sometimes takes off his CI and does not seem to be getting much access to spoken language from it.

The AVT completed the *Preschool Language Scale* (PLS-5; Zimmerman, Steiner, & Pond, 2011; see Appendix B), which is intended for children from birth through 7 years of age. For auditory comprehension Liam had a *standard score* of 50, placing him in the first percentile, meaning that 99% of children who complete this test score higher than Liam, which demonstrates his low auditory comprehension. His expressive communication standard score was 61, again placing him in the first percentile and showing his delayed *expressive language*.

The AVT also helped his parents complete a *MacArthur Communicative Development Inventory for American Sign Language* (ASL-CDI; Anderson & Reilly, 2002; see Appendix B) for Liam to measure his vocabulary. He scored at 12–13 months based on the CDI, showing that he is delayed by about a year in his expressive language. He scored at 12–14 months for "actions and gestures," again showing a delay.

Observational assessment demonstrated that Liam did not consistently turn to his name but would turn to loud environmental sounds (e.g., drums, cowbell, hand clapping). Further, Liam could not successfully identify the *Ling sounds*. After reviewing his *audiogram* and his audiological case history, the AVT also discovered that Liam had not been back to see the *audiologist* since his initial CI *mapping* appointment and could not consistently respond to sound in the booth at 2000 or 4000 hertz (Hz). Liam's language development was consistent with his listening skills, and his assessments showed that he had expressive language commensurate with a 1-year-old.

The AVT explained to his parents that without consistent audiological follow-up, Liam will likely not benefit from his CI. Unless his CI is *mapped* often in conjunction with consistent *auditory habilitation*, like that which comes from an AVT, he will likely not have access to sounds and spoken language in his environment. Because a typically hearing child develops *phonemes* and sounds in words in the first years of life, and listening is the precursor to spoken language development, Liam does not currently have the necessary foundation for spoken language. Liam will need audiological intervention (i.e., mapping of his CI) to facilitate access to all speech sounds so that he can develop adequate listening skills and, eventually, develop spoken language.

Without *audiological access*, his auditory representation of language will be incomplete.

Discussion Questions

1. What follow-up recommendations should the AVT make if Liam's family continues to attend appointments sporadically?
2. What kind of information can the AVT and audiologist share to create more specific CI programming/mapping information to best meet Liam's LSL needs? (See Figure 3.1. Audiology Observation Report in Additional Resources.)
3. What are the various ways to help parents of a deaf child become fully informed of the realities of post-CI procedures?
4. How might Liam's AVT help Liam identify and connect other meaningful sounds in his environment (e.g., Someone important knocking at the door who is very important to Liam, like Mommy and Daddy. Or common phrases that are very motivating to him, such as "Time to eat!" or "Night, Night time")? Why is this an important early listening skill?
5. Consider a child such as Liam who is unable to distinguish between his name and other sounds in the environment that have a two pattern rhythm (such as "mommy" or "choo choo"). Write a script of what you might say to this child's parent as they question, "Why doesn't our child respond to his name when we call him?"

Activities

1. Investigate the process for receiving a CI. Write a summary of the process and share with your classmates.
2. Research one empirical article on outcomes for children with CI. What factors are predictors for success?
3. Create two activities for families focused on conversations around routines to meet the goal of 25–35 hours of conversation per week. Consider the extended family and primary caregivers.
4. Design an informative brochure explaining the function of a CI and listing the advantages and the disadvantages of a young child obtaining and wearing a CI.
5. Explore the Early Speech Perception Test, an assessment used to identify a child's early listening skills (https://cid.edu/professionals/shop/cid-esp-early-speech-perception-test/). Write a detailed narrative of how the assessment results can aid an AVT in planning instruction to help a learner advance through four primary levels of listening: (1) Detection, (2) Discrimination, (3) Identification, and (4) Comprehension.

ADDITIONAL RESOURCES

Success for Kids with Hearing Loss www.successforkidswithhearingloss.com
Suskind, D. (2015). *Thirty million words: Building a child's brain.* New York, NY: Dutton.
   www.hearingfirst.org
White, E. & Voss, J. (2016). *Small talk.* St. Louis, MO: Central Institute for the Deaf.

SUPPORTING DOCUMENTS

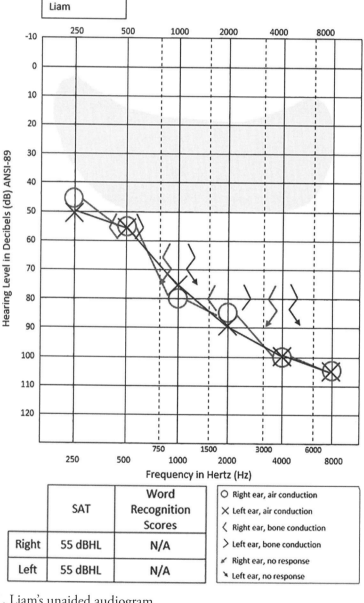

Figure 3.1. Liam's unaided audiogram.

Audiology Report

Reliability: ☑ Good ☐ Fair ☐ Poor
Method: ☑ VRA ☐ Play ☐ Conventional ☐ Inserts ☐ Headphones
Audiometer: ☑ GSI-61 ☐ MA-40

Name: _Liam #4_ Pt. # _____
DOB: _4/1/14_ Date: _4/16/16_

Diagnosis: _bilateral sensorineural_ Code: _#90.3_

Right Ear

Left Ear

AIR CONDUCTION		BONE CONDUCTION			No Response	Sound Field	S
Unmasked	Masked	Unmasked	Masked	Unspecified		Aided	A
R	O	Δ	<	[	Λ	↙	Could Not Test	CNT
L	X	□	>	]		↘	Did Not Test	DNT

R Ear : med El Opus 2
L Ear : none

SPEECH AUDIOMETRY

CD ☐ MLV ☐	PTA	SRT/ SAT	Speech Discrimination			Speech Material
Right			%	dB HL	M	
Left			%	dB HL	M	
S O U N D	F I E L D	Unaided		%	dB HL	M	
		Aided	20	%	dB HL	M	

IMMITTANCE MEASUREMENTS

Tympanometry
Right Ear: _____ Volume: _____
Left Ear: _____ Volume: _____

Type A: Normal middle ear pressure and mobility
Type B: Reduced tympanic membrane mobility
Type C: Normal tympanic membrane mobility with negative middle ear pressure
Type As: Reduced tympanic membrane movement with normal middle ear pressure
Type Ad: Increased tympanic membrane movement

Visit Summary: _Good responses today. Remapped for high frequencies_

Recommendations: _① return in one month for audiogram ② consider 2nd CI ③ continue to follow up with parent education w/ AV therapist to address troubleshooting issues ④ increase wear time_

Results were discussed with _mother_

Audiologist: _____ GA License #: _au_

Figure 3.2. Liam's aided audiogram.

Audiology Observation Report

Student: _____Liam Archer_____   Date: ____4/1/16_____

Person Completing Form: ____Lori Martin_____   Role: _Audiologist_

EQUIPMENT CONCERNS

Do you have any concerns related to the student's hearing devices?

Liam wears one CI. His mother reports that he does not always turn to sound and frequently removes his CI. His CI appears to be working but has not been remapped since receiving it more than 12 months ago, thus it is unlikely that Liam will be comfortable wearing this device.

MEDICAL CONCERNS

Do you have any medical concerns related to the student's ears (i.e., cerumen, middle ear function, ear drainage, cochlear implant site, etc.)?
None.

HEARING/LISTENING CONCERNS

1. Have you noticed obvious changes in hearing though equipment appears to be working properly?

None. Liam has not yet established consistent device use, nor does he appear to receive functional benefit from the CI at this point.

2. Have you noticed a change in Listening for the following Ling Sounds:

__ ah   __ m __oo __sh   __ s __ee

Liam was unable to consistently respond to (detect) any of the Ling sounds.

3. Have you noticed any difficulties with detection or discrimination of any other speech sounds?

Liam currently is inconsistent with detection and discrimination of any sounds.

4. Do you have concerns related to the child's educational progress that you believe may be related to hearing?

Liam is only 2 years of age; however, his lack of language skills is concerning related to his educational progress.

ADDITIONAL INFORMATION

Please describe the student's general performance and anything else you would like to share with the audiologist:

Liam's mother is concerned about Liam's lack of both receptive and expressive language. He inconsistently turns to his name and spoken language; he appears to turn more consistently to loud environmental sounds. She noted the difficulty they have had with maintaining follow-up appointments. His parents are seeking information on the benefits of Liam receiving a second bilateral CI.

Figure 3.3. Audiology observation report.

4

Dashawn

Key Topics

Assessment; Collaboration; Early Intervention; IEP/IFSP/504; Inclusion; Parent Involvement; Placement

Dashawn is a 3-year-old toddler who is *deaf*, born to hearing parents. Information regarding his birth mother's pregnancy and birth is unclear because Carola and Mitt Jacobs adopted Dashawn as a newborn. Dashawn's *hearing loss* was identified using *Universal Newborn Hearing Screening* (UNHS), and he was referred to a pediatric *audiologist* who conducted an *auditory brainstem response* (ABR) test. Results indicated that Dashawn had a *profound bilateral sensorineural* hearing loss. Carola and Mitt worked with Dashawn's pediatrician, audiologist, *Ear, Nose, and Throat physician* (ENT), and an *early intervention* service agency to determine the most effective communication and education path for Dashawn. While Dashawn began wearing *hearing aids* when he was 2 months old, he didn't appear to receive much benefit given his *hearing level*. His parents and educational team concluded Dashawn may benefit from a *cochlear implant* (CI) so they began the process of *CI implant evaluation*, including examination of medical, audiological, and *psychosocial criteria*, at the local children's hospital (ASHA Technical Report: Cochlear Implants, 2003). A series of appointments, the *CI team*, consisting of audiologists, a *Speech Language Pathologist* (SLP), an ENT, and a social worker, evaluated Dashawn's *unaided and aided audiometric thresholds*, examined his overall health status, and interviewed his parents and therapists to examine the social factors that may contribute to his success in habilitation after surgery. Based on the comprehensive evaluation and the motivation of his parents, the team determined that Dashawn could benefit from this technology. Dashawn received a CI at 8 months of age, earlier than Federal Drug Administration's (FDA) standard, through a clinical trial. Dashawn's CI surgery was deemed successful, and he began vocalizing his wants and needs and attended to sounds within the environment following several months of *post-activation habilitation services*. His parents consistently met with the audiologist to adjust and refine the programming or *mapping* on Dashawn's CI. Because of these factors, his CI team recommended that Dashawn's family consider a second CI. After consultation with his therapists and the team, and approval from his insurance company, Dashawn received a second bilateral CI when he was 1 year, 2 months of age. Based on the Gallaudet Research Institute survey (2011) of 37,800 children, about 24% of children with a CI have a second CI.

Dashawn's educational team established an *Individual Family Service Plan* (IFSP) that included early intervention services through the local early intervention agency. Additionally, Dashawn and his parents began *Auditory-Verbal Therapy* (AVT), which they carried over to the home setting through play, family routines, and targeted listening and language activities. By 2 years of age, Dashawn and his parents engaged in sessions with a certified *Listening and Spoken Language Specialist* (LSLS) and SLP. Dashawn also participated in playgroups in a classroom setting three times per week.

Now Dashawn is 3 years old. His *receptive language* includes following two-step commands, pointing to pictures in a book when prompted, and listening to simple songs and stories. Expressively, Dashawn uses two- and three-word utterances, including the use of *carrier phrases*, can label most basic objects in his home and school environments, and can express his basic wants and needs. Dashawn's *early intervention provider* (EI) has begun to ask questions about his transition from early intervention to preschool. Dashawn's parents recently divorced and disagree on Dashawn's school placement. Mitt feels that Dashawn has made enough progress to go to the neighborhood childcare center, and Carola believes that Dashawn should stay in a *self-contained, small group* program.

DISCUSSION QUESTIONS

1. When Dashawn transitions to preschool, what are some appropriate placement options? Describe the population, environment, available instructional supports, and *mode of communication* used within your placement(s) of choice.
2. How might Dashawn's *Individualized Education Program* (IEP) differ from his current IFSP (see Supporting Documents)? What type of family-centered questions can you ask Dashawn's parents to help determine the best goals and objectives, *accommodations*, and services for *inclusion* in his IEP? Consider the perspectives of both parents.
3. Draft four objectives that will address Dashawn's current educational needs as he begins preschool.
4. Which aspect(s) of Dashawn's case study is most likely to be a strong predictor of his successes or challenges during his academic career?
5. How might having a Deaf role model/consultant who uses a CI on the *IFSP/IEP team* impact the family's communication and placement decisions?
6. Consider how the educational providers might facilitate collaboration with Dashawn's parents who are divorced and might have divergent opinions about decisions related to communication and intervention.

ACTIVITIES

1. Role-play Question 1 as if you are educating Dashawn's parents on the advantages and disadvantages of various preschool placement options. Keeping in mind the psychosocial aspects of the situation for Dashawn, role-play how you will assist his parents in the creation of a plan that meets Dashawn's needs in preschool.
2. Create an IEP team for Dashawn based on his preschool placement. Who will be involved in Dashawn's team? What will be their roles and responsibilities?
3. Visit two potential placement options (e.g., *inclusive* preschool and self-contained preschool) and compare them. Describe what you saw, the strategies used, and which setting you believe would be the best fit for Dashawn. Support your decision with concrete examples. Consider the Hands & Voices resource listed under Additional Resources as you evaluate these placements.
4. It is a good idea for parents to watch for early childhood milestones. How can a parent or an educator tell the difference between a child who is taking his or her time and one who has a true developmental delay? Identify the main categories of certain tasks that young children should accomplish at a certain age.
5. Research LEAD-K, a visual-right movement to end the nationwide epidemic of language deprivation of deaf children. Discuss how this campaign could benefit Dashawn's parents. Check out http://www.lead-k.org.

ADDITIONAL RESOURCES

Explore resources available to aid in evaluating educational placement settings. http://www.handsandvoices.org/articles/early_intervention/V8-4_transition.htm

Know and understand the difference between an IFSP and an IEP. Learn how to make a smooth transition between these two documents. http://idea.ed.gov/

Learn how to create meaningful early childhood goals and objectives for an IEP. http://kskits.dept.ku.edu/ta/Packets/CreatingMeaningfulIEP_2011/index.html

SUPPORTING DOCUMENTS

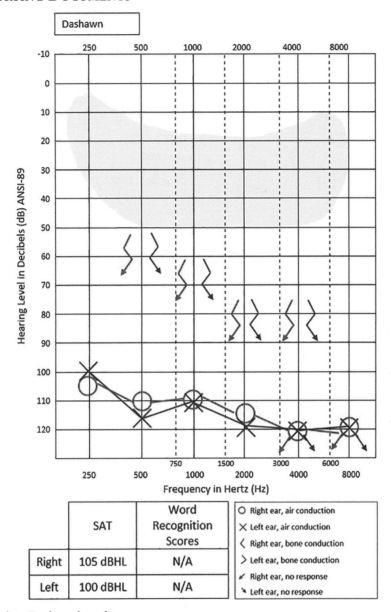

Figure 4.1. Dashawn's audiogram.

Individualized Family Service Plan

Goals	Strategies
Parents' Priority: "To make sure that Dashawn is able to fit in with his peers, listen and speak clearly, and know what is expected of him in social situations."	Schedule weekly appointments with Jennifer (LSLS Cert. AVT) to continue to focus on auditory, speech, language, and social goals. Age-appropriate games and activities will be used during sessions, and strategies and suggestions will be provided to the parents for home practice.
Understanding Language (Receptive): ○ Dashawn will appropriately respond to questions about events that have taken place within his home or school environments (e.g., "what happened?"). ○ Dashawn will indicate understanding of the names and function of familiar objects or actions during mealtimes and play by obtaining them when requested and using them appropriately.	Carola, Mitt, and Jennifer will discuss ways to help Dashawn answer questions about what has happened. Carola and Mitt will use Dashawn's calendar system to talk about past and future events. Use of Dashawn's Phonological Awareness Literacy Screening (PALS) home-book may also be useful to recall events that have happened. Motivating, age-appropriate games and activities will be used in weekly sessions to target Dashawn's language goals.
Using Language (Expressive): ○ Dashawn will spontaneously use multi-word phrases (i.e., more than three words) to make requests or answer questions during daily routines, including mealtime and play. ○ Dashawn will use personal pronouns (I, me, my, you, your) as well as names of family members when expressing wants and needs.	Jennifer will encourage expressive language development through the use of toys, games, and activities. Strategies such as finger pacing, tapping, and/or visual cues will be used in sessions to encourage Dashawn's use of expanded vocabulary in his utterances. Carola and Mitt will model the targeted language forms on a regular basis with Dashawn in both natural and structured situations. Jennifer will provide strategies and/or materials to practice at home.
Listening: ○ Carola and Mitt will monitor the listening environment at home by reducing background noise.	Carola and Mitt will continue to: 1. keep background noise to a minimum when communicating with Dashawn; 2. be close to Dashawn (3–6 feet) when speaking; and

○ Dashawn will learn to discriminate the Ling six sounds at distances of 3, 6, and 9 feet to help his caregivers ensure his CIs are functioning properly.	3. position themselves, relative to Dashawn, during conversation, book sharing, and play to optimize auditory input.
Speech: ○ Dashawn will clearly produce developmentally appropriate speech sounds when speaking so others may understand him. ○ Dashawn's parents will understand what speech sounds are developmentally appropriate and what sounds might be challenging for Dashawn given his hearing level and access to sound.	Carola and Mitt will: 1. report on observations of Dashawn's individual phoneme production development over time; 2. use games and activities to stimulate and model the production of specific speech sounds; 3. ask Dashawn to look at their mouths when they produce sounds in isolation and within words; 4. highlight and repeat the correct sound production when communicating with Dashawn; 5. break words down into syllables and produce each syllable slowly and gradually with Dashawn; and 6. use play activities wherein Dashawn can produce the target word and they can select and choose items/objects.
Goals	**Strategies**
Social Communication: ○ Dashawn will use his spoken language to communicate his wants and needs in social situations. ○ Carola and Mitt will rehearse/role-play social situations with Dashawn prior to attending. ○ Dashawn and his parents will identify appropriate communication and behavior when presented with real or simulated situations involving peers	Carola and Mitt will encourage Dashawn to use his expressive language at home and in social settings. Carola and Mitt will provide Dashawn with opportunities to practice his social communication through play dates and other structured and unstructured playtime with his peers. Jennifer will use games and role-play to increase Dashawn's vocabulary regarding social activities and to practice appropriate behaviors.

Auditory Technology:	Carola and Mitt will make a special place in Dashawn's room to keep the implants, batteries, chargers, etc. and make sure that spare batteries are always available to Dashawn when away from home.
o Dashawn will wear his bilateral implants, including all external components, during all waking hours.	
o Dashawn will inform an adult when the battery is dead on either implant.	Jennifer will review care and maintenance with Dashawn during each visit to emphasize the importance of the equipment.
o Carola and Mitt will maintain the implant, including all external components, and provide Dashawn with training on care and maintenance appropriate for his age.	Carola and Mitt will display a checklist in Dashawn's room and check off each day that he wears his implants, alerts an adult if the battery is dead, and returns them to their special place in his room. After three stickers in a row, Dashawn will receive an extra privilege.

Services:

X Individual Session ___ Parent Group **X** Parent to Parent ___ Baby Group ___ Consultation___ Partners and Playmates **X** Parents and Language Stimulation ___ Sign Language ___

Figure 4.2. Dashawn's IFSP.

5
Celeste

Key Topics

Accommodations; Assessment; Deaf with a Disability; Early Intervention; IEP/IFSP/504; Modality; Placement; Transition

Celeste is a 3-year-old who is transitioning from her family's participation in *early intervention* services to an early childhood program beginning in the fall. Celeste has a diagnosis of *CHARGE syndrome*, which is a syndrome presenting as a constellation of *congenital* malformations and medical conditions that vary greatly among individuals with this diagnosis. The name is an acronym standing for coloboma, heart defect, atresia choanae (also known as choanal atresia), delayed growth and development, genital abnormality, and ear abnormality (resulting in *hearing loss*). CHARGE affects one in every 8,000–10,000 births, though every person with CHARGE has a unique set of features as there is a wide variation in physical presentation and cognitive ability (CHARGE Syndrome Foundation, 2017). In 80–90% of cases, the cause is attributed to genetic mutations on chromosome 8. The family became aware of the possibility of this diagnosis after Celeste was born when she presented with some significant medical challenges, including coloboma (similar to a cleft of the eye resulting in *vision loss*), choanal stenosis (narrowing of the passages from nose to back of throat, resulting in early breathing difficulty), and difficulty swallowing. Her *severe mixed bilateral hearing loss* was initially identified on the newborn *hearing screening*, and a combination of behavioral and objective testing confirmed it. The tests included *auditory brainstem response* (ABR), *otoacoustic emissions* (OAE), *behavioral observational audiometry* (BOA), and *visual reinforcement audiometry* (VRA). Celeste was fit with *behind-the-ear hearing aids* at 3 months of age. She now consistently wears her hearing aids all waking hours, even requesting them from her parents by pointing and gesturing when she wakes in the morning.

The local children's hospital has a *multidisciplinary team* of professionals that run a CHARGE clinic to serve children and families with this diagnosis. The family is also connected with a *parent liaison* from their regional chapter of the national CHARGE Syndrome Foundation. With the support of the medical team and *early intervention providers* (EIs) from Part C of the *Individuals with Disabilities Education Improvement*

Act (IDEIA), the family has been working to promote Celeste's development. Celeste primarily uses simple sentences, often starting with *carrier phrases* or stringing vocabulary together to make her wants and needs known. She isn't consistently engaging in conversational *turn-taking*. Celeste gets frustrated when others don't understand some of her communication attempts. She appears to express this frustration by calling out, throwing materials, and disengaging in communication attempts. When using spoken language to communicate with non-familiar partners, some people have experienced difficulty understanding her speech due to *misarticulations*, poor vocal quality (*hypernasality*), and errors and confusion in her syntax.

The family speaks very highly of their entire experience in the early intervention system. They feel supported by a team of experts (*Speech Language Pathologists* [SLPs], *teacher of the d/Deaf and hard of hearing* [TODHH], *Occupational Therapists* [OTs], *Physical Therapists* [PTs], and *teacher of students with Visual Impairments* [TSVI]). They also find support from their medical team. While these services have been supportive and resulted in dramatic advances in Celeste's development, she qualifies for the *Part B program of the IDEIA*, school age services, given her complex diagnosis and her ability to access the educational curriculum.

Celeste has global delays of note in addition to concerns related to communication development. In the area of motor development, Celeste was a late walker and continues to be challenged by gross motor tasks, such as climbing on and off the couch and efficiently navigating play equipment and playground surfaces at the neighborhood park. Her poor balance led the *early intervention team* to introduce a walker and gait trainer to Celeste. Celeste is also identified as being *deafblind*, as she has limited vision due to the coloboma of the optic nerve. While wearing corrective lenses and bilateral hearing aids, Celeste does have sufficient visual and *auditory access* to learn from her environment.

Celeste uses a *gastric tube* (G-tube), receiving nutrition in this manner for the majority of her caloric intake. The G-tube feedings were initiated when Celeste was an infant given the impact of her *orofacial anomalies* on her ability to receive nutrition by mouth. The family and team have plans to begin phasing out use of the G-tube between 4 and 6 years of age. They are currently working on increasing her feedings by mouth and decreasing the use of formula through the G-tube. At this point Celeste is licking and tasting foods. The family has just started introducing a soft diet but is afraid of Celeste's safety as she has demonstrated some significant pocketing of the foods presented to her (e.g., getting food stuck in her cheek instead of swallowing). They have been working with an OT from the *early intervention team* but are concerned about how this support will continue in the transition to an early childhood program. They are also very concerned about her physical safety at school in regards to her physical movement in the building and around the play spaces, as well as her safety when eating.

Celeste does best with very consistent routines, and her mother describes observing Celeste undergoing significant anxiety when there are changes to her daily routine. These are most observable on the weekends, which are less predictable/structured, and around holidays or special occasions. Celeste is supported by *visual schedules*, which seem to provide some security and predictability. Her parents make these in the form of flipbooks, which they create for special circumstances and predictable routines.

The early intervention team has been working closely with the family's local school district as they transition from Part C of IDEIA to Part B of IDEIA. A portfolio-type assessment, including a review of records, review of current developmental milestones, review of progress towards goals and functional assessments of her vision and hearing, as well as scores from a standardized global developmental assessment helped the team determine her eligibility. There is an upcoming meeting to develop her initial *Individualized Education Program* (IEP).

The family wants Celeste to attend preschool at the neighborhood school but with the necessary supports to keep her safe and support her development. The school district is recommending a half-day placement in one of their early childhood classrooms with 10 students (half of whom are IEP eligible, half of whom qualify for early childhood education because they are at-risk). The class is co-taught by an early childhood educator and early childhood special educator with two additional *paraprofessionals*. The district suggests Celeste could receive additional support from her TSVI, TODHH, OT, and SLP in the form of *pull-out* or *push-in service delivery* during her school day.

Discussion Questions

1. What questions or concerns might you have about the district's placement recommendation for Celeste?
2. Discuss collaboration among professionals and how this may be especially important for children with CHARGE.
3. Discuss strategies to support children who experience anxiety and benefit from clear and consistent routines (i.e., visual schedule).
4. Celeste and many children with CHARGE syndrome face significant challenges with feeding and mealtimes. How might this impact a child's ability to access instruction in the public school? What support can nursing and other staff provide to ensure equal access for all children?
5. Because Celeste becomes frustrated when others do not understand her communication attempts, what are some tips to encourage and support language while also reducing frustration for both communicative partners?

ACTIVITIES

1. The medical and health challenges faced by children with CHARGE vary greatly. Thus, it is not a surprise that the degree and impact of hearing and vision loss will vary greatly across the population. Explore the packet for professionals available from the CHARGE Syndrome Foundation, and identify those areas where you would like additional professional development in order to best serve a child with this diagnosis. http://www.chargesyndrome.org/for-professionals/education-professional-packet/

2. Explore several blogs, podcasts, or personal reflections written by parents and educators of children with CHARGE syndrome. How might these perspectives inform your practice? Get started here:

   http://theoneinamillionbaby.com/category/special-needs/charge-syndrome/
   https://onthepositiveside.wordpress.com/
   http://thejellychronicles.blogspot.com/p/about-charge-syndrome.html
   http://lessonsfrommatthew.com/
   https://sites.google.com/site/alicjanowickacharge/

3. Using your state or district's early childhood learning standards, create a standards-based lesson plan for a group of three to five preschoolers (with at least one learner who has CHARGE). Indicate the ways you will differentiate instruction to meet the needs of a group of diverse learners. Consider access to instruction both auditorally, visually, and for learners with varying levels of cognitive capacity.

4. Consider similarities and differences between children with CHARGE and *Autism Spectrum Disorders* (ASDs). What strategies might benefit both populations? How might assessment and identification of children with these challenges prove difficult? What should professionals keep in mind relative to assessment, diagnoses, and educational placements?

ADDITIONAL RESOURCES

Genetics Home Reference: CHARGE Syndrome
    https://ghr.nlm.nih.gov/condition/charge-syndrome
CHARGE Syndrome Foundation http://www.chargesyndrome.org/
Understanding Deafness and Disability http://understandingdad.net/

Supporting Document

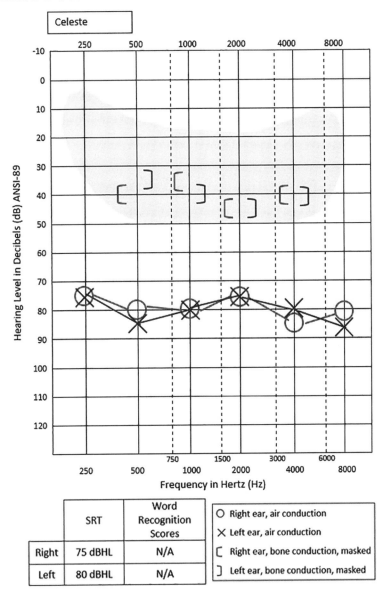

Figure 5.1. Celeste's audiogram.

6
Spencer

Key Topics

Assessment; Audiological Management; Deaf of Deaf; Inclusion; Literacy; Multilingual; Parent Involvement; Psychosocial

Spencer is a 3-year-old boy who was born with a *profound sensorineural hearing level* to *deaf* parents, Brenda and Raul. His parents raised him using *American Sign Language* (ASL) from birth, and he began using expressive signs at 9 months of age. When tested at 3 years of age using the *MacArthur Communicative Development Inventory for American Sign Language* (ASL-CDI; Anderson & Reilly, 2002; see Appendix B), his language was within the average range, and Spencer was forming four- and five-word sentences. Spencer spent much of his time at home with his family where his mother and father frequently read books to him using the 15 principles of the *Shared Reading Project* (Schleper, 1995), which allowed him to engage in rich storytelling and conversations around text.

Spencer also had numerous language experiences in spending a great deal of time with his extended family since numerous grandparents, uncles, aunts, and cousins lived in the same town in the Midwest. All of Spencer's extended family was hearing, as both of his mother and father were born to hearing parents with no other deaf relatives on either side of the family. The extended family used ASL to interact with Spencer and his parents and facilitated communication well at large family gatherings. Spencer's maternal grandfather and paternal grandmother are both retired and share childcare duties with his parents when they are working. Spencer's parents both work outside the home. Brenda is a phlebotomist at a research lab where she draws and examines blood samples, and Raul is a graphic designer for a company that makes decals for motorcycles and race cars.

Spencer's parents and family were extremely curious about the options available for him as he begins to prepare for his entry into the local school system. Both of Spencer's parents attended the state residential *school for the deaf* during elementary school and were then *mainstreamed* in their local middle and high schools. Options in Spencer's state no longer included a school for the deaf, as it closed over 15 years ago. Seeking guidance from outreach services for the *d/Deaf* and *hard of hearing* (d/Dhh), Spencer's parents asked about available options. The outreach coordinator explained that there was a range of services available from certified *teachers of the d/Deaf and hard of hearing* (TODHHs). These services included *itinerant* (traveling TODHH that visits the school two to four times per month to collaborate with the general education teacher and work with the student), *resource* (TODHH housed at the school would meet with Spencer in a separate classroom one to five times per week to focus instruction on language and/or academics), *inclusive* (TODHH collaborates with the general education teacher and is present in the classroom for a certain period/all day to provide instruction to the whole class, support *accommodations* in the classroom, and provide focused instruction for Spencer and others in the class who may need it), or a combination of any of these services. The consultant also explained to Brenda and Raul that accommodations (ASL *interpreter*, *closed captioning* on all videos, *soundfield systems*, etc.) could be provided in any setting.

After learning more about the future school options available to Spencer, the outreach coordinator recommended his parents investigate their local chapter Hands & Voices Guide By Your Side program because his parents also wanted to learn more about *amplification* options for children with profound hearing levels. Their local Hands & Voices Guide By Your Side program paired them with Louise who provided them with information about amplification devices such as *cochlear implants* (CI) and hearing aids. Louise explained that Spencer's *first language* (L1), ASL, put him at a great advantage for developing spoken English (*second language* [L2]) with the use of amplification because he already had a visual language foundation to map the English words onto. Louise also explained that new research shows us that brain and language development between birth and age 3 can be visual or auditory (Visual Language and Visual Learning Science of Learning Center, 2012). Even though Spencer already has a robust *sign language*, she explained that the process of developing sufficient auditory and spoken language skills will take time (12–18 months) and significant support should they chose to use amplification. Children who receive CIs benefit from extensive *auditory habilitation* through work with *Listening and Spoken Language Specialists* (LSLS), audiologists, *Speech Language Pathologist* (SLPs), and TODHHs.

Louise also recommended Spencer's parents might find it helpful to meet and communicate with other hearing and deaf parents about the decisions they made for their own deaf children, especially their fears, hopes, and dreams for their children from a parent's perspective. Brenda and Raul used social media, video chatting, and local, in-person events to meet a variety of parents of *d/Deaf* and *hard of hearing* (d/Dhh) children using multiple avenues to language and communication, including several who use hearing aids and CIs along with ASL. Spencer's parents appreciated the exposure to a wide community of people and felt they now had enough facts to begin to make an informed decision about their son's future.

Now Spencer's parents have some choices to make. Should they consider an inclusive setting? Should they consider hearing aids (if they are beneficial considering his hearing level) or a CI? Brenda and Raul see pros and cons to each decision. It is important to them that Spencer continues to experience *Deaf culture* within their community of friends, has good communication with all members of his extended family, and thrives in an educational environment that will allow him multiple future opportunities.

Discussion Questions

1. What are some of the cultural, educational, and language considerations that will influence Spencer's parents' decision regarding possible amplification devices?
2. What role do other parents and family members play in supporting Brenda and Raul's decision?
3. Regardless of Spencer's parents' decision about amplification technology, what approaches to literacy, communication, family, and culture should Spencer's parents continue to utilize to prepare him for school? How are all these areas (literacy, communication, family, and culture) vital to Spencer's language development in ASL and English (via print or *through-the-air*)?
4. What are the pros and cons of each service model (itinerant, resource, inclusive) for Spencer? How might the possibility of adding amplification devices at this point in Spencer's development change those items in each column?

Activities

1. Use the Additional Resources to investigate Shared Reading and its benefits for children who are d/Dhh. Record yourself attempting to use the 15 principles of the Shared Reading strategy when reading a storybook to a child who is d/Dhh and share with at least two classmates.
2. Trends of schools for the deaf and teacher training programs for TODHHs closing throughout the United States and Canada have been on the rise. Investigate the

schools for the deaf and teacher training programs for TODHHs in your immedi-ate and surrounding area and determine if there are similar trends. How does the increase of inclusive school environments and low enrollment influence these trends? Does this limit the options for students and families? What service models would allow the most efficient use of resources, especially in rural areas, and pro-vide the *Least Restrictive Environment* (LRE) for all d/Dhh students? What could you do to be an advocate for all service models in your local districts/state/province?

3. Watch the TEDx Talk of Heather Artinian, a young deaf woman raised using ASL who eventually got a CI: https://www.youtube.com/watch?v=jhm5OaXJVMQ and write a response.

4. Read Research Briefs #6: The Implications of Bimodal Bilingual Approaches for Children with Cochlear Implants (http://vl2.gallaudet.edu/research/research-briefs/). Summarize each section with what new information you learned. If you already knew the information in a section, summarize how you would explain this to parents like Spencer's who are trying to make informed decisions while respect-ing their beliefs and values.

ADDITIONAL RESOURCES

Barrett, F. L. (1982). *A teacher's guide to shared reading.* New York, NY: Scholastic.

Garate, M. (2000, Spring). Reading to children . . . guided reading and writing . . . shared reading and writing . . . independent reading: Program modifications for ESL students. *Odyssey, 1*(2), 7–10.

Guide By Your Side http://www.handsandvoices.org/gbys/

Parent Resources, Hands & Voices http://www.handsandvoices.org/

Shared Reading Project, Laurent Clerc National Deaf Education Center http://www3.gallaudet.edu/clerc-center/our-resources/shared-reading-project.html

Visual Language and Visual Learning VL2 http://vl2.gallaudet.edu/labs/brain-and-language-lab/

Supporting Document

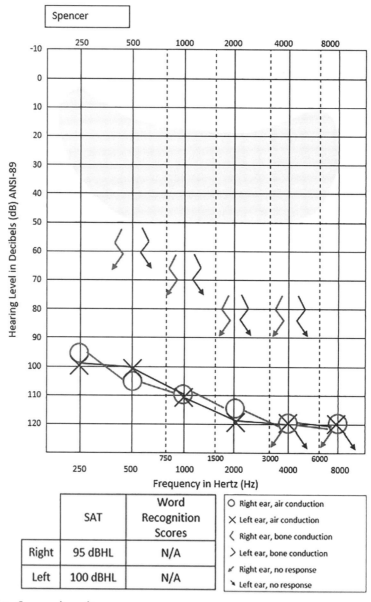

Figure 6.1. Spencer's audiogram.

7
Isabella

KEY TOPICS

Collaboration; Culture; Early Intervention; Parent Involvement; Psychosocial; SES

Isabella, currently 4 years of age, was born in a large city to hearing parents who had a history of *hearing loss* with various members of their extended family. She was screened at birth and soon after diagnosed with a *moderate* to *severe unilateral hearing level* in her left ear. An *early intervention provider* (EI) talked with the family about their daughter's hearing loss and *amplification* options, but her parents misunderstood that they were expected to follow up with professionals. Subsequently, they missed regular appointments with their service providers, such as the *early interventionist* (EI), the pediatrician, the *audiologist*, and the *Ear, Nose, and Throat physician* (ENT). Additionally, when contacted by the follow-up coordinator, Isabella's mom did not understand many of the field-related jargon words that he used, such as unilateral, *intervention*, and amplification. Isabella's parents did not pursue in-home services or enroll her in any *early intervention* programs. When Isabella was almost 2 years old, her mother became concerned that she had very limited speech and, given the family history and her newborn *hearing screening* results, she decided to contact the audiologist. Isabella was fitted with a *hearing aid* and the audiologist recommended a follow-up appointment with the ENT to discuss *fluid build-up* in Isabella's right ear.

After Isabella was fitted with a hearing aid, an EI was assigned to Isabella's family. The EI began working with her family on language techniques and strategies that they could use at home to increase Isabella's speech production and encourage her language development (see Appendix C for instructional strategies related to language acquisition and development). These activities included a list of suggestions for books and toys that would help Isabella label and identify familiar objects, such as a barn with farm animals and *touch and feel books*. The EI also suggested that Isabella and her mother go outside for nature walks and talk about their journey. However, every time the EI visited Isabella, the materials were not visible and her family had not practiced the activities. Frequently, Isabella's mother seemed irritated with the EI. The EI tried to get Isabella's mother involved by showing Isabella's language scores and explained that Isabella might be at risk for some delays. Isabella's mother did not seem to be responsive and hardly looked at the test scores.

The EI consulted with her supervisor who suggested some strategies for use with Isabella and her family. After some time, the EI asked Isabella's mother what they liked to do together as a family. First, Isabella's mother reported that she enjoyed sitting with Isabella and looking through old family photos and advertisement mailers, talking about what they have done and activities they would like to do. She also reported that it was not safe for her to go for walks outside in their neighborhood, but they could take the bus to the other side of town where there was a library and a park. Next, the mother told the EI that Isabella's grandmother was usually the person who cared for Isabella during the day, and the grandmother frequently took Isabella to the grocery store for the weekly shopping. Finally, Isabella's mother told the EI that the family could not afford to buy most of the items on the list. After the conversation, the EI noticed a change in Isabella's mother's willingness to participate. The EI also noticed that when she changed content-specific jargon such as *expressive language* to "words that people say," Isabella's mom seemed more receptive to intervention information.

DISCUSSION QUESTIONS

1. From the information given in this case study, what can you discern about the effects of Isabella's hearing loss?

2. What kind of early language development activities are Isabella and her mother already doing? How can they expand these activities across settings to continue to develop her language?

3. What are the socio-economic and/or cultural issues that might influence the relationship between the parent and EI? Describe them. What can be done to reduce these issues and foster a positive relationship?

4. What are some of the possible repercussions Isabella might experience because she did not receive consistent early intervention services? What actions can the mother and EI take to help remediate some of those potential repercussions?

5. Early intervention services often include visits from a Deaf role model/consultant. How might Isabella's early home visits have changed with the addition of a Deaf role model/consultant?

6. Extended members of Isabella's family have been identified with hearing loss. Think of ways that Isabella's extended family could be actively involved in Isabella's life. How could this assist Isabella's mother in becoming more receptive to her daughter's intervention?

ACTIVITIES

1. List the qualities of an effective EI. In what ways could Isabella's EI improve her strategies and be more effective with Isabella's family?

2. Plan a safe and free outing for Isabella and her mother. If you were the EI, how could you involve Isabella's mother in the planning? How would you encourage her to make this outing a language development activity? Describe the outing plans, list the steps, and bullet the possible vocabulary to be targeted during the outing.

3. Create a family-focused handout of the possible *assistive listening devices* (ALDs) and resources that could benefit Isabella or other families with children like Isabella across various settings (home, school, community, etc.). Describe and provide a picture of the various *assistive technologies* available, and provide references to additional online and local agencies that can assist in acquiring more information.

4. Write two brief transcripts of a "conversation" between the mother and the EI. Begin by writing a transcript of the current relationship. Write the second transcript from a culturally sensitive and parent-friendly terminology viewpoint that illustrates the family and interventionist participating in a collaborative relationship.

5. The Home & Family Oriented Program Essentials (HOPE) Company distributes quality state-of-the-art materials for children with special needs, their families, and the service providers who work with them. Many of the materials are for use in *family-centered early intervention* programs, including materials for children who are d/Dhh, *visually impaired, deafblind*, have multiple disabilities, and have special needs. The materials have also been used in settings other than the home, including day care, preschool, school, hospital, and clinic settings. Visit HOPE's website and identify the different materials that you think would be beneficial to a family like Isabella's, and substantiate your choice of materials (http://hopepubl.com/index.php).

6. Research and discuss different communication barriers that occur between professionals and parents of children with disabilities. In this case study, Isabella's mother experienced a communication barrier with one of the professionals. Discuss educational jargon and devise a list of acceptable words for professionals to use with parents.

Additional Resources

Foundations exist to help people with sight and/or sound loss. Learn how these foundations can help fund the technological hearing devices needed by families who are unable to afford such technology.

- Help America Hear http://foundationforsightandsound.org/help_america_hear_program.html?gclid=CJzvscjxnbcCFZFr7AodWwoAdQ
- Hearing Loss Association of America http://www.hearingloss.org/content/financial-assistance-programs-foundations
- John Tracy Clinic http://www.jtc.org/

Professor Yanhui Pang discusses how to address common challenges professionals face when involving families who are *culturally and linguistically diverse* in the *Individualized Family Service Plan* (IFSP)/*Individualized Education Program* (IEP) process. Explore some of her solutions: Pang, Y. (2011). Barriers and solutions in involving culturally linguistically diverse families in the IFSP/IEP process. *Making Connections: Interdisciplinary Approaches to Cultural Diversity, 12*, 42–51.

SUPPORTING DOCUMENT

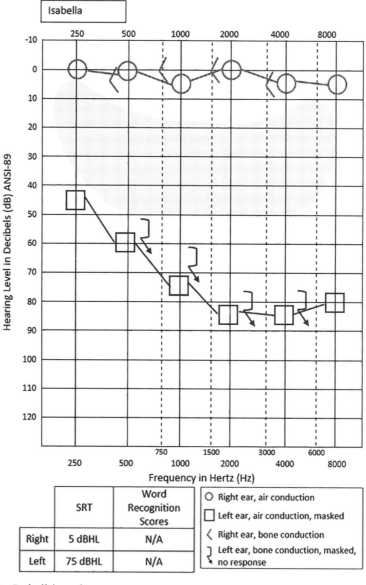

Figure 7.1. Isabella's audiogram.

8
Faith

Assessment; Assistive Technology; Audiological Management; IEP/IFSP/504; Inclusion; Language Development; Literacy; Parent Involvement; SES

Faith is a 4-year-old girl identified with a *profound bilateral sensorineural hearing level* at birth. Faith is a surviving twin and was born premature at 25 weeks. She spent almost six months in the *Neonatal Intensive Care Unit* (NICU) before she was stable enough to go home with her parents. She currently wears bilateral *cochlear implants* (CIs), but her left ear only has a *partial insertion* due to *ossification of the cochlea*. Faith received her first CI at the age of 1 year, 2 months and her second at 2 years of age. Faith uses *listening and spoken language* (LSL) to communicate. Faith's parents worked with a *CI team* (parents, pediatrician, audiologist, otolaryngologist surgeon, *Speech Language Pathologist* [SLP], *early interventionist provider* [EI] for the *d/Deaf* and *hard of hearing* [d/Dhh], social worker) during the process of receiving both CIs. Her parents took advantage of family support services (advice, information, counseling services, parent mentors and support groups/organizations) and worked with their *early intervention team* (parents, SLP, EI, *Auditory Verbal Therapist* [AVT]) to develop an *Individualized Family Service Plan* (IFSP) for Faith.

During this time the team documented that at 1 year of age Faith was having difficulty sitting up without assistance and continued to have balance issues, which contributed to her delay in learning to walk until she was almost 2 years old. The family also reported that when they transitioned from a bright outdoor setting to an indoor building or when Faith played in her bedroom, which did not receive much sunlight and had one small lamp, Faith became agitated, rubbing her eyes. Upon the recommendation of her early intervention team, her parents took Faith to an *ophthalmologist* who prescribed her glasses at 2 1/2 years of age. As a result of her vision and balance concerns, the team then recommended further testing and Faith was recently identified as having *Usher syndrome* Type 1.

Faith's parents experienced a significant period of change and adjustment during her first 2 years of life. Not only were they grieving over losing Faith's twin sibling, they also had to adjust to the fact that Faith is profoundly deaf, has gross motor issues, and has now been identified with vision problems. They also experienced financial pressures from Faith's extended hospital stay in the NICU and struggled to meet all of the follow-up care appointments and accompanying instructions. Faith's mother works part-time in a cafeteria at a local elementary school, and her father pours concrete for a local company and helps with his cousin's moving business on the weekends, yet it is difficult for the family to pay their monthly bills. They also resided in a rural area and owned only one vehicle. The gas and wear and tear on their older car to travel to appointments as well as the time off of their hourly wage jobs presented multiple challenges, but they were able to consistently work with the expanded early intervention team (EI for children who are *visually impaired* and d/Dhh; SLP; AVT; *Occupational Therapist* [OT]; *Physical Therapist* [PT]; audiologist; *Orientation and Mobility Specialist* [O&M]) to provide Faith with the services she needed to thrive.

She received early intervention services from her team primarily at home, consistent with *Individuals with Disabilities Education Improvement Act* (IDEIA) guidance on service delivery in the natural environment, from age 6 months until 3 years of age when she began attending a preschool for students with special needs (IDEIA, 2004). A *teacher of the d/Deaf and hard of hearing* (TODHH) and a *teacher of students with Visual Impairments* (TSVI) collaborated with her special education preschool teacher to ensure that Faith received *intervention* services and *accommodations* to meet her needs.

Faith will enter kindergarten next year. Her family and preschool teachers are planning for this transition, preparing goals and recommendations to present at the upcoming *Individualized Education Program* (IEP) meeting. Faith has made progress in the small preschool classroom environment of six classmates, one teacher, and two *educational assistants*, but kindergarten poses new challenges.

Her current *IEP team* (parents, TODHH, TSVI, SLP, OT, PT, educational assistants, special education preschool teacher, O&M specialist, *deafblind consultant*) is concerned about the future decline in her vision and would like to determine what senses Faith uses most to gain information from her environment. Faith's parents are also very focused on her early literacy skills and would like advice about whether to introduce *braille* as she begins to read more. The TOVI, O&M specialist, and deafblind consultant collaborated to complete an initial Learning Media Assessment (LMA; see Additional Resources) to determine her best learning medium (regular print, regular print with low vision devices, large print, braille, audio materials to supplement one of the other mediums). They also conducted a Functional Vision Assessment (FVA; see Additional Resources) to ascertain how she uses vision in her current preschool environment. This included looking at visual acuity, visual field, and light and color sensitivity. Recommendations presented at the IEP team meeting included using large print in the kindergarten classroom and introducing braille (based on the LMA) and *modifications* to the classroom environment's lighting and seating arrangements (based on the FVA).

Additionally, Faith seems to be struggling to make new friends in her neighborhood, and the family hopes attending her neighborhood school will help improve this situation. The IEP team also arranged for Faith to video chat with another kindergartener who has Usher syndrome and lives in another part of the state. They will now video chat weekly and work with their TODHH to increase their communication skills and practice peer interactions. The team also arranged for a woman who has Usher syndrome and lives in a neighboring district to come to the school and eat lunch with Faith once a month.

DISCUSSION QUESTIONS

1. How did the members of the intervention teams (CI, early intervention, IFSP, IEP) change as Faith's special needs developed? List the importance of each member to Faith's overall development.
2. What challenges do a kindergarten classroom and a large elementary school setting pose for a student like Faith? How can her team assist in meeting these challenges?
3. How can the use of peer and adult role models benefit Faith's social-emotional development?

ACTIVITIES

1. Use the Additional Resources to investigate and learn more about the LMA and the FVA. Why do you think the results of Faith's LMA determined large print?
2. Investigate and design a classroom for a student like Faith who is deaf, has a vision loss, and has balance and/or mobility challenges. Create a visual model for this ideal classroom and present it to your classmates.
3. Investigate Usher syndrome; describe the characteristics of the three types and how they are diagnosed.
4. Locate local training on the screening process for different types of Usher syndrome to increase your knowledge of all three types and ways TODHHs can assist in identification.

ADDITIONAL RESOURCES

American Federation for the Blind http://www.afb.org/default.aspx
Center for Visually Impaired: http://www.cviga.org/
Functional Vision Assessment http://www.familyconnect.org/info/education/assessments/functional-vision-assessment-fva/135
Learning Media Assessment http://www.afb.org/info/education/assessments/learning-media-assessment-lma/235
National Center on Deafblindess https://nationaldb.org/

Orientation and Mobility Specialist http://www.tsbvi.edu/orientation-and-mobility-items/
    2110-the-role-of-the-orientation-and-mobility-teacher-in-the-public-schools-1
Usher syndrome:
    http://www.usher-syndrome.org/
    https://www.nidcd.nih.gov/health/usher-syndrome

Supporting Document

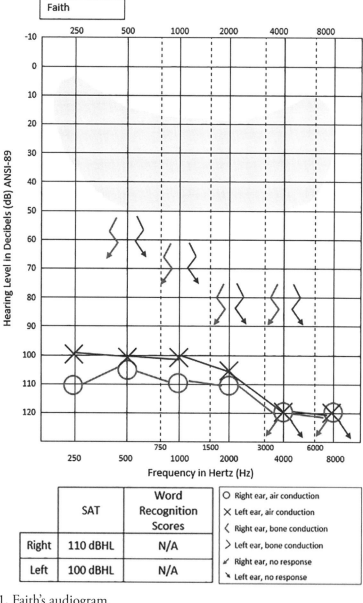

Figure 8.1. Faith's audiogram.

9

Drake

KEY TOPICS

Accommodations; Audiological Management; Collaboration; IEP/IFSP/504; Inclusion; Literacy; Placement; Transition

Drake is a 5-year-old boy with a *profound bilateral sensorineural hearing level*. His hearing level was identified after two referrals from the *Universal Newborn Hearing Screening* (UNHS) in the hospital and an *auditory brainstem response* (ABR) at 1 month of age. Drake's parents' pursued genetic testing to determine the *etiology* and results indicated a Connexin 26 mutation. His parents chose to have Drake receive bilateral *cochlear implants* (CIs). The *simultaneous CI* surgery was scheduled at 9 months of age, but Drake had fluid in his ears at the time of the appointment. Three months later, the *CI team* successfully completed the surgery at 12 months of age.

Drake's parents were committed to providing him with a language-rich environment, using all *modes of communication*. Before and after this CI surgery, his mom and dad used *sign language* and spoken English to communicate and narrate their actions throughout their day to encourage Drake's language development. By the time Drake received his CI, he was approximating 20 words expressively in sign language, including "milk," "eat," "more," and "mommy," as well as the gestures for the words "up," "no," "bye-bye," and more. Once he received his CI, his parents continued to support Drake's language development using a combination of sign and spoken language. Drake declined in his use of signs and increased his use of spoken words at around 18 months of age. During Drake's infant and toddler years, his family received *early intervention* services from Part C of the *Individuals with Disabilities Education Improvement Act* (IDEIA, 2004). At age 3 Drake transitioned to Part B of IDEIA, receiving services from a *teacher of the d/Deaf and hard of hearing* (TODHH) two times a week at a general education preschool. The TODHH collaborated with the preschool teachers to ensure Drake had the best acoustic environment by measuring background noise (with no one present in the classroom) of his preschool classroom. The initial results of 50 *decibels* (dB) were above the American National Standards Institute (ANSI) standards for classroom acoustic environments, which states that background noise should not exceed 35 dB. They worked together to add modified tennis balls to the bottom of all the classroom chairs, weather stripping around windows and doors to reduce outside noise pollution, rugs around the classroom, and some acoustic ceiling tiles. When the TODHH measured the background noise again it was reduced to 40 dB, still above the ANSI recommendation but an overall improvement.

Drake's preschool teachers also collaborated with the TODHH on their program's intentional focus on the development of early literacy skills throughout the day. The teachers worked together to organize their early literacy instruction around five key elements or blocks: (1) story read-alouds, (2) *phonological awareness*, concepts of print, and *alphabetic knowledge*, (3) experiences with nonfiction or informational text, (4) conversational language opportunities, and (5) emergent writing. As a result of the intentional instruction, the preschool teacher was aware when Drake had difficulties hearing certain sounds during *phonological awareness* and *alphabetic knowledge* activities and made classroom adjustments recommended by the TODHH to improve auditory and visual access (see Appendix C for instructional strategies related to literacy acquisition and development).

As a result of this collaboration and intense literacy focus, Drake completed preschool with language and literacy levels commensurate with his typically hearing age-level peers. At his *IEP team* meeting in preparation for kindergarten, the team determined that Drake no longer meets the two requirements (hearing loss and impact on learning) necessary to qualify for IEP services due to his high performance levels. Instead, the team decided that Drake's accommodations needs could be met in the general education classroom through a *Section 504 plan*. The team worked to explain the technical differences between the two types of eligibility criteria. The team agreed that they would collaborate to make all accommodations recommended for Drake, Drake's current TODHH will monitor him and provide the Section 504 plan services, and the team will meet again in three months to determine if the Section 504 plan is meeting his needs.

The team assured the parents' that the acoustic environment in Drake's new school will be met. The class size will be increasing from 10 students to 24 students, and his family would like to explore the available *assistive listening devices* (ALDs) for increased access to sound and the curriculum in Drake's new classroom environment. The following notes from Drake's most recent team meeting describe the new kindergarten environment:

> Drake's parents are worried about the noise in the classroom. Drake's current classroom has been modified to absorb sound and reduce sound reverberation. His new class, with additional students, has tile floors, and the teacher uses a small group instructional model where students rotate among multiple learning groups within the classroom. If there is background noise during phonological awareness or reading instruction, it may be a challenge for Drake to perceive the acoustic information or spoken language given the poor signal to noise ratio.

Drake's team recommended working with the district *audiologist* and TODHH to use a *soundfield system* and an *FM/DM system* to reduce *signal-to-noise ratio* in the classroom to support the instruction and access. Other recommended classroom accommodations included reducing the space between Drake and the teacher during instruction and making similar acoustic *modifications* completed at his preschool. These should be completed not only in his classroom but in all the school environments (including auditorium, lunch room, gymnasium, etc.).

DISCUSSION QUESTIONS

1. How can the educational team acoustically modify his new school environment based on the description of the classroom provided and the typical set up of school buildings?
2. Drake's team determined he did not meet the criteria for eligibility for IEP services and changed to a Section 504 plan instead. Do you think this decision was justified based on the information provided?
3. Drake had a positive preschool experience that supported his continued growth in language and early literacy. What elements of language (e.g., phonology, morphology, semantics, syntax, and pragmatics) were covered in the five key blocks utilized in his preschool? How do these align with the National Reading Panel's recommendations (i.e., Phonemic Awareness, Alphabetic Principle, *Fluency*, Vocabulary, and Comprehension) for beginning readers?
4. Drake's educational team worked and collaborated well together to provide him with the supports he needed to be successful in preschool. If you were Drake's new kindergarten teacher, what questions would you ask the team in order to replicate their collaborative nature?

ACTIVITIES

1. Investigate information about improving acoustic environments from your resources and those links listed under Additional Resources. Create a diagram of a kindergarten classroom, detail the accommodations listed for Drake and any that should be added.
2. Review the resources about Parts B and C of IDEIA and Section 504 plans in Additional Resources, and develop a chart or paragraph summarizing each for a parent or general educator. Practice explaining this with a partner in or outside of class.
3. Use an app for acoustic environment, and measure the decibel levels in two to three classroom environments in your area and list ways that sound levels could be decreased to increase communication access for all.

4. If you were Drake's teacher, what kind of accommodations would you provide for this child to ensure he has full access to the classroom routine?
5. Create an alternative scenario where Drake is placed in a deaf program or a school for the deaf beginning in kindergarten. Discuss his auditory needs and the benefits of a sign language and/or spoken English environment for Drake.

ADDITIONAL RESOURCES

Classroom acoustics:

Acoustic Standards http://successforkidswithhearingloss.com/classroom-acoustics-standard/

Preparing the classroom http://successforkidswithhearingloss.com/classroom-acoustics-impact/

Early Literacy resources:

www.readrightfromthestart.org
www.readaloud.org

Information about Part B and C of IDEA for parents and teachers:

Part B http://www.parentcenterhub.org/repository/schoolage/
Part C http://www.parentcenterhub.org/repository/partc/
Section 504 plan vs. IEPs (Part B) information https://www.understood.org/en/school-learning/special-services/504-plan/the-difference-between-ieps-and-504-plans

National Reading Panel: 5 Big Ideas in Beginning Reading:

http://reading.uoregon.edu/big_ideas/

SUPPORTING DOCUMENT

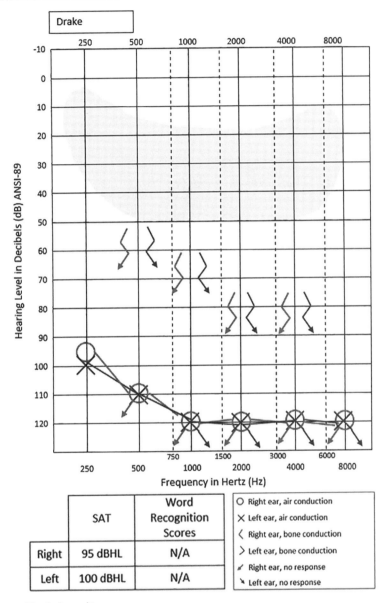

Figure 9.1. Drake's audiogram.

10

Bianca

KEY TOPICS

Assessment; Culture; Deaf with a Disability; Early Intervention; IEP/IFSP/504; Multilingual; Transition

Bianca is a 5-year-old female who recently immigrated to the Northeast region of the United States from Manila, Philippines, with her hearing parents. Bianca has two siblings (one younger and one older brother), and due to complications during birth, Bianca was born with a *moderate* to *severe sensorineural hearing level* and moderate *spastic cerebral palsy* (CP; caused by lack of oxygen, illness, or injury during or after birth and results in tightness and spasms of muscles in the body that cause involuntary movement and might interfere with gait and mobility in all extremities). Although her hearing level was detected at birth, Bianca did not receive *early intervention* services because there were no available programs in Manila at the time her family lived there.

In Manila, Bianca's parents were both teachers (her mother a second grade teacher and her father a high school math teacher) who spoke Filipino and English and provided her with an enriched home environment that promoted visual language and communication by labeling items in the home. The whole family learned and used a modified form of *Filipino Sign Language* (FSL), which is heavily influenced by *American Sign Language* (ASL) and used within *schools for the deaf* in Manila. The family also used *home signs* and highly encouraged communication with her siblings and extended family members. Her parents are bilingual, in Tagalog and English. Bianca recently began using an electric wheelchair for mobility. She has limited use of her left arm, and the electric chair gives her more independence and mobility than her previous manual wheelchair. Bianca expresses herself using limited intelligible speech with her primary *mode of communication* as FSL and home signs due to her mobility issues, which limit her to some sign approximations. Bianca receptively understands *sign-supported speech* best, by moving signs in her visual proximity. As a result of her CP, Bianca cannot hold her head up straight for more than a few seconds so she holds it to the side, but this makes following an *interpreter* or prolonged signed conversations tiring.

Because her family recently moved from Manila, Bianca's parents were asked to come for an initial placement and eligibility meeting at her local elementary school where Bianca will begin kindergarten at the beginning of the next school year. Her parents were advised to bring a *cultural broker* to the meeting to make sure they fully comprehend all the information and questions during this important decision-making discussion (Cannon & Luckner, 2016). This transition to the U.S. school system where Bianca will attend classes for the first time is an enormous stress as well as an exciting opportunity for the family and Bianca. The process can be overwhelming because a student like Bianca may be eligible for services from a *teacher of the d/Deaf and hard of hearing* (TODHH), an *Occupational Therapist* (OT), a *Physical Therapist* (PT), an expert in *Augmentative Alternative Communication* (AAC) devices, an *Adaptive Physical Education* specialist, a *Speech Language Pathologist* (SLP), and/or an *educational assistant*. In addition, the general education teacher, principal, school nurse, and fellow classmates will be a part of Bianca's community, and her parents will get to know and interact with all these individuals during Bianca's school career. Collaboration among these professionals is key to Bianca's success in her new environment, and the cultural broker will assist the family with the referral to the *Individualized Education Program* (IEP) process.

Gathering the appropriate information during this transition time is essential to Bianca's acclimation to her new environment. There are no school records regarding her academic performance, and the professionals will have to rely on Bianca's parents to gain an understanding of the goals/objectives and best placement options for Bianca. When they lived in Manila and her parents were at work, Bianca stayed with her maternal aunt and older brother. Therefore the team will request information from the aunt and brother as well. The preliminary meeting with the family revealed that, with the use of *binaural hearing aids*, Bianca is able to follow verbal directions and comprehend some auditory information (she was provided with personal hearing aids from an organization in Manila). Bianca also uses a digital tablet that her family purchased; it has personal augmentative communication device applications that communicate her ideas by "speaking" for her when she is in the community and/or trying to express something to her family and friends. She presses the picture/symbol, and the device voices a word or sentence for her. Her parents also report that Bianca requires one-on-one assistance during all daily activities, including transition times, mealtimes, and in the bathroom.

Bianca's parents then completed the *MacArthur Communicative Development Inventory for American Sign Language* (ASL-CDI; Anderson & Reilly, 2002; see Appendix B) with the assistance of the TODHH, a Filipino interpreter, and their cultural broker. This questionnaire/checklist asks parents to identify words their child expresses through speech or *sign language*. The ASL-CDI includes vocabulary regarding things in the home, people, action words, description words, pronouns, prepositions, question words, sentences, and grammar. This will provide her initial *IEP team* (TODHH, PT, OT, SLP, augmentative communication district representative, *Adaptive Physical Education* specialist) with some information to collaborate to decide what assessments are necessary to determine goals and accommodations for Bianca's multiple needs.

DISCUSSION QUESTIONS

1. What categories of assessments would you begin with in order to get a picture of Bianca's present levels of performance?
2. What accommodations would you recommend to support Bianca's mobility needs due to her CP?
3. How were Bianca's team supportive of her parents while they completed the ASL-CDI? What challenges might the team have faced in providing Bianca's parents with support in completing this questionnaire, considering they live in a rural area and have a different cultural and linguistic background?
4. What do you know about mobility issues for students with CP, and what do you need to learn more about before you could provide Bianca with appropriate services? How do some of Bianca's mobility issues interfere with her access to language?

ACTIVITIES

1. Investigate the Additional Resources about CP, and learn more about the issues some students with CP face in communication, mobility, and self-help skills. Develop a plan to train the service providers working with Bianca about CP and to learn from their expertise. Collaboration is vital across multiple individuals who will provide Bianca with services, and this process can be overwhelming for teachers and parents. Developing a clear, documented plan will reduce this issue and provide transparency for Bianca's services.
2. Identify two to three organizations (public and/or private), local services, and *Disability Resource Centers* (DRCs) that provide parents with assistance acquiring equipment and adaptations. Call at least one agency and inquire about the cost of services and resources and the types of resources available for students like Bianca.

3. Read Guardino and Cannon (2016), and write a one-page summary about what we know, what we don't know, and what you want to learn more about regarding d/Dhh students who are multilingual and have a disability.

4. As outlined in Guardino and Cannon (2016), minimal research and information is available about students who are d/Dhh and diverse, especially those who are d/Dhh multilingual learners and have a disability. Complete a literature search for up-to-date research, and compile a reference list. Based on the information you located, what are some of the challenges in conducting research with this unique population, and what should be the field's future research direction to determine evidence-based practices and train preservice teachers?

ADDITIONAL RESOURCES

Augmentative communication devices for students with CP http://cpfamilynetwork .org/assistive-devices-abound-for-helping-with-communication-for-cerebral -palsy-kids/

Cerebral Palsy

https://www.cerebralpalsyguide.com/
http://www.cerebralpalsy.org/
http://cpfamilynetwork.org/cerebral-palsy-diagnosis/

IEPs: A Guide for Families http://www.parentcenterhub.org/repository/pa12/
Resources for parents, teachers, and other professionals working with students who are d/Dhh and diverse:

http://understandingdad.net/
https://www.cerebralpalsyguide.com/cerebral-palsy/coexisting-conditions/

Supporting Document

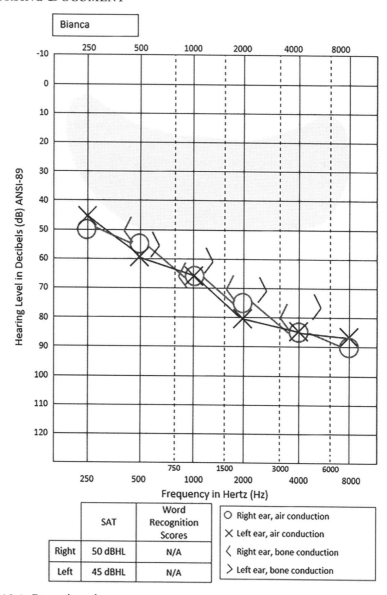

Figure 10.1. Bianca's audiogram.

11
Ava

KEY TOPICS

Assessment; Assistive Technology; Audiological Management; Collaboration; Deaf with Disability; Inclusion

Ava is a 6-year-old girl who is the youngest of five children and was identified with a *profound bilateral sensorineural hearing loss* at birth. She received *binaural hearing aids* at 4 months of age. Ava did not appear to tolerate her hearing aids well, and her parents struggled to keep them in her ears. Unsure that Ava benefitted from the hearing aids, her use of them was inconsistent. Her family lives in a rural area so travel to *early intervention* services was a challenge; therefore, the *early intervention provider* (EI) made an initial visit to the family's home and established *tele-practice* for weekly *intervention* services. The EI connected them with a parent-to-parent program, encouraged Ava's family to explore online *American Sign Language* (ASL) resources, and provided them with information about *cochlear implants* (CIs).

The parents and siblings began using ASL with Ava in the home. Because all of the children were homeschooled, Ava had many language models. The family attempted to engage Ava in interactions via songs, games, finger-plays, and books using both spoken and *sign language*; however her responses seemed inconsistent (e.g., limited shared joint attention and eye contact). Her family felt she might benefit from increased access to spoken language. When Ava was around 1 year of age, they began to discuss the possibility of Ava receiving a CI. For religious reasons, the family was uncertain and spent a considerable amount of time consulting with their religious leaders about the surgery. After two months of deliberation, the family decided to move forward with the surgery. At 18 months of age, Ava received bilateral CIs and the addition of weekly *Auditory-Verbal Therapy* (AVT) via *tele-practice*. These therapy services aimed to teach Ava's caregivers how to help Ava access and use sound to develop spoken language. Similar to the use of ASL, the older siblings were able to implement and support the listening, language, and auditory therapies for Ava.

After a year of listening time, Ava sporadically used one-word utterances (signed and spoken) for requests and demands. However, she did not appear to consistently respond to her name, rarely made eye contact or engaged in reciprocal play, and began to engage in repetitive behaviors when playing with her toys. She seemed to become overwhelmed easily within her large family, often having tantrums or leaving loud situations to sit in her closet. In addition, Ava would become frustrated and hit her family members in an effort to get her needs met (e.g., to get candy or play with a certain toy). Despite continued early intervention services, these behaviors did not diminish during the next six months. At her final *Individual Family Services Plan* (IFSP) meeting, the team recommended that Ava transition to a special education preschool program. Her family discussed this option but felt that placement was inappropriate for Ava because she was already overwhelmed at home and feared a new environment would only increase her challenging behaviors. Ava's mother consulted with her network of homeschool families who suggested that she seek additional support from a homeschool Specialized Education Program (SEP). This program provided her with a list of educational consultants and developmental specialists. With these resources, Ava's family decided to continue homeschooling.

By the time Ava was 4 years of age, her behaviors remained the same and she made minimal progress in her *expressive language*. The family located a developmental specialist through the SEP. After in-home observations, consultation with Ava's pediatrician, and completion of the Modified Checklist for Autism in Toddlers (M-CHAT; see Supporting Documents and Additional Resources) by the specialist and her parents, Ava was identified with *Autism Spectrum Disorder* (ASD). The family realized that the homeschool environment was insufficient to meet Ava's needs and contacted their local school system to pursue education within the local school system.

Ava's eligibility was established, and the *Individualized Education Program* (IEP) team met to discuss her educational placement options. The team determined that a separate class at the local preschool was the *Least Restrictive Environment* (LRE) and most appropriate educational placement for Ava. She received weekly services from an *Occupational Therapist* (OT) for sensory integration; a *Speech Language Pathologist* (SLP) who focused on the use of the *Picture Exchange Communication System* (PECS) for learning language functions as well as *listening and spoken language* (LSL) skills; and an *Applied Behavior Analysis* (ABA) therapist who worked with Ava and her team to positively change her behaviors. Her parents collaborated with the teachers to ensure her CIs were closely monitored. This combination of services helped Ava gradually increased her vocabulary and social interactions. She remained in this placement until she turned 6 years old. Now that she is ready to transition to kindergarten, the family has to make a decision about the next educational setting. They are deliberating about whether to send her to their local public school to receive special education services in a *self-contained classroom* with *inclusion* opportunities or to homeschool her with the rest of the siblings.

DISCUSSION QUESTIONS

1. What do you think would be the best educational placement for Ava based on the evidence stated within the case study?
2. What questions should the *IEP team* consider to demonstrate their respect and understanding of Ava's family values?
3. How can Ava's family and therapists maximize her audiological access in the home and educational settings?
4. Considering a child similar to Ava at the age of 3 years old, with sporadic one-word utterances, what communication goals might the educational team develop to increase his or her express and receptive communication skills?

ACTIVITIES

1. Create a list of questions that Ava's parents can ask to evaluate the appropriateness of a given educational setting for Ava.
2. Learn more about early intervention services for children with ASD. Create a guide or pamphlet for families.
3. Family values influence educational placement and decision-making for children with special needs. How have Ava's family values influenced decisions for Ava? Research and write three to five paragraphs on culturally responsive practices relative to religious values and considerations.
4. Investigate ABA therapy and its potential to increase the communication skills of students with ASD. Find an ABA resource to provide to parents of children with ASD.

ADDITIONAL RESOURCES

The Modified Checklist for Autism in Toddlers (M-CHAT) https://www.m-chat.org/

SUPPORTING DOCUMENTS

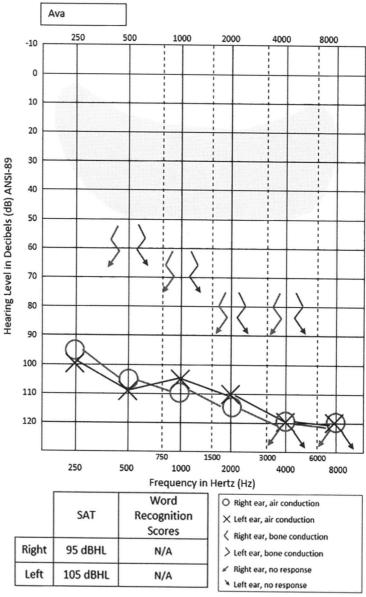

Figure 11.1. Ava's audiogram.

M-CHAT-R/F (Modified Checklist for Autism in Toddlers, Revised with Follow-Up)

1. If you point at something across the room, does your child look at it? (FOR EXAMPLE, if you point at a toy or an animal, does your child look at the toy or animal?)

   ○ Yes ● No

2. Have you ever wondered if your child might be deaf?

   ○ Yes ● No

3. Does your child play pretend or make-believe? (FOR EXAMPLE, pretend to drink from an empty cup, pretend to talk on a phone, or pretend to feed a doll or stuffed animal?)

   ● Yes ○ No

4. Does your child like climbing on things? (FOR EXAMPLE, furniture, playground equipment, or stairs)

   ● Yes ○ No

5. Does your child make unusual finger movements near his or her eyes? (FOR EXAMPLE, does your child wiggle his or her fingers close to his or her eyes?)

   ○ Yes ● No

6. Does your child point with one finger to ask for something or to get help? (FOR EXAMPLE, pointing to a snack or toy that is out of reach)

   ○ Yes ● No

7. Does your child point with one finger to show you something interesting? (FOR EXAMPLE, pointing to an airplane in the sky or a big truck in the road. This is different from your child pointing to ASK for something [Question #6.])

   ● Yes ○ No

8. Is your child interested in other children? (FOR EXAMPLE, does your child watch other children, smile at them, or go to them?)

   ● Yes ○ No

9. Does your child show you things by bringing them to you or holding them up for you to see - not to get help, but just to share? (FOR EXAMPLE, showing you a flower, a stuffed animal, or a toy truck)

   ● Yes ○ No   Copyright 1999 Robins, Fein, Barton

Figure 11.2. Ava's M-CHAT.

12
Dwayne

Collaboration; Inclusion; Psychosocial

Dwayne is a 6-year-old boy who experienced *post-lingual deafness* at the age of 3 after having contracted *bacterial meningitis*. He has a *profound bilateral sensorineural hearing level*. While he has *digital hearing aids*, he often refuses to wear them at school and "misplaces" them when at home. Dwayne attends a self-contained classroom for students who are *d/Deaf* and *hard of hearing* (d/Dhh) at the local public school. He lives with his single mother who has had several unstable relationships during Dwayne's childhood. Although Dwayne spoke prior to contracting meningitis, his current speech is nearly unintelligible, as he rarely uses speech to communicate at school or home and is learning *American Sign Language* (ASL) at school.

Midway through the school year, Dwayne's mother acquired a boyfriend and invited him to live with them when he was looking for employment. Traditionally, Dwayne would attend after school care, but to save money, she started letting her boyfriend care for him instead. Although Dwayne's mother knows basic vocabulary in ASL (e.g., eat, sleep, drink, bed, toilet, more), her boyfriend does not and often becomes frustrated with Dwayne. He yells at Dwayne when he doesn't respond to his requests and physically grabs him when he wants him to go somewhere or do something such as clean up or go to bed. Dwayne's mother returns after midnight and is regularly too tired to wake in the morning to get Dwayne to school. Dwayne has learned not to wake his mother because this angers her boyfriend. He has learned to get himself dressed and to the bus stop on most days.

Dwayne's teacher began to notice a change in Dwayne's overall appearance and behavior. He frequently arrives at school disheveled and hungry. He has been difficult toward the end of the school day, refusing to ride the bus home. She recalled from her *deaf education program* that the incidence rates of abuse to children with disabilities, including neglect, physical, emotional, and sexual abuse, is more than 25% higher than reported by the hearing population (Johnson, 2012; Jones et al., 2012). Abused children tend to withhold their trauma unless specifically asked; this is especially true for *deaf* children. Furthermore, children in general, are often conditioned to comply with authority, and they know that if they break the rules, they may be punished.

If abused, they may fear rejection, punishment, loss of parental love, or blame for the abuse. This problem can be complicated by the fact that approximately 95% of deaf children have hearing parents who often struggle to communicate with their child and may leave communication issues to the school and the teachers. Dwayne's teacher knew that she needed to respond to his behavioral changes, as they might be warning signs of child abuse and neglect.

Immediately, his teacher started to document Dwayne's situation, noting his clothing and hygiene, as well as the days he struggled to get on the bus. After three weeks of documentation, she noticed he had a bruise on his forearm, which at first glance she had mistaken for dirt. It was then that his teacher decided to call the authorities to report what she had observed over the last few weeks.

First, Dwayne's teacher went to the school principal who told her that she should continue to document the situation. If more bruises appeared or if Dwayne reported violence, then they should call the police. However, his teacher knew that she was a *mandatory reporter*, which means professionals who have frequent contact with children are obligated by law to report incidences or suspicion of abuse or neglect. She kindly informed her principal that if they were not going to make the call together, she would have to make the call herself. The principal conceded, and together they called the authorities.

DISCUSSION QUESTIONS

1. Do you think the teacher reacted professionally and appropriately? Why or why not?
2. What does it mean to be a mandatory reporter?
3. Who is considered an authority when reporting suspected or confirmed child abuse or neglect?
4. When you report abuse or neglect, does that mean the child will be taken away from his or her home?
5. When reporting abuse, can you remain anonymous?

ACTIVITIES

1. Use the Child Welfare Information Gateway website and search "state statues" (https://www.childwelfare.gov/topics/systemwide/laws-policies/state/). Locate your state and local authority for reporting child abuse or neglect. Provide contact information, a link to their website, and any pdf documents they provide for parents and professionals.
2. Create an informative visual that you could handout to parents and/or post on your classroom website that defines the different types of abuse: neglect, physical, emotional, and sexual. List three to four signs of each abuse. Provide contact

information for reporting abuse. Utilize this resource "Recognizing Child Abuse and Neglect: Signs and Symptoms (2007)" as a starting point: https://www .childwelfare.gov/pubPDFs/signs.pdf

3. Does your school or school district use a prevention curriculum to keep children safe? If so, provide the name of the curriculum. If not, seek out a curriculum (e.g., *Good Touch & Bad Touch*, Monique Burr Foundation) used in another state. After identifying the curriculum, provide a citation and link (if possible) to the curriculum. Write a one-page summary that reviews the curriculum and its accessibility to children who are d/Dhh.

4. What local agencies in your area provide education to parents and/or training to teachers about child abuse and neglect prevention?

5. Watch the 7 Kidpower Strategies for Keeping Your Child Safe video at https:// www.youtube.com/results?search_query=7+kidpower+strategies. How might you adapt these strategies for students who are d/Dhh?

6. Determine the possible reasons for the higher rates of abuse and neglect for deaf children as compared to hearing children. List the indicators, besides a deaf child's overall appearance (bodily marks), that indicate abuse or neglect might be occurring to the child.

7. Create an artifact (e.g., presentation, brochure, poster) that describes the communication difficulties children who are d/Dhh encounter. Describe at least three ways we can help d/Dhh children become more empowered and feel safe reporting the abuse that is happening to them. Discuss the impact that child abuse and neglect may have on their mental health functioning.

ADDITIONAL RESOURCES

Child Abuse and Neglect: Recognizing the Signs and Making a Difference https:// www.helpguide.org/articles/abuse/child-abuse-and-neglect.htm

ChildHelp Hotline 1-800-4-A-CHILD and reporting information at https://www .childhelp.org/hotline/

Crosson-Tower, C. (2003). The Role of Educators in Preventing and Responding to Child Abuse & Neglect. https://www.childwelfare.gov/pubPDFs/educator.pdf

Johnson, H. (2012). Protecting the Most Vulnerable from Abuse. http://leader.pubs .asha.org/article.aspx?articleid=2280650

Johnson, H. (2015). Prevention of abuse as experienced by children with disabilities: A U.S. model for policy, planning, professional development and collaboration. http://www.deafed.net/Forms/HJohnsonUSModel.pdf

Jones, L., Bellis, M., Wood, S., Huges, K., McCoy, E., Eckley, L., & Officer, A. (2012). *Prevalence and risk of violence against children with disabilities: A systematic review and meta-analysis of observational studies.* Lancet, published online July 12. DOI: 10.1016/S0140-6736(12)60692-8

Protective Factors to Promote Well-Being https://www.childwelfare.gov/topics/
preventing/promoting/protectfactors/?hasBeenRedirected=1

Safety Checklist http://www.deafed.net/Forms/03_22_16_Safety_Checklist_Document.pdf

The Risk and Prevention of Maltreatment of Children with Disabilities (2012) https://
www.childwelfare.gov/pubPDFs/focus.pdf

Supporting Document

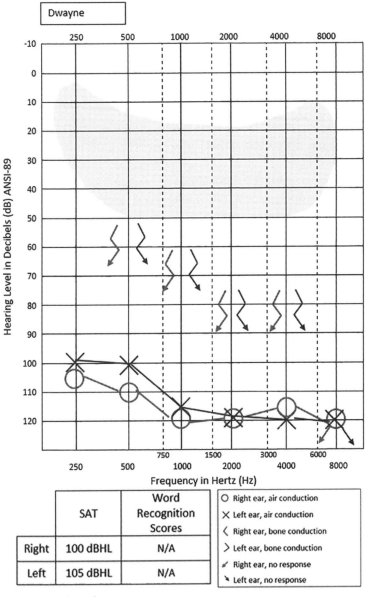

Figure 12.1. Dwayne's audiogram.

13
Olivia

Content Area Instruction; Culture; Literacy; Placement

Olivia is a 7-year-old student currently placed in her local public school with an *educational interpreter*. Olivia was identified with a *moderate* to *severe sensorineural hearing level* at two years of age. Her parents are from Mexico and use spoken Spanish at home. Olivia has three older siblings who use both spoken Spanish and English at home. Olivia was born at home, and her parents did not follow up with *Universal Newborn Hearing Screening* (UNHS). When she was younger, her parents noticed that Olivia did not meet the same language milestones as her siblings. For example, she was delayed in *babbling* and her vocalizations were difficult to understand. They took her to a pediatrician who referred them to an *audiologist*. To establish Olivia's *hearing level*, the audiologist used *conditioned play audiometry* (CPA), a form of *pure tone audiometry* (PTA) often used with children. When using CPA, the audiologist taught Olivia to place blocks in a basket when she heard a tone from the pure tone audiometer (i.e., the machine used to present sounds during a hearing test). After the session, Olivia was identified with a moderate to severe *bilateral* hearing level and fitted with *binaural behind-the-ear hearing aids*. Olivia benefitted from the hearing aids and quickly began verbalizing more with her parents and siblings. The audiologist also referred Olivia's parents to the local *early intervention provider* (EI) who worked with her parents to complete eligibility paperwork to receive special education services.

Olivia and her family received in-home *early intervention* services. Her parents and EIs developed goals for Olivia, such as increasing Olivia's functional vocabulary related to family routines. Their EI was fluent in both Spanish and *American Sign Language* (ASL). Olivia's family chose to combine spoken Spanish and English with sign language to support Olivia's communication needs. Her siblings also participated in the *intervention* sessions and quickly learned the targeted *sign language* vocabulary (i.e., bath, hungry, more, bedtime, book, TV, eat). Additionally, Olivia's oldest sister borrowed sign language dictionaries from the school library and showed her parents available online sign language dictionaries, such as Signing Savvy, ASLPro, Handspeak, and spreadthesign.com, and her parents downloaded ASL apps on their phones. When

Olivia turned 3 years old, she transitioned to a local preschool program for children with varying special needs where she received services from an itinerant *teacher of the d/Deaf and hard of hearing* (TODHH), an *educational interpreter*, and a *Speech Language Pathologist* (SLP) who all worked with the special education teacher. Her *Individualized Education Program* (IEP) *team* agreed that this type of educational setting allowed Olivia access to language, academic, and social skills, and her assessment data indicated that Olivia was making appropriate progress. For instance, she acquired both spoken Spanish and English vocabulary in addition to corresponding signs. She transitioned to a general education setting at her local elementary school for kindergarten and first grade and received similar services.

Now that she is in second grade, her *IEP team* is discussing how to take advantage of Olivia's language skills within her *content area* instruction. Her TODHH has investigated evidence-based instructional strategies and suggested weekly one-on-one instructional time to address explicit instruction in these strategies so that Olivia can generalize their use across her content classes (i.e., English/language arts/reading, science, social studies, and math). For writing, her TODHH plans to use Strategic Interactive Writing Instruction (Wolbers, 2008), in which she records Olivia's *codeswitching* language behaviors, or use of spoken Spanish, spoken English, and ASL, during idea generation for writing activities. The TODHH will record Olivia's Spanish, ASL, and English ideas on separate easels and provide direct instruction in translating these generated ideas into written English on the dedicated English easel (see Appendix C for instructional strategies related to language and literacy acquisition and development).

Specific to science and social studies, the TODHH will provide mini-lessons on the organization of Olivia's textbooks and the purpose for each part of the text to assist Olivia in her mental organization and recall of the information (Howell & Luckner, 2003). Finally, to assist with *content area vocabulary* learning, the TODHH will pair *chaining* with *mental imagery*. For *chaining*, the teacher models a relationship among the printed word, its corresponding sign, and *fingerspelling* (Padden & Ramsey, 1998). For *mental imagery*, Olivia creates a picture in her mind for a given vocabulary concept based upon her personal life experience, such as a tadpole developing pulmonary breathing and morphing into a frog as an example of the concept of a life cycle.

DISCUSSION QUESTIONS

1. How long should teachers expect Olivia to be able to attend to an interpreter in kindergarten versus second grade? What are some of the difficulties d/Dhh students face when using an interpreter at school? What can teachers do to help alleviate some of those challenges?

2. What is codeswitching? How do you use codeswitching with different groups of people (e.g., students, families, friends, colleagues)? Why is codeswitching important for d/Dhh learners?

3. In what ways do content area and literacy instruction overlap? How might strategies such as chaining and mental imagery assist in each instructional area?
4. Reflect upon the range of communication situations a deaf child is likely to encounter. Include how you as an educator might prepare the child to communicate successfully in these various situations.
5. Is ASL/Spanish/English trilingualism possible? In the United States it is common to find monolingual school teachers who are unfamiliar with trilingualism and therefore are unprepared to implement ASL/Spanish/English instruction. Discuss what needs to be done to remove this barrier to meet the needs of students like Olivia.

Activities

1. Read Pizzo, L. (2016). d/Deaf and hard of hearing multilingual learners: The development of communication and language. *American Annals of the Deaf, 161*(1), 17–32. Discuss how you might use Pizzo's three recommendations for practice, including family engagement in early language experiences, targeted and intentional language instruction, and utilizing language–culture connections of multicultural learners such as Olivia.
2. Discuss how you can address Olivia's development of both *basic interpersonal communicative skills* (BICS) and *cognitive/academic language proficiency* (CALP).
3. Discuss how you might introduce the sign language dictionary sources that appear under Additional Resources with parents of a signing d/Dhh student. How would you suggest parents and siblings use these resources?
4. Read Andrews, J. F., & Rusher, M. (2010). Codeswitching techniques: Evidence-based instructional practices for the ASL/English bilingual classroom. *American Annals of the Deaf, 155*(4), 407–424. Develop a content area lesson plan (i.e., ELA/reading, science, or social studies) and explicitly describe how you will embed codeswitching instructional strategies within the lesson.
5. Generate a list of five vocabulary words. Practice chaining and mental imagery with a partner. Discuss how these techniques made you feel, understand, and comprehend the words.

Additional Resources

Conditioned Play Audiometry:
    https://www.childrens.com/specialties-services/specialty-centers-and-programs/
    ear-nose-and-throat/programs-and-services/audiology/conditions-and-treatments/
    conditioned-play-audiometry
    https://www.youtube.com/watch?v=_eKn-lrGYZo

Online sign language dictionaries:
   https://www.signingsavvy.com
   http://www.handspeak.com/word
   http://www.aslpro.com/cgi-bin/aslpro/aslpro.cgi

Supporting Document

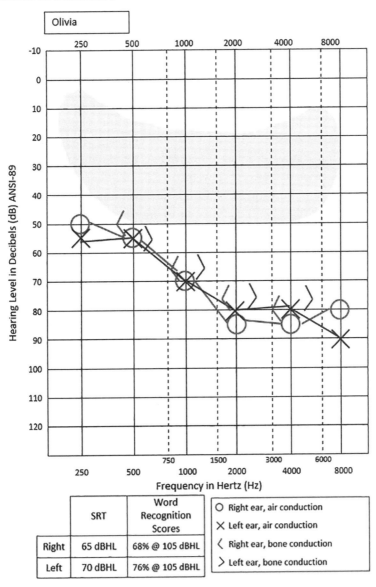

Figure 13.1. Olivia's audiogram.

14
Santiago

KEY TOPICS

Assessment; Culture; Language Development; Literacy; Multilingual; SES

Santiago is a shy and eager-to-please 7-year-old second grader at a local elementary school in a rural community in the Midwestern part of the United States. He comes from a home where Spanish is the primary spoken language. Several factors related to low socio-economic status (SES) have impacted his development thus far. His family earnings have fluctuated between "low income" and "extreme poverty" (National Center for Children in Poverty, 2017; Office of the Assistant Secretary for Planning and Evaluation [OASPE], 2017). At the time of this publication, the yearly income to be classified as earning below the federal poverty level for a family of three was $20,420 (OASPE, 2017). This level has remained essentially unchanged since it was established in the mid-1960s and applies all across the United States, without consideration of cost of living differences by region (National Center for Children in Poverty, 2016).

Contributing additional stress into the home, Santiago's parents are consistently concerned about their immigration status. Santiago's parents emigrated from Mexico before he was born. His mother is employed and holds a current visa that allows her to work full-time. She speaks sufficient English to communicate with her employer. Santiago's father has an expired temporary visa. He has done seasonal work in the past and has limited English skills, consisting of limited vocabulary and simple phrases used for greetings. In general, Santiago's father is leery of engaging with public systems where someone in authority might question his immigration status.

While Santiago had a newborn *hearing screening*, he was *lost to follow-up* testing. Santiago's *mixed hearing level* was identified at 2 years and 10 months after a pediatrician completed an in-office developmental screening and indicated concern about his auditory responsiveness. Santiago receives health care from a community-based family clinic (not a consistent *medical home*) rather than a pediatrician who can provide consistent support. He has *mild* to *moderate bilateral hearing loss*. While he was fitted with *bilateral hearing aids* just before his third birthday, he has never fully established consistent use of his hearing aids. Given that Santiago was not diagnosed until close to his third birthday, his family did not receive *early intervention* services beyond the hearing assessment and fitting of devices. His parents did not receive parent coaching or *family-centered early intervention* services emphasizing the importance of establishing use of his hearing aids during all waking hours. Santiago began attending a Head Start preschool at age 3 and was eligible for an *Individualized Education Program* (IEP). A *Speech Language Pathologist* (SLP) who had no background working with children were *d/Deaf* and *hard of hearing* (d/Dhh) was assigned to work with him, visiting at the Head Start facility. This Head Start program was situated in a part of town with a strong community of other Spanish-speaking parents and early educators who use spoken English and spoken Spanish in the classroom. However, the staff did not receive any in-service or support on the importance of providing consistent access to sound. Thus, they were not vigilant about promoting hearing aid use because they didn't fully understand the need nor value the benefit technology might provide relative to Santiago's general development. Because Santiago has a mild to moderate hearing loss, he appeared responsive to much of the classroom instruction, so his teachers were unaware that he might have been missing important conversation and content.

When Santiago transitioned from the Head Start program to his elementary school, a *teacher of the d/Deaf and hard of hearing* (TODHH) joined his *IEP team*. In spite of her oversight and consultation with classroom teachers, his hearing device use remained inconsistent. When he was in the first grade, the TODHH recognized an opportunity to collaborate with his classroom teacher to put a system of daily device and listening checks in place. The classroom teacher took on the responsibility of conducting daily *Ling sounds* check. She also kept data on whether or not he presented at school wearing his devices and whether or not they were in good working order. While his classroom teachers have consistent expectations for him to wear his devices, sometimes he does not bring them to school. Other times, when he does have the hearing aids, they aren't in good working order; they are in need of batteries, cleaning of the *earmolds*, or repair.

Because the parents' first language is spoken Spanish, Santiago's IEP indicates that his parents will need a Spanish language *interpreter* for IEP meetings and school conferences. While the school ensures an interpreter is present for these official meetings, they do not regularly have a Spanish interpreter available for school events. Occasionally an older relative or family friend is able to interpret for Santiago's parents. Subsequently, the family is relatively non-participatory in any extracurricular activities, including school social events, reading incentive programs, holiday programs, and parent conferences given the language barrier. The educators perceive his parents to have relatively low literacy skills. Even when official documents are translated into Spanish, it is unclear if they are being provided at a literacy level that is accessible to the parents, which causes an additional language barrier to parental participation.

Prior to a recent *multidisciplinary team evaluation*, Santiago's SLP requested that her bilingual Spanish-speaking colleague participate in his evaluations. This was

Table 14.1. CELF-4 – Spanish.

Core Score/Index	Standard Score	Percentile Rank
Core Language	53	.1
Receptive Language Index	60	.1
Expressive Language Index	61	.25

important as the team administered a *Clinical Evaluation of Language Fundamentals, Fourth Edition* (CELF-4; see Appendix B), Spanish, to evaluate Santiago's general language ability in Spanish. This assessment revealed the scores in Table 14.1.

Results from assessment of Santiago's spoken Spanish language skills suggest below average expressive and receptive skills for his age. Santiago appeared to have particular difficulty in vocabulary, following directions, and sentence construction. The diagnostic team has concluded that Santiago's Spanish language skills are in a similar range as his English language skills, concluding that he does not have significantly different language competency in English or Spanish, but is currently below age-level proficiency in both languages.

Current educational goals for Santiago focus on the IEP team's concerns about his literacy development. As Santiago's hearing loss is mild to moderate, he should, theoretically, receive sufficient access to spoken language with his hearing aids. However, the time that he actually wears his hearing aids outside of school appears limited at best. With inconsistent hearing aid use, resulting in variable access to spoken language, Santiago struggles in his mainstream first-grade classroom. He receives 30 minutes of individual instruction with a TODHH who specializes in serving children using *listening and spoken language* (LSL) daily. He also receives *small group* SLP services for 30 minutes two times per week.

Concerns to be addressed in the next annual IEP include the following:

• Inconsistent use of hearing technology. Santiago has not yet achieved consistent wear time though he has had hearing aids since he was 2 years, 10 months. Additionally, Santiago will likely require a new pair of hearing aids since his are out of warranty and are utilizing out-of-date technology nearing the end of their life span. This makes it difficult for the district audiologist to troubleshoot, or to connect with a personal DM system. Because Santiago receives public health insurance, it is likely that he will be eligible to receive new devices during the next academic year.

• Concerns about literacy/cognition. Based on most recent evaluations, there is a gap between Santiago's English and Spanish skills, with both being behind what would be expected of typically hearing peers (see Appendix C for instructional strategies related to language and literacy acquisition and development).

- Psychosocial factors. Santiago seems to have friends and peer relationships with several cousins who are close in age and a neighborhood with a strong community of Spanish speakers. However, his classroom teachers are unsure of how well he understands conversation in social environments within his home community, as he isn't likely wearing his hearing aids at those times. In classroom group activities, during lunch, and at recess, it does not appear that Santiago uses language to communicate with his peers. He tends to sit quietly and nod along with the more vocal leaders in the group. It does not appear that Santiago advocates for himself when he cannot hear or understand instruction. Occasionally he recounts these instances of confusion when meeting with the TODHH in a *pull-out* session, but for the most part, he is unaware that he has missed classroom instructions or discourse.

DISCUSSION QUESTIONS

1. Discuss strategies the team might use to ensure the concerns listed in this case study, including hearing technology, literacy and cognition development, and the psychosocial factors. Consider the value of collaboration in addressing these concerns.
2. Consider the impact over the course of a child's development when a family does not receive high-quality family-centered early intervention services. What knowledge and skills, on the part of the parents, might have been missed as compared to if they had received family-centered early intervention when their child was between the ages of birth and 3 years old? How will this gap in services impact their ability to engage with their child and educational providers for years to come? What are some possible ways current school professionals might provide family education and increase engagement within the context of a school system?
3. Reflect on *implicit bias*. How could your personal values and biases as a TODHH influence the service delivery you provide to Santiago and his family?
4. Given the limited minutes determined in the IEP, prioritize what the TODHH and the SLP should work on during their weekly instructional time.

ACTIVITIES

1. Look up the role of a *cultural broker*. https://nccc.georgetown.edu/culturalbroker/ 5_brokers/index.html. Identify the ways a cultural broker might aid school professionals in supporting Santiago and his family. Compare and contrast the roles of a language interpreter and cultural broker. Consider how these professionals might support greater family engagement in the school environment and IEP team.

2. Do a quick internet search to identify a free hearing level simulator. Explore one of these simulators or demonstrations, focusing on the degrees of mild to moderate. Try spending several hours wearing foam earplugs that might grossly simulate a mild to moderate *conductive* hearing loss. Based on your experience with the simulations and demonstrations cited below, answer the following questions:

   http://www.starkey.com/hearing-loss-simulator

   http://www.hearinglikeme.com/hearing-loss-simulator/

   http://successforkidswithhearingloss.com/demonstrations/

   a. What situations and environments might prove most challenging?

   b. What are the educational and social implications of a hearing loss of this nature?

   c. How would inconsistent hearing aid use further perpetuate these challenges?

   d. How might age of onset of a hearing loss in the mild to moderate range impact potential challenges/outcomes?

3. Explore the Worldwide Parent Education opportunities offered by the John Tracy Clinic: http://www.jtc.org/worldwide-parent-education/. Take note of those online learning options and the summer program for Spanish-speaking families.

   a. Would you recommend this type of training and support for Santiago's family?

   b. Which aspects?

   c. Why or why not?

4. Investigate *frequency modulation* (FM), *digital modulation* (DM), and *soundfield systems*. How might this type of technology support children with hearing loss in their inclusive educational environments? Which would you recommend for Santiago's case? Provide justification for your recommendation. http://successforkidswithhearingloss.com/fm-systems/

5. How might a teacher or service provider check and maintain records of Santiago's daily hearing aid assessment? Consider both device checks as well as listening checks (e.g., Ling sound test). Design a form to track this data. Who should take responsibility for these checks?

   http://www.hear-2-learn.com/pages/links.html

   http://successforkidswithhearingloss.com/

ADDITIONAL RESOURCES

Teaching Tolerance: A Project of the Southern Poverty Law Center. See online resources related to Hidden and Implicit Bias. http://www.tolerance.org/Hidden-bias

Voss, J., & Lenihan, S. (2015, December). Fostering resilience for children living in poverty: Effective practices & resources for EHDI Professionals Journal of Early Hearing Detection and Intervention. *Issues Briefs for Early Hearing Detection and*

Intervention. Logan, UT: National Center on Hearing Assessment and Management. Available at http://www.infanthearing.org/issue_briefs/Fostering_resilience_in_children_living_in_poverty.pdf

Voss, J. M., & Lenihan, S. (2016). Professional competence to promote resilience for children living in poverty. *Journal of Early Hearing Detection and Intervention, 1*(1), Article 7. Available at http://digitalcommons.usu.edu/jehdi/vol1/iss1/7

Supporting Document

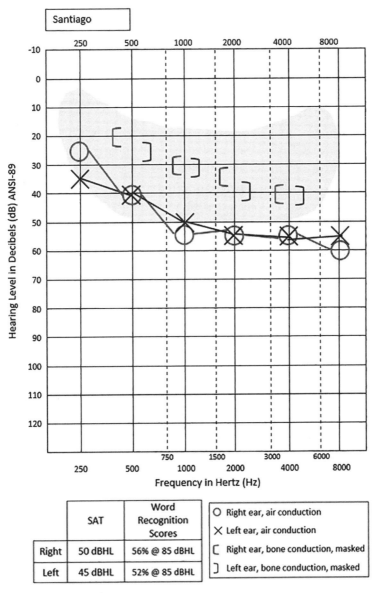

Figure 14.1. Santiago's audiogram.

15
Xavier

KEY TOPICS

Assistive Technology; Audiological Management; Inclusion; Modality; Placement

Xavier Casabianca is 7 years old and lives with his family in a suburban community. Xavier was born with *Treacher Collins syndrome*, a rare condition that affects bone and tissue development. In Xavier's case, this syndrome caused an absence of the right *pinna (i.e., microtia)* as well as *atresia* (small ear canal); thus he did not pass his newborn *hearing screening*. Xavier's parents, Jimenez and Dora, could recall no other family members who were *deaf* in their family lineage. When Xavier was approximately 3 months old, his *hearing loss* was determined to be a *severe bilateral conductive hearing loss*. The conductive loss is a characteristic with children who have *Treacher Collins syndrome*. Xavier's parents were referred to and actively participated with all *early intervention* recommendations, including the use of *hearing aids*.

At 6 months of age Xavier was fitted with *softband bone-conduction* hearing aids. At approximately 12 months old, Xavier began to *babble* and vocalize single utterances such as "da da" and "ba ba." Xavier's language development continued on a steady path of growth over the course of the next year and a half. At the age of 3, Xavier expressed over 100 words, which represented a language delay of approximately 6–12 months compared to his typically hearing peers. When Xavier transitioned to preschool, the Casabiancas chose an *inclusion* setting so he would be exposed to as much spoken language as possible during the school day.

Xavier attended an inclusive preschool classroom within the local public elementary school. The classroom was diverse with approximately 12 typically developing hearing peers and 3 children with special needs, including Xavier. During his preschool program, Xavier received consistent services from a *Speech Language Pathologist* (SLP) as well as a *teacher of the d/Deaf and hard of hearing* (TODHH). Because Xavier had a language delay upon entering preschool, the pace of the inclusive setting was challenging. Furthermore, the level of constant noise in the preschool setting made it difficult for Xavier to have good language *uptake*. Xavier made adequate linguistic progress over the course of the next two years. When he transitioned from preschool to kindergarten, Xavier was functioning linguistically at a 4-year-old level. Xavier's parents opted to keep him at the preschool for an additional year in hopes that he might increase his language skills to a level comparable with his peers before entering kindergarten.

At the age of 5, Xavier was eligible for *bone-anchored hearing aids*. However, his parents were fearful of putting Xavier through surgery and felt that the *softband bone-conduction hearing aid* was sufficient for his age. Both Jimenez and Dora agreed that they would reconsider this option once Xavier reached an older age.

Following Xavier's sixth birthday, an *Individual Education Program* (IEP) meeting was held to determine if the current inclusive elementary school was the best kindergarten setting for Xavier. Other educational settings the team considered were a *self-contained* classroom for students who are *d/Deaf* and *hard of hearing* (d/Dhh) in a different public elementary school or a private school specializing in *listening and spoken language* (LSL) located two hours from the Casabianca's residence. The self-contained classroom teacher used *American Sign Language* (ASL) to support the students' learning. Jimenez and Dora were worried that introducing *sign language* would further complicate Xavier's language progress, and the private school was too far from home. His parents decided to keep Xavier in his current setting with some educational and service changes.

Xavier's speech and language therapy was increased to 180 minutes per week. Instead of staying in the inclusion setting all day, Xavier would now go to a *resource* room for one hour every day to receive intensive and individualized language instruction by a special educator.

The summer before Xavier entered first grade, his parents decided to move ahead with the *bone-anchored hearing aid* surgery. Xavier recovered quickly from the surgery and is in the middle of first grade successfully benefitting from the use of his new hearing aids.

DISCUSSION QUESTIONS

1. Examine Xavier's *audiogram*. How would you describe Xavier's hearing loss in audiological terms? What is his hearing status aided versus unaided? Using the *speech banana*, describe the access to sounds Xavier has with his aids compared to without them.

2. Use the American Speech-Language-Hearing Associations (ASHA) language development charts (see Additional Resources) to compare Xavier's language development to a typically developing hearing child. How does his language development differ?
3. What does "Xavier was functioning linguistically at a 4-year-old level" mean? Use a language development milestone chart to support your answer.
4. Xavier's parents "were worried that introducing sign language would further complicate Xavier's language progress." Examine the research by the Visual Language and Visual Learning Center (search: VL2 and bilingualism), Dr. Petitto and her research team from The Brain and Language Laboratory (see References), and Davidson, Lillo-Martin, and Pichler's (2013) *Spoken English language development amongst native signing children with cochlear implants*. Is there evidence to suggest that Xavier's parents have a valid concern supported by research?

ACTIVITIES

1. Create a brochure that outlines the similarities and differences between a bone-conduction hearing aid and a *behind-the-ear* or *in-the-ear digital hearing aid*. Include diagrams. Explain the maintenance of both assistive technology devices.
2. Use the ASHA language milestone chart (see Additional Resources) to trace Xavier's development compared to a typically developing child. Choose another case study in this text and chart their language development as well. Write a professional statement (two to three paragraphs) comparing and contrasting the language development of the two case studies. Discuss the implications of the age a child was identified and the type of early intervention received on their language development.
3. Most children with Treacher Collins syndrome have an abnormality with the external ear. Research Treacher Collins syndrome, and describe the difficulties children affected with this syndrome experience. Describe other symptoms such as sleep apnea. What abnormalities can be corrected with surgery, such as reconstruction?

ADDITIONAL RESOURCES

American Speech-Language-Hearing Associations (ASHA) language development charts http://www.asha.org/public/speech/development/chart/

Genetics Home Reference: A guide to understanding genetic conditions https://ghr.nlm.nih.gov/condition/treacher-collins-syndrome

SUPPORTING DOCUMENT

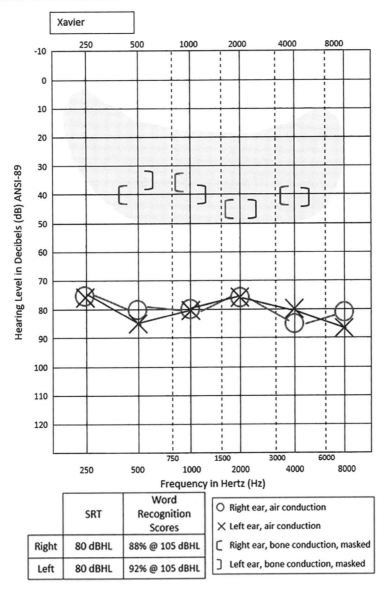

Figure 15.1. Xavier's audiogram.

16
Sam

Accommodations; Assessment; Content Area Instruction; IEP/IFSP/504; Inclusion; Literacy; Modality; Placement

Sam is an 8-year-old boy born at home with the aid of a midwife to hearing parents in a rural section of the Midwest. Sam's family had no history of *hearing loss*, but Sam's parents became concerned when Sam, at almost 2 years of age, said none of the words that his two older siblings said at a similar age. Sam also did not seem to understand communication directed to him. Sam's pediatrician referred his mother to an *audiologist* based on his lack of communication. The audiologist diagnosed Sam with a *severe bilateral sensorineural hearing loss*. The audiologist discussed a *cochlear implant* (CI) with Sam's family, but Sam's mother and father did not know anyone who had received a CI and did not feel comfortable with surgery. Shortly after his second birthday, Sam was fitted with *digital hearing aids* and received gains up to 45 *decibels* (dB) in both ears. Sam began receiving services from a *Speech Language Pathologist* (SLP) at a center-based setting three times per week. He also began receiving home-based services from the state *early intervention* program once a week. With a *Speech Reception Threshold* (SRT) of 45 dB aided and *Speech Discrimination* (SD) of 55%, the SLP and *early interventionist* (EI) set goals for improving Sam's (1) ability to make the best use of his *residual hearing* through auditory training activities; (2) language development through language-rich activities at the center and at home; and (3) speech production through *articulation* activities (see Appendix C for instructional strategies related to language and literacy acquisition and development).

When Sam turned 3 years old, he entered a multi-categorical preschool program for children with various disabilities. The classroom setting made it difficult for the teachers to meet Sam's hearing loss-related needs, but there was no preschool classroom in or near his town for children who are *d/Deaf* or *hard of hearing* (d/Dhh). After his first year, his teachers assessed him using the *MacArthur Communicative Development Inventory* (CDI; Fenson et al., 2007; see Appendix B), which indicated that Sam's *expressive language* was delayed by more than two years. Sam began to exhibit negative behavior, usually when he was trying to communicate. He would become frustrated and throw toys at clean-up time and hit other children during work time when he wanted a turn. His *Individualized Education Program* (IEP) *team* and his parents decided to incorporate visual support to help Sam communicate and to build a stronger language foundation. Sam's mother began *American Sign Language* (ASL) classes at the local college and incorporated *sign language* at home when communicating with Sam. His father and siblings learned basic signs as taught by their Sam's mother and Sam. They did not attend any formal sign language classes. During his last year of preschool, Sam's parents visited the kindergarten classroom at the *school for the deaf* that was in the next town. They decided this would be the best placement for Sam upon his transition from preschool to kindergarten.

After a few months in a kindergarten program with ASL instruction, Sam's receptive and expressive English and ASL language skills increased as measured by the *Peabody Picture Vocabulary Test, Fourth Edition.* (PPVT-4; Dunn & Dunn, 2007; see Appendix B) and the CDI (Fenson et al., 2007), respectively. By the end of first grade, Sam enjoyed reading books with simple sentences and picture support. He could read and understand phrases at the simple sentence level.

Before second grade, the *IEP team* met to determine Sam's placement options. Sam's father expressed the importance including Sam in general education classrooms as much as possible and having the opportunity to interact with hearing students in his local school district through extracurricular activities. Therefore, his team decided to place him in a *resource* classroom at his local elementary school for children who are d/Dhh. The *teacher of the d/Deaf and hard of hearing* (TODHH) used *sign-supported speech* to ensure all students had access to visual and spoken languages. The new placement provided him opportunities for *inclusion* in some academic classes and special activities with an *educational interpreter*. Sam's current achievement test scores show challenges in the areas of *expressive* and *receptive language*, reading comprehension, and *decoding* skills as shown by his results on the *Basic Reading Inventory* (BRI; Johns, 2017; see Appendix B).

DISCUSSION QUESTIONS

1. Name three to five specific behaviors that indicate Sam will benefit from sign-supported speech. Explain how access to language might change those behaviors.
2. Describe Sam's current areas of relative strength and how they will impact his future learning. Explain two instructional strategies that you believe could increase Sam's literacy skills.

3. Describe information from the assessments that Sam's team used to make appropriate placement decisions.
4. In kindergarten, Sam demonstrated growth based on two assessments, and this could indicate that the school for the deaf was an appropriate placement for him. When he was transferred to his local school district, his test scores showed evidence of weak literacy skills. Discuss the advantages and disadvantages of being in a school for the deaf versus a general education inclusive program for Sam.

ACTIVITIES

1. Interview a *school psychologist* or reading coach in a program with students who are d/Dhh. Identify two different assessments used to measure reading comprehension (see Appendix B), other than the ones used already, and describe how they can be used to determine appropriate placement and additional IEP goals for a student.
2. With another individual, role-play an interaction between a TODHH and the classroom teacher to monitor Sam's progress on reading comprehension over a 12-week period. For students enrolled in an online course, record a three-minute role-play session.
3. Examine research on reading comprehension for students who are d/Dhh. Based on your research, generate a list of effective practices and strategies to develop reading comprehension, specifically for children who are d/Dhh, like Sam.

ADDITIONAL RESOURCES

Hands & Voices is an organization of parents and professionals working to create unity, strength, and understanding amongst the *Deaf community*. They present placement options for children who are d/Dhh from a non-biased standpoint. Read their review of placement options. http://www.handsandvoices.org/needs/placement.htm

Reading and understanding an *audiogram* can be a daunting task; however, plenty of resources exist to assist in the process. Hearing professionals provide an overview of how to read an audiogram on their website. Within the website, under "hearing tests" scroll down to "Understanding an audiogram." http://www.hearingpro.com.au/index.html

Watch this helpful video to learn a step-by-step process of reading and understanding an audiogram: http://www.youtube.com/watch?v=ie1SdWdWErg

Supporting Document

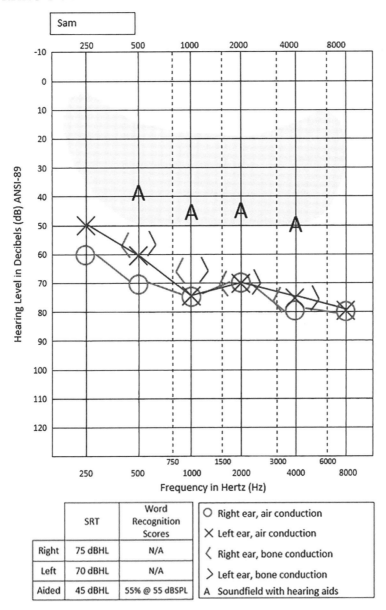

Figure 16.1. Sam's audiogram.

17
Dylan

Key Topics

Content Area Instruction; Inclusion; Language Development; Psychosocial

Dylan is an 8-year-old with a *profound bilateral hearing loss*. He wears bilateral *cochlear implants* (CI) and is a confident, consistent user of his devices. Dylan is a twin born at 30 weeks gestation. Dylan and his twin brother spent the first six weeks of life in the *Neonatal Intensive Care Unit* (NICU). Dylan required high levels of oxygen at birth as well as *ototoxic medicine* to treat a serious infection. These early medical interventions were likely responsible for his hearing loss. His twin, who was generally healthier and underwent less medical intervention, has typical *hearing levels*. Dylan's hearing level was identified at 2 months of age, and he began using initial *amplification*, in the form of bilateral *hearing aids*, at 3 months of age. Dylan's parents began receiving *early intervention* services for both boys as soon as they were discharged from the hospital. Dylan received *simultaneous* CIs at 14 months of age. His family participated in weekly early intervention sessions through the summer when he turned 3 years old.

Dylan's *early intervention provider* (EI), who came to the family home for weekly coaching sessions, was a *Listening and Spoken Language Specialist* (LSLS) employed by an *OPTIONSchool,* a *listening and spoken language* (LSL) program, in the family's community. When the boys were 20 months old, they both started attending a half-day *inclusion* toddler class at this OPTIONSchool where instruction was focused on promoting the development of LSL for children who are *d/Deaf* or *hard of hearing* (d/Dhh). Dylan's mother would stay and observe at the window in the classroom while Dylan and his brother participated in early language experiences and play-based *intervention* in a group of six to eight children. Dylan and his twin remained at the OPTIONSchool for preschool. Dylan's twin served as a hearing peer and was integrated in small and larger group interactions. Dylan's parents felt very grateful for having an educational setting that could meet both boys' needs, even at these early stages. They began kindergarten at their local parochial school where they are now in third grade.

The private parochial school has a reading specialist and *Speech Language Pathologist* (SLP) on staff, and Dylan has an *Individualized Education Program* (IEP) through the public school district. While private parochial school is not required to provide services outlined in an IEP, educators from the private school and the public district collaborate and consult often to ensure they are meeting Dylan's needs. Dylan receives support to enhance his *auditory skills* (in listening in noise, *dichotic listening*), to promote *self-advocacy*, and for content area vocabulary.

Dylan's mother takes him to the local public school for 60 minutes per week to meet with the itinerant *teacher of the d/Deaf or hard of hearing* (TODHH). While this teacher is not a certified LSLS, she has attended workshops and professional development from the OPTIONSchool. She is motivated to keep her knowledge and skills current and keeps in close collaboration with her *deaf education program* colleagues through membership in her local *Alexander Graham Bell Chapter* and participation in an online community called Hearing First. Dylan's current educational goals focus on providing the supports necessary to keep him on track with the grade-level curriculum.

Dylan uses a personal *digital modulation* (DM) *system* that connects directly to his CI, though sometimes he forgets to use it. His *itinerant* TODHH is really beginning to focus on developing Dylan's *self-advocacy* skills. She also spends time *pre-teaching vocabulary* and concepts for upcoming math, science, and social studies units (see Appendix C for instructional strategies related to language and literacy acquisition and development). Dylan enjoys playing on soccer and basketball teams with his schoolmates. He also attends an after school Science Technology Engineering and Math (STEM) club. He is generally very social with his peers. As there are not many children at Dylan's school with specialized learning or health care needs, the family and itinerant teacher's goals are to support Dylan's self-advocacy to ensure his needs are being met in all of the spaces where he learns and plays.

DISCUSSION QUESTIONS

1. Discuss the self-advocacy goals you would define for Dylan. Why are these important? Looking forward to the next several years, what do you hope Dylan will do for himself in educational and social settings?

2. What are the ways you might facilitate collaboration between public and private providers to ensure support for Dylan? What systems and individual characteristics make this type of collaboration challenging? What characteristics promote this type of collaboration?

3. Dylan meets weekly with an itinerant TODHH to get support for vocabulary related to content area instruction. What are some strategies the TODHH might

employ to *pre-teach vocabulary*? What information would the TODHH need from Dylan's classroom teacher to guide her instruction?

4. What are the variables in the case study that have supported Dylan's successful psychosocial development? How might Dylan's teachers and parents capitalize on his positive social relationships to increase his self-advocacy in academic and social settings? Given his experiences, how might Dylan mentor others who are working on their own self-advocacy skills?

ACTIVITIES

1. Draft a presentation or in-service you would give to the faculty and staff at Dylan's private school. What are your goals for this type of professional development offering? What key points will you be sure to include? Why?

2. Call an independent or private school (parochial, religious, or otherwise, not specializing in serving children who are d/Dhh), and ask what infrastructure they have to support children with special needs. Ask if they have ever collaborated with a public district to provide supports for learners with specials needs. In what ways do private programs collaborate with public schools to support students? What is parent responsibility in these types of situations?

3. Explore the OPTIONSchools website to locate an OPTIONSchools program near you. Describe the children they serve. Do they collaborate with public programs in their region? How do OPTIONSchools fund their program? What are qualifications or certifications of the program staff?

4. Explore the *Alexander Graham Bell* Academy for Listening and Spoken Language website to learn about the certification for LSLS (*Auditory-Verbal Therapist*s [AVTs] and Auditory Verbal Educators).

5. Now that Dylan is in the third grade at his parochial school, what are some IEP goals you would develop for him? Write instructional goals that Dylan needs to learn and what action you want to see. How would you measure progress toward Dylan's goals? Are the goals specific, measurable, and realistic for Dylan?

ADDITIONAL RESOURCES

Alexander Graham Bell Academy for Listening and Spoken Language https://www.agbell.org/AcademyDocument.aspx?id=541

OPTIONSchools, Inc. https://www.optionschools.org/
     Hearing First https://hearingfirst.org/

Self-advocacy for d/Dhh students: Hands & Voices http://www.handsandvoices.org/needs/advocacy.htm

SUPPORTING DOCUMENT

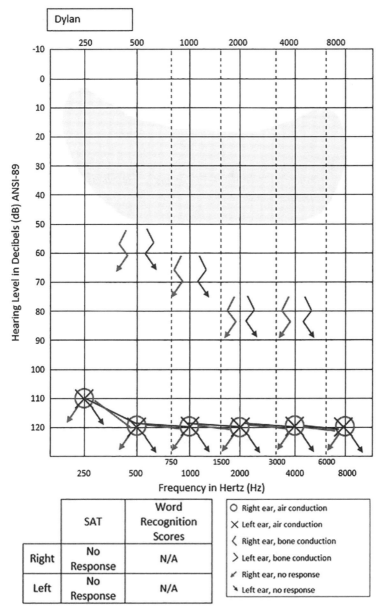

Figure 17.1. Dylan's audiogram.

18
Megumi

KEY TOPICS

Accommodations; Culture; IEP/IFSP/504; Language Development; Literacy; Modality; Multilingual; Parent Involvement

Megumi is a 9-year-old girl who recently immigrated to the Pacific Northwest from Okayama, Japan, with her hearing parents. Megumi has no siblings and was born with a *severe to profound sensorineural hearing level*. She was identified at birth through the *Universal Newborn Hearing Screening* (UNHS) program that began in the Okayam Prefecture, Japan, in 1999 (Ohmori et al., 2015). Her mother had a maternal aunt (Suki) who was also *deaf* and utilized *Japanese Sign Language* (JSL; recognized as an official language with 2011 legislation and influenced by the Japanese writing system). Suki worked with Megumi and her family so that they could acquire JSL from the time Megumi was identified as deaf. Megumi began wearing *binaural hearing aids* at 6 months of age, but the family did not pursue *listening and spoken language* (LSL) *interventions*. Therefore Megumi has grown up in a bilingual home environment where her parents use JSL (her *first language* [L1]) and Japanese spoken and written language (her *second language* [L2] via print). Her father is an investment banker, and her mother is an engineer and both have graduate degrees.

When Megumi was in kindergarten her family relocated to Tokyo, and her parents decided to enroll her in a *school for the deaf* that promotes a *bilingual/bicultural environment* with JSL and written Japanese. She continued at this school, making above average progress in all academic and social areas. When Megumi was 9 years old and in fourth grade her mother accepted a company job transfer to a position in the Canadian Pacific Northwest, and the family immigrated to Canada. The family wanted to enroll Megumi in a school for the deaf in their new location but struggled to understand the procedures for referral within the Canadian education system and had never been exposed to the *Individualized Education Program* (IEP) process in Japan. Therefore the professionals assisting them with the transition to the school for the deaf provided Japanese *interpreters* for the parents to make sure they understood all of the terminology utilized in paperwork and the IEP content and procedures as well as their role in the process as parents. In addition to an interpreter, the family was provided with a *cultural broker* (Ayantoye & Luckner, 2016; Cannon & Luckner, 2016). Information regarding community agencies that assist families that are recent immigrants was also provided.

Megumi's teachers at the school for the deaf realized that she would be utilizing four languages (JSL, written Japanese, *American Sign Language* [ASL], and written English) across two modalities (spoken and *sign language*) to acquire two new languages (ASL and English). A teacher for *English Language Learners* (ELLs) who works full-time at the school for the deaf will assist Megumi by working with her parents and teachers and by going in to Megumi's classes and providing one-on-one assistance as needed. Her ELL teacher and *teacher of the d/Deaf and hard of hearing* (TODHH) knew she would first need to begin by increasing her everyday conversational language in ASL, which draws on *basic interpersonal communicative skills* (BICS) within social settings (Cummins, 1979; see Pizzo, 2016, Table 18.1 for techniques). These skills can take six months to two years to acquire. Then the teachers worked on increasing her *cognitive/academic language proficiency* (CALP) in ASL, which requires more cognitively demanding language to complete academic tasks for school success and takes five to seven years to acquire (Collier, 1987; Cummins, 1979; Grosjean, 1982; Klesmer, 1994; Pizzo, 2016). Her acquisition of CALP concepts and vocabulary in ASL will then assist her in mapping L1 (JSL) and L3 (ASL) onto her L2 (Japanese) onto her L4 (English) via print to increase her English literacy skills.

Megumi's teachers first completed a language profile to determine which language is most developed (L1) and how they can use it to assist her in acquiring English and ASL (Pizzo, 2016). Multiple language samples (written and *through-the-air* transcriptions) across multiple settings (and multiple languages) were collected. The ELL teacher is fluent in Japanese and will assist Megumi's TODHHs in analyzing her written Japanese language samples. None of the teachers at the school are fluent in JSL, so determining Megumi's current language level isn't possible. Although collecting a language sample of her present level of ASL performance will provide baseline data to be used as a comparison for future progress in language acquisition. For example, interactions during recess time could be recorded between students to capture Megumi's understanding of ASL. Megumi's teachers will also use techniques to connect language and culture by using her cultural background to facilitate language experiences that allow her to learn new vocabulary and concepts (Pizzo, 2016; see Appendix C for instructional strategies related to language and literacy acquisition and development).

DISCUSSION QUESTIONS

1. What are some ideas for Megumi's teachers to facilitate language experiences and tie them to her home culture? What resources could they begin with to better understand the culture she comes from?

2. Develop a progress monitoring system that utilizes language samples to document Megumi's language acquisition. How often will samples be collected? From what settings? Which languages? How will you analyze them?
3. What activities could the TODHHs and the ELL teacher do with Megumi to increase her BICS and CALP?
4. What activities could the TODHH encourage the parents to do to assist Megumi in mapping Japanese print to English print?

ACTIVITIES

1. Synthesize purposes and steps of the IEP process using a visual organizer that could be shared with the parents so they understand the "big picture" and rationale for each procedure.
2. Find resources and informal assessments that will assist the TODHHs in documenting Megumi's language acquisition skills in her L1, L2, L3, and L4.
3. Create a lesson plan with ELL strategies and modify them for d/Dhh students who are multilingual. Identify two resources used to create this lesson plan.
4. Read the articles provided in additional resources (or others) and synthesize what is currently known about students who are d/Dhh multilingual learners. What theoretical frameworks support their instruction? What evidence-based and/or best practice strategies can teachers use to increase their language acquisition?

ADDITIONAL RESOURCES

Cannon, J. E., Guardino, C., & Gallimore, E. (2016). A new kind of heterogeneity: What we can learn from d/Deaf and hard of hearing multilingual learners. *American Annals of the Deaf, 161*(1), 8–16.

Pizzo, L. (2016). d/Deaf and hard of hearing multilingual learners: The development of communication and language. *American Annals of the Deaf, 161*(1), 17–32.

SUPPORTING DOCUMENTS

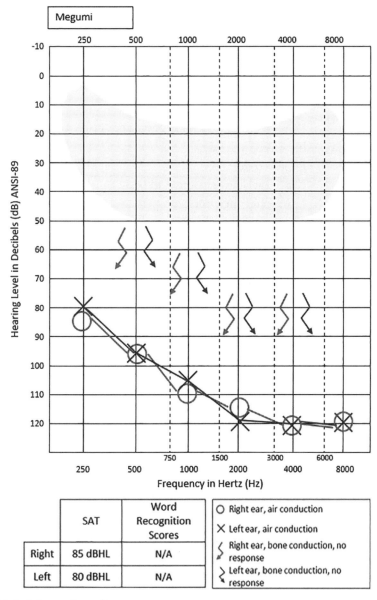

Figure 18.1. Megumi's audiogram.

Table 18.1. High Quality ASL Input Learning from Adult-Child Interactions.

Category	Characteristics
Language Accessibility and Joint Attention	Use of repetitive movements in storytelling
	Waiting until the children are looking at you before using language
	Attention-getting strategies
	Altered location of the sign to accommodate line of sight
	Using pointing as a replacement for a sign
	Increased cyclicity
	Increased duration
	Use of facial expressions and body language to demonstrate characters in a book
Attending to ASL as a separate language system from English and home language	Clearly articulated signing
	Lack of advanced grammatical structures
	Use of "lone signs"
	Drawing attention to the hands and formation of signs
	Use of fingerspelling to point out various word parts
	Attaching a fingerspelled word to a printed word
	Attaching the fingerspelled word to a sign
Shared Reading Strategies (Shared Reading Project; Schleper, 1996)	Deaf readers expect the child to become literate
	Deaf readers translate stories using ASL
	Deaf readers keep both languages visible (ASL and English)
	Deaf readers are not constrained by the text
	Deaf readers re-read stories on a storytelling to story reading continuum
	Deaf readers follow the child's lead
	Deaf readers make what is implied explicit
	Deaf readers adjust sign placement to fit the story
	Deaf readers adjust signing style to fit the story.
	Deaf readers connect concepts in the story to the real world
	Deaf readers use attention maintenance strategies
	Deaf readers use eye gaze to elicit participation
	Deaf readers engage in role-play to extend concepts
	Deaf readers use ASL variations to sign repetitive English phrases
	Deaf readers provide a positive and reinforcing environment

19

Susanna

Assistive Technology; Collaboration; Inclusion; Placement

Susanna, 9 years old, attends a regional day program for children who are *d/Deaf* or *hard of hearing* (d/Dhh), housed in a large suburban public school. This program serves children from many local school districts. Students are bussed to the elementary school where a team of *teachers of the d/Deaf and hard of hearing* (TODHH), *Speech Language Pathologists* (SLP), *educational interpreters*, and *paraprofessionals* serve children from kindergarten through fifth grade. Susanna has a *severe sensorineural hearing loss*. She is a *bimodal device user*, wearing a *hearing aid* at one ear, since age 8 months, and a *cochlear implant* (CI) on the other, which she received at age 2 years. Susanna spends the majority of her day in her general education third grade classroom, visiting a TODHH in the *resource* room for reading and language arts support 45 minutes daily. She also works with an SLP on language, *auditory habilitation* and *speech articulation* for 30 minutes twice a week in a *pull-out* one-on-one setting.

Susanna has many peer relationships and presents as an outgoing, energetic child. She struggles to read but is motivated to please her teacher. Susanna has yet to show independence and responsibility for her hearing devices. While she consistently wears the devices, she is not reliable at reporting if the battery fails or if the device is malfunctioning. When Susanna goes to the resource room, the TODHH routinely conducts a *Ling sounds* check prior to beginning instruction. However, sometimes Susanna doesn't go to the resource room until late afternoon, so less than ideal access to sound can occur. The classroom teacher does not have a plan in place to maintain devices nor does she view this as one of her primary responsibilities.

Susanna's family and educational team have primarily focused on supporting Susanna's spoken language development. Recently, Susanna has expressed interest in learning *sign language* because she has been interacting with peers in school who use sign to communicate. Susanna's parents have approached her *Individualized Education Program* (IEP) team to inquire about whether this is something that they could address in the IEP. The family has expressed interest in developing their *American Sign Language* (ASL), so they might introduce sign language to support Susanna's development as well. They have not yet had an opportunity to take formal instruction in signed language, but they enjoy borrowing Signing Times videos from the state resource lending library. Susanna seems to enjoy the videos, despite the fact that they may be juvenile for her, but after several months, she is not yet showing any real indication of comprehension or use of signs. The family admits the exposure to these videos has been inconsistent and limited thus far. The family has requested that Susanna be allowed to spend more time in the *self-contained* classroom setting so that she can use a classroom interpreter and learn more sign language.

The *case manager* and TODHH have tried to explain that Susanna will need formal sign language instruction, not just exposure to an interpreter, to develop competency in ASL. At this time, Susanna is making adequate progress on her IEP goals, and the TODHH is concerned that she could not substantiate the need for an interpreter. The case manager has called an upcoming IEP team meeting with the primary objective to discuss a significant revision to her *communication plan* (see Supporting Documents) and subsequent re-examination of her educational goals and services.

At the team meeting, Susanna's communication plan was reviewed. It was determined that a significant change in placement was not appropriate as Susanna's primary *mode of communication*, or the way she was to access instruction, remained unchanged. However, the team identified opportunities to include Susanna with *Deaf* peers who sign by having her attend her electives (e.g., art, music, physical education, etc.) with this group of learners. The TODHH also suggested Susanna participate in an after school ASL club to increase her opportunity to develop her ASL skills. The family felt satisfied with these changes and were pleased with how the IEP meeting addressed their concerns.

There have been many positive examples of collaboration in Susanna's educational experience. These include grade-level team meetings with the general education teacher and the TODHH. Her classroom teacher would send weekly emails to the TODHH, previewing content and general plans for the following week. The resource room TODHH would provide *push-in services* every other week to probe Susanna's generalization and maintenance of skills and collect data on her performance related to curriculum standards. Two challenges to collaboration was that there were no built-in systems for communication nor opportunities for joint planning between the teachers of the elective classes (e.g., art, music, PE) and the TODHH.

Discussion Questions

1. What are the examples of successful collaborations? How can other collaborations improve?

2. What types of *assistive technology* were used? Were there opportunities to use alternative technologies? Were these technologies managed and maintained

appropriately? What suggestions do you have for supporting the use of Susanna's hearing technology?

3. How does a communication plan impact a student's educational placement? How did the IEP team acknowledge the parent concerns regarding Susanna's communication and utilize the IEP process to satisfy those concerns?

ACTIVITIES

1. Many states have lending libraries to provide assistive technology and materials that are captioned or accessible for individuals with disabilities. Explore the resources available for families and educators from your state's lending library. Consider materials that would support students who are d/Dhh who utilize a variety of communication modalities.

2. Explore the website and discussion forums on The Radical Middle http://radicalmiddledhh.org/. Based on the information in Susanna's case study, do you recognize any "radically middle" ideas or attitudes amongst these professionals? How might these beliefs have altered Susanna's experience if they were practiced to a greater or lesser extent? Do you identify with the basic tenets of being "radically middle"? Why or why not?

3. Drawing from another case study or using information about a student you know, complete a communication plan form. Use guidance from Hands & Voices. http://www.handsandvoices.org/articles/education/law/complan_faq.htm

4. Create a list of questions a parent might ask as they evaluate what placement options are available and most appropriate for their child who is d/Dhh.

ADDITIONAL RESOURCES

Exploring Communication Choices http://successforkidswithhearingloss.com/communication-choices/

Communication Considerations http://www.handsandvoices.org/comcon/index.html

Supporting Documents

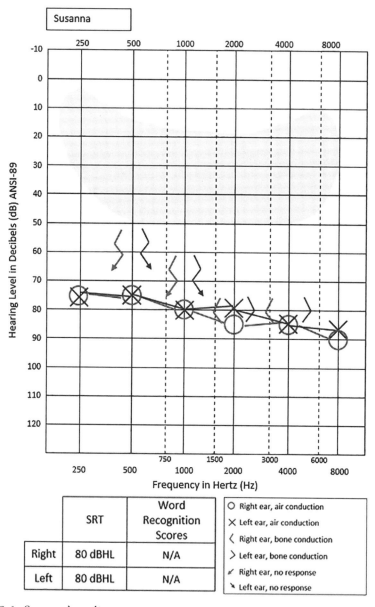

Figure 19.1. Susanna's audiogram.

Administrative Unit Name	Date

Susanna		
Legal Name of Child/Student	Child/Student ID	DOB

Communication Plan
for Child/Student who is Deaf/Hard of Hearing

The IEP team has considered each area listed below, and has not denied instructional opportunity based on the amount of the child's/student's residual hearing, the ability of the parent(s) to communicate, nor the child's/student's experience with other communication modes.

1. The child's/student's primary communication mode is one or more of the following:
   (check those that apply)

   ☑ Aural, oral, speech-based   ☐ English based manual or sign system

   ☐ American Sign Language

   Issues considered:

   Susanna's family communicates using listening and spoken language. They would like her to communicate in the same way so she can speak with her family and friends (in church, school, and the neighborhood)
   Action plan, if any:

2. The IEP team has considered the availability of deaf/hard of hearing adult role models and peer group of the child's/student's communication mode or language.
   Issues considered:

   Susanna would like to meet children who are deaf and also use listening and spoken language to communicate. She subscribes to "Hearing Our Way", a newsmagazine featuring children who wear cochlear implants and hearing aids. Her family is exploring summer camp options for
   Action plan, if any:

   Consider placement opportunities where Susanna might interact with other children who are deaf/hh, some of whom use listening and spoken language to communicate.

3. An explanation of all educational options provided by the administrative unit and available for the child/student has been provided.
   Issues considered:

   The Regional Deaf and Hard of Hearing Program has an elementary school program in the district where Susanna resides. She can attend a school that is not her home elementary school, but one where there are a range of educational options for children with hearing loss.
   Action plan, if any:

   Susanna will be educated in a mainstream classroom so she can learn and play with typically hearing peers who use listening and spoken language to communicate. This building placement will allow her to access the resource room for children with hearing loss.

4. Teachers, interpreters, and other specialists delivering the communication plan to the child/student must have demonstrated proficiency in, and be able to accommodate for, the child's/student's primary communication mode or language.
   Issues considered:

   The third grade teacher uses listening and spoken language in her classroom environment. The teacher of the deaf is available for additional support as needed.
   Action plan, if any:

5. The communication-accessible academic instruction, school services, and extracurricular activities the child/student will receive have been identified.
   Issues considered:

   When Susanna is wearing her hearing devices (a cochlear implant and a hearing aid), she is able to access spoken language. She may have difficulty in noisy environments.
   Action plan, if any:
   Consider acoustic modifications to classroom and learning environments to optimize listening conditions and decrease signal to noise ratio.

Must be reviewed at all IEP meetings for children/students with a hearing disability.

COMMUNICATION PLAN for
CHILD/STUDENT WHO IS DEAF/HARD OF HEARING
(Form 7b, Page 1 of 1)

1. The Plan must include a statement identifying the child's primary communication mode as one or more of the following: Aural, Oral, Speech-based, English Based Manual or Sign System, American Sign Language. The IEP team cannot deny instructional opportunity based on the amount of the child's residual hearing, the ability of the parent(s) to communicate, nor the child's experience with other communication modes [ECEA Section 4.02(4)(k)(I)].

When discussing these issues, the following questions may be helpful to clarify the child's needs: When considering the child's primary communication mode, is there just one? Does the child use a combination of modes? What mode do the parents use with their child? What mode does the child use to communicate with his/her friends?

2. The Plan must include a statement documenting that an explanation was given of all educational options provided by the school district and available to the child [ECEA Section 4.02(4)(k)(ii)].

When considering all educational options, are the options available in your school district? What about statewide options including the Colorado School for the Deaf & the Blind, the Magnet School for the Deaf in Denver and open enrollment in other schools or districts? Encourage the family to check out the **Colorado Program Directory for Students who are Deaf or Hard of Hearing** and the **Resource Guide** if they are interested in pursuing those kinds of options for their child. These resources will also prove helpful in locating peers and adult role models.

3. The Plan must include a statement documenting that the IEP team, in addressing the child's needs, considered the availability of Deaf and Hard of Hearing role models and a Deaf/Hard of Hearing peer group of the child's communication mode or language [ECEA 4.01 (4)(k)(iii).

Because of the low incidence of a hearing disability, many students who are Deaf or Hard of Hearing find themselves without contact with other Deaf/Hard of Hearing children. Combine that with the fact that 95% of these children are born into families with normal hearing, and you have the potential for serious isolation. How about some time during the week to "chat" on-line with other Deaf/Hard of Hearing kids? Does the family know about the various regional activities, which occur during the year for Deaf/Hard of Hearing children? Explore all known opportunities.

4. The Plan must include a statement that the teachers, interpreters, and other specialists delivering the Communication Plan to the student must have demonstrated proficiency in, and be able to accommodate for, the child's primary communication mode or language [ECEA 4.02 (4)(k)(iv)].

Discuss the communication proficiency of the child/student's service providers and write a statement of the needs of the staff. Is training/inservice/mentoring a possibility? Is there an accommodation not being utilized? Review the IEP Checklist: Recommended Accommodations and Modifications that is available through CDE and addresses frequent accommodations used with children with a hearing loss.

5.The Plan must include a statement of the communication-accessible academic instruction, school services, and extracurricular activities that the student will receive [ECEA 4.02(4)(k)(v)].

These questions may help to clarify the student's needs: Is the student enjoying full access to academic instruction and services? To extra-curricular activities? The IEP checklist for Recommended Accommodations and Modifications (for students with a hearing loss) may be a useful resource for this discussion. Are TTY's, captioned television, interpreters for field trips, etc. being utilized?

Figure 19.2. Susanna's communication plan. From www.handsandvoices.org/pdf/ communication_plan.pdf

Administrative Unit Name	Date

Legal Name of Child/Student	Child/Student ID	DOB

Communication Plan
for Child/Student who is Deaf/Hard of Hearing

The IEP team has considered each area listed below, and has not denied instructional opportunity based on the amount of the child's/student's residual hearing, the ability of the parent(s) to communicate, nor the child's/student's experience with other communication modes.

1. The child's/student's primary communication mode is one or more of the following:
    (check those that apply)

    ☐   Aural, oral, speech-based   ☐   English based manual or sign system

    ☐   American Sign Language

    Issues considered:

    Action plan, if any:

2. The IEP team has considered the availability of deaf/hard of hearing adult role models and peer group of the child's/student's communication mode or language.
    Issues considered:

    Action plan, if any:

3. An explanation of all educational options provided by the administrative unit and available for the child/student has been provided.
    Issues considered:

    Action plan, if any:

4. Teachers, interpreters, and other specialists delivering the communication plan to the child/student must have demonstrated proficiency in, and be able to accommodate for, the child's/student's primary communication mode or language.
    Issues considered:

    Action plan, if any:

5. The communication-accessible academic instruction, school services, and extracurricular activities the child/student will receive have been identified.
    Issues considered:

    Action plan, if any:

Must be reviewed at all IEP meetings for children/students with a hearing disability.

COMMUNICATION PLAN for
CHILD/STUDENT WHO IS DEAF/HARD OF HEARING
(Form 7b, Page 1 of 1)

1. The Plan must include a statement identifying the child's primary communication mode as one or more of the following: Aural, Oral, Speech-based, English Based Manual or Sign System, American Sign Language. The IEP team cannot deny instructional opportunity based on the amount of the child's residual hearing, the ability of the parent(s) to communicate, nor the child's experience with other communication modes [ECEA Section 4.02(4)(k)(I)].

When discussing these issues, the following questions may be helpful to clarify the child's needs: When considering the child's primary communication mode, is there just one? Does the child use a combination of modes? What mode do the parents use with their child? What mode does the child use to communicate with his/her friends?

2. The Plan must include a statement documenting that an explanation was given of all educational options provided by the school district and available to the child [ECEA Section 4.02(4)(k)(ii).

When considering all educational options, are the options available in your school district? What about statewide options including the Colorado School for the Deaf & the Blind, the Magnet School for the Deaf in Denver and open enrollment in other schools or districts? Encourage the family to check out the **Colorado Program Directory for Students who are Deaf or Hard of Hearing** and the **Resource Guide** if they are interested in pursuing those kinds of options for their child. These resources will also prove helpful in locating peers and adult role models.

3. The Plan must include a statement documenting that the IEP team, in addressing the child's needs, considered the availability of Deaf and Hard of Hearing role models and a Deaf/Hard of Hearing peer group of the child's communication mode or language [ECEA 4.01 (4)(k)(iii).

Because of the low incidence of a hearing disability, many students who are Deaf or Hard of Hearing find themselves without contact with other Deaf/Hard of Hearing children. Combine that with the fact that 95% of these children are born into families with normal hearing, and you have the potential for serious isolation. How about some time during the week to "chat" on-line with other Deaf/Hard of Hearing kids? Does the family know about the various regional activities, which occur during the year for Deaf/Hard of Hearing children? Explore all known opportunities.

4. The Plan must include a statement that the teachers, interpreters, and other specialists delivering the Communication Plan to the student must have demonstrated proficiency in, and be able to accommodate for, the child's primary communication mode or language [ECEA 4.02 (4)(k)(iv)].

Discuss the communication proficiency of the child/student's service providers and write a statement of the needs of the staff. Is training/inservice/mentoring a possibility? Is there an accommodation not being utilized? Review the IEP Checklist: Recommended Accommodations and Modifications that is available through CDE and addresses frequent accommodations used with children with a hearing loss.

5.The Plan must include a statement of the communication-accessible academic instruction, school services, and extracurricular activities that the student will receive [ECEA 4.02(4)(k)(v)].

These questions may help to clarify the student's needs: Is the student enjoying full access to academic instruction and services? To extra-curricular activities? The IEP checklist for Recommended Accommodations and Modifications (for students with a hearing loss) may be a useful resource for this discussion. Are TTY's, captioned television, interpreters for field trips, etc. being utilized?

Legal Name of Student	State Student ID (SASID)	Date of Birth	Date

COMMUNICATION PLAN FOR STUDENT WHO IS DEAF/HARD OF HEARING OR DEAF-BLIND

The IEP team has considered each area listed below, and has not denied instructional opportunity based on the amount of the child's/student's residual hearing, the ability of the parent(s) to communicate, nor the child's/student's experience with other communication modes. To the extent appropriate, the input about this child's/student's communication and related needs as suggested from adults who are deaf/hard of hearing has been considered. 300.324(a)(2)(IV) 4.03(6)(A)

1. **Language and Communication**
1. **a.** The child's/student's **primary language** is one or more of the following.
   Check all that apply.

Receptive   **Expressive**

☐   ☐   English
☐   ☐   Native language (ASL, Spanish etc), specify _____
☐   ☐   Combination of several languages
☐   ☐   Minimal language skills; no formal primary language

Describe:

Action Plan, if any:

1. **b.** The child's/student's **primary communication mode** is one or more of the following. Supports 300.116(e).
   Check all that apply and if more than one applies, explain.

Receptive:

☐ Auditory   ☐ Signing Exact English/Signed English
☐ Speechreading   ☐ Conceptual signs (Pidgin Signed English or Conceptually
☐ Fingerspelling   Accurate Signed English)
☐ Tactile/objects
☐ Home signs   ☐ American Sign Language
☐ Other, please explain _____   ☐ Cued Speech/Cued English
                                              ☐ Gestures
                                              ☐ Picture symbols/pictures/photographs

Expressive:

☐ Spoken language   ☐ Signing Exact English/Signed English
☐ Conceptual signs (Pidgin Signed English   ☐ Gestures
   or Conceptually Accurate Signed English)
☐ Tactile/objects   ☐ American Sign Language
☐ Cued Speech/Cued English   ☐ Fingerspelling
                                              ☐ Home signs
                                              ☐ Pictures symbols/pictures/photographs
                                              ☐ Other, please explain _____

Explanation for multiple modes of communication, if necessary:

1/16/08

Legal Name of Student	State Student ID (SASID)	Date of Birth	Date

1. c. What supports are needed to increase the proficiency of parents and family members in communicating with the child/student? Parent Counseling Training 300.34(8)(i) and (iii)

Issues considered:

Action Plan, if any:

2. Describe the child's/student's need for deaf/hard of hearing adult role models and peer groups in sufficient numbers of the child's/student/s communication mode or language. Document who on the team will be responsible for arranging for adult role model connections and opportunities to interact with peers. (Section 3. 22-20-108 CRS II) 300.116

Placement Determination
Opportunities considered: ECEA proposed 4.03(6)(a)(iii)

Action Plan, if any:

3. An explanation of all educational options provided by the administrative unit and available for thechild/student has been given. Placement determination 300.115 and 300.116

Placements explained:

Describe how the placement options impact the child's communication access and educational progress:

4. Teachers, interpreters, and other specialists delivering the communication plan to the child/student must have demonstrated proficiency in, and be able to accommodate for, the child's/student's primary communication mode or language. ECEA 3.04(1)(f)

Considerations:

Action Plan, if any:

5. The communication-accessible academic instruction, school services, and extracurricular activities the child/student will receive have been identified. The team will consider the entire school day, daily transition times, and what the child/student needs for full communication access in all activities.
Considerations 300.324(a)(2)(iv) Communication plan; 300.107 Non-academic settings. 300.101 FAPE:

Action Plan, if any:

1/16/08

Figure 19.3. A blank communication plan.

20
Rosie

KEY TOPICS

Assessment; Collaboration; Content Area Instruction; Deaf with a Disability; Language Development; Literacy

Rosie is a 9-year-old third grader who was diagnosed with congenital *Cytomegalovirus* (CMV) in the *Neonatal Intensive Care Unit* (NICU) due to concerns of microcephaly (e.g., smaller than typical head size) and low birth weight. The medical team explained that CMV can cause *mild* to *profound hearing loss* as well as health concerns, including *vision loss, intellectual disability*, fine and gross motor delays, and/or seizures. Rosie was identified with a *mild sensorineural hearing level* shortly after birth.

As Rosie developed, she displayed delays in language that were inconsistent with her level of hearing and the extensive support from her parents and *early intervention providers* (EIs). Her parents and EIs were concerned and confused. Full evaluation and work-up by the *audiologist* ruled out *Auditory Neuropathy Spectrum Disorder* (ANSD) following *Otoacoustic Emissions* (OAE) and *auditory brainstem response* (ABR) testing. *Hearing aids* were an appropriate fit for her stable *mild hearing level*. Her *audiologist* reported consistent hearing aid use based on the *data logging* from the hearing aids. Her EI observed that Rosie's parents frequently talked to her and initiated conversations. Rosie did not consistently engage in *turn-taking* and was primarily pointing and using gestures to communicate. She had limited *expressive language* and was not consistently responding to her name. Rosie's behaviors prompted her EI to recommend that the family pursue an evaluation from a *Developmental Behavioral Pediatrician* (DBP). The evaluation determined that Rosie's lack of eye contact and delayed language development was not likely due to *Autism Spectrum Disorder* (ASD).

Rosie transitioned from an *Individualized Family Service Plan* (IFSP) to an *Individualized Education Program* (IEP) when she turned 3 years old. She qualified for early childhood special education services due to her hearing level and limited expressive language skills. From the ages of 3 to 5 years old, Rosie attended preschool in an early childhood special education classroom. The classroom teacher had early childhood special education certification and consulted with an itinerant *teacher of the d/Deaf and hard of hearing* (TODHH) on a regular basis to ensure that Rosie's accommodations were met. When Rosie transitioned to full-day kindergarten, she was placed in a general education classroom with her same-age peers. The *itinerant* TODHH worked with her early childhood educator in preschool and continued to provide *consultative services*. Rosie's IEP also indicated services from a *Speech Language Pathologist* (SLP) for 100 minutes/week to support her language acquisition.

Just after Rosie's sixth birthday, she began experiencing frequent petit mal seizures (also called absence seizures). These seizures often caused brief periods of loss of consciousness. Following the seizures, Rosie's teacher reported that she appeared inattentive and would send Rosie to the nurse's office to rest. Rosie required repeated visits to the physician to check her medical status, which resulted in frequent absences from school and missed instructional time. In spite of these health concerns, Rosie was highly motivated to participate in classroom activities on days she was present and felt well. Yet, due to her frequent absences, it was rare that she received the full instructional time each week.

In first and second grade, because Rosie's learning profile was unique, her teachers and SLP used data to determine how she learned best. They used *summative assessment* scores from standardized assessments to evaluate Rosie's progress over time as compared to her typical peers as well as overall growth or challenges in particular areas. After identifying particular target areas to create goals and objectives, they used *formative assessments* to collect data for a 12-week time period, adjusting instruction based on Rosie's progress. They used checklists and charts to measure Rosie's ability to acquire academic skills (e.g., letter-sound correspondences), attention and memory skills (e.g., attending to a book in a small group setting and answering questions), behavior and self-regulation skills (e.g., teacher redirection strategies), and language (e.g., vocabulary acquisition). The teachers used a combination of *summative* and *formative assessments* to plan their weekly lessons.

For example, Rosie was two *standard deviations* behind her same-age peers in receptive vocabulary based on her *standard score* of 70 on the *Peabody Picture Vocabulary Test-4* (PPVT-4; see Appendix B). In second grade her teacher and SLP, upon reviewing the school to home communication journals, noticed that Rosie remembered words better when her mom did activities with her using the same book at home. Her teachers collected data using a teacher-made targeted vocabulary checklist from instructional materials to measure her proficiency weekly. After analyzing data collected across several weeks, Rosie's teachers were able to show that Rosie was, on average, able to use three more words per week with supplemental instruction. They implemented a take-home backpack literacy program. With these materials, Rosie heard and interacted with the same books she saw in class repetitively through video, digital books, and home activities. Rosie's vocabulary acquisition rate increased; however, she still was unable to make more than a year's progress in a year's time. Her proficiency in vocabulary remained lower than average (see Appendix C for instructional strategies related to language and literacy acquisition and development).

In preparing for her third grade year, the *IEP team* met to consider Rosie's progress. Her parents agreed with the team's recommendation to have Rosie evaluated by a *school psychologist*. This psycho-educational evaluation will help the team determine if her challenges stem from her CMV, mild hearing level, or complex medical needs.

DISCUSSION QUESTIONS

1. What is the difference between a formative and summative assessment? What is the benefit of each assessment type? Using formative and summative assessments, how do educators measure growth and proficiency for academics and language?
2. Discuss the meaning of an "average" score on a standardized assessment. What does a standard score that is two standard deviations below the mean imply? How would this performance level affect Rosie's participation in her current inclusion setting? In contrast, what does a standard score two standard deviations above the mean imply? What kind of services might a student at this performance level receive?
3. What would be the benefit of changing the TODHH's current role from consultative services to provision of direct instruction to support Rosie's language development?

ACTIVITIES

1. Create a lesson plan that includes a formative assessment. Include information on how to measure progress and criteria for mastery.
2. Create a learning profile for Rosie that will go to her third grade teacher. What questions do you still have about Rosie's academic performance and potential annual goals?
3. Read and summarize two peer-reviewed articles on how lack of vocabulary knowledge impacts language acquisition and literacy comprehension. From that review and summary create a visual organizer that illustrates the reciprocal relationships between vocabulary and literacy.
4. To encourage the home–school literacy connection Rosie's teachers implemented a take-home backpack literacy program. Explore online resources and ideas for a similar program and outline an action plan for implementation with students who are d/Dhh.
5. Research different types of vocabulary resources and list benefits of each resource for a student who is d/Dhh.

ADDITIONAL RESOURCES

Centers for Disease Control and Prevention https://www.cdc.gov/cmv/

SUPPORTING DOCUMENT

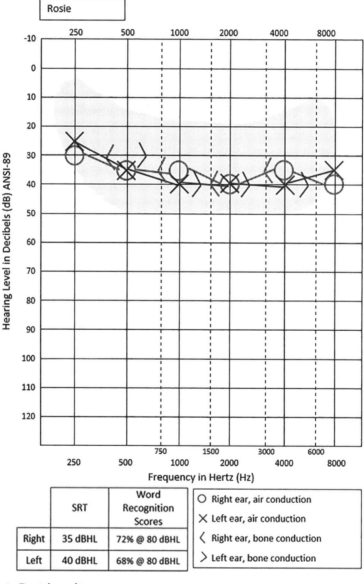

Figure 20.1. Rosie's audiogram.

21
Jayden

Accommodations; Assessment; Deaf of Deaf; Deaf with a Disability; IEP/IFSP/504; Placement; Psychosocial

Jayden is 10 years old and in the fifth grade. He was born *profoundly deaf*, due to a *genetic trait* inherited by both of his parents who are also profoundly deaf. The family uses *American Sign Language* (ASL) to communicate within the home. Jayden has attended the residential *school for the deaf* from the age of 5 and has performed at the top of the class. He is currently reading and writing at the seventh grade level. At the end of first grade, Jayden's parents consented to have his *IQ* tested to see if he was qualified as *gifted and talented* (GT). The *school psychologist* tested Jayden across three domains to determine his GT status: intellectual, academic, and creative. The psychologist used the *Wechsler Intelligence Scale for Children* (WISC-IV; Wechsler et al., 2003) to test Jayden's intellect and academic levels. He scored 136, which is two *standard deviations* above the mean. Jayden was tested using the *Torrance Tests of Creative Thinking* (Torrance, E.P., 1984) as well as teacher and parent observational reports to determine his creativity and motivation to learn in the classroom. The results of this testing showed Jayden performed above the mean and within the qualifying range for children who are GT. Although Jayden qualified as GT, he struggled emotionally.

Jayden often had difficulty making friends and interacting with other children. During recess or free play, he was easily frustrated and would break down in tears when the game didn't go his way. In the classroom, when doing small group or paired work, Jayden would argue with his classmates when they didn't agree with his suggestions or answers. Jayden qualified for special educational services at the residential school, not because of his GT but rather because his *emotional and behavioral challenges*. Jayden's worked with the school counselor one hour a week to address his challenges.

Because the residential school didn't have a GT program, once a week Jayden was transported to the local elementary school to attend a two-hour class for children who were GT. This elementary school was the *magnet program* for children who are GT; it also provided programming for GT children who attended other local public schools without GT support to fulfill the requirements of their *educational plan* (EP). An EP is a plan for students who are GT without a disability. However, because Jayden has *emotional and behavioral challenges*, Jayden has an IEP that covers both his GT and psychosocial goals. This model seemed to work throughout Jayden's elementary school years.

Now that Jayden is about to enter the sixth grade, a *transition meeting* must be held to determine his middle school placement. Jayden has discussed with his parents the possibility of leaving the residential school to attend the local public middle school where Jayden would be fully included in the general education classrooms with the support of an *educational interpreter*. There are several issues and details to be considered prior to making this decision.

DISCUSSION QUESTIONS

1. What *genetic traits* are linked to deafness?
2. Prior to the transition meeting, what would you suggest the parents do to prepare Jayden? What information (e.g., quality of interpreters, visit school sites) can you gather to help the family in making their decision?
3. What *accommodations* would the transition team include in his IEP to ensure Jayden's success if he decides to move to a public school setting?
4. How might being GT affect Jayden's *social identities* within the hearing and deaf communities? How might Jayden's emotional and behavioral challenges affect his social identity within the hearing and deaf communities?
5. How could the *itinerant* teacher, GT teacher, and general education teacher work together to ensure Jayden is successful in an *inclusive* setting?

ACTIVITIES

1. What does it mean to fall a standard deviation below the mean? Referring to this case study, what does it mean to fall two standard deviations above the mean? Draw a *bell curve* and explain what it means to deviate from the mean. Highlight where Jayden falls.
2. What are some of the social emotional implications of a student who attends a public school with the full-time support of an interpreter? Support your answer with three citations of research from a peer-reviewed journal. Create an annotated bibliography that summarizes your references.
3. Find two online resources to support teaching students who are GT in an inclusive classroom. Based on your resources, develop a lesson plan for students who are GT. How does this lesson plan differ from a lesson for typically developing students?

4. Is it common for students who are GT to have psychosocial challenges? Find two online resources as well as two peer-reviewed resources that support your answer. Make sure to include a reference list in APA format for your four resources.

5. Look up your state plus one additional state's definition, identification policy, and special programs designated for student who are GT. Describe how these state laws and regulations converge and diverge.

6. Form groups of three to four students. Use the *Behavior Intervention Plan* (BIP) to brainstorm a plan to help Jayden work on his emotional and behavioral challenges. The information given in the case study narrative will not be enough to complete the form. Your group must create information to address the problem areas with a BIP.

ADDITIONAL RESOURCES

Centers for Disease Control and Prevention, A Parent's Guide to Genetics & Hearing Losshttps://www.cdc.gov/ncbddd/hearingloss/freematerials/parentsguide508.pdf

Gifted and Talented advanced learning site developed by Stanford University https://giftedandtalented.com/

National Society for the Gifted and Talented. http://www.nsgt.org/

McIlroy, G., & Storbeck, C. (2011). Development of deaf identity: An ethnographic study. *Journal of Deaf Studies and Deaf Education, 16*(4), 494–511. doi: 10.1093/deafed/enr017

Supporting the Emotional Needs of the Gifted (SENG). http://sengifted.org/

Supporting Documents

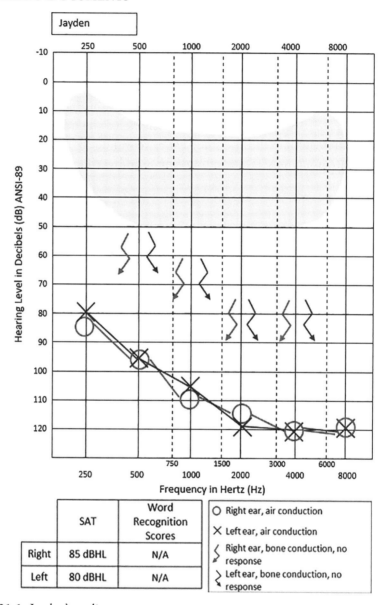

Figure 21.1. Jayden's audiogram.

Behavior Intervention Plan

Student Name: _____ Grade:_____ DOB:_____

Functional Behavior Assessment

If this is a Special Education Behavior Plan, Copy and Paste this information directly into the IIEP. You may also upload this Word file as an attachment to the IEP, in addition to copying into the IEP.

Behaviors of Concern:

Participants:

1. What is the specific behavior of concern and how does it interfere with learning? (list only 1 behavior)
2. When, where, and with whom does the behavior occur? Be specific.
3. How often does the behavior occur, and how long does it last?
4. What things seem to trigger the behavior?
5. What usually happens when this behavior occurs; reactions of peers/adults, consequences of the behavior?

Academic accommodations, environmental modifications, positive reinforcement and/or discipline:

6. What interventions have NOT been effective?
7. What interventions have helped improve behavior?
8. In what situations does the student behave most appropriately?
9. What reinforcers would the student prefer to support compliance in school?

Functions of Behavior:

1. Identify the predominant purpose/function the problem behavior appears to serve for the student:
   Choose One:
   To gain
   To avoid
   To communicate
   Other
2. Assess the student in these areas: (Needs Instruction, Needs Support to Use, Performs Adequately)
   - Demonstrates appropriate coping responses
   - Able to use self-control
   - Makes and keeps friends at school
   - Has formed an appropriate relationship with one or more school staff
   - Able to function adequately in classroom setting (can concentrate, retain information, satisfactory attendance, etc.)

Conference Date: _____   2/2/18

Student Name: _____ SBCSC ID#: _____ STN#: _____

Positive Strategies/Instructional Experiences:

1. Replacement Behavior:

2. Successive Teaching Steps: (Include WHO will teach, WHERE and HOW OFTEN)

3. Positive Programming and Reinforcement Strategies:

4. Redirection and De-escalation Strategies:

5. Environmental Modifications:

6. Progress Monitoring:

7. Consequences: Student will follow the Student Code of Conduct unless otherwise noted. You may want to consider the following:

8. Crisis Management Plan:

Conference Date: _____   2/2/18

Figure 21.2. Behavior Intervention Plan.

Student: _____
DOB: _____ **Age:** _____ **Grade:** _____ **Gender:** _____

| **Accommodations:** |

Please record all accommodations selected for state assessment purposes and additional accommodations if appropriate:
(All accommodations selected for assessment purposes must be provided on a regular basis.)

_____
_____
_____
_____
_____
_____
_____

| **Services and other Provisions:** |

Transition Services (if necessary)

Description	By Whom	To Support	Completion Date

(Transition IEP only) Please document the written information presented to the parent and student regarding available adult services provided through state and local agencies and other organizations to facilitate student movement from the public agency to adult life:

_____
_____
_____
_____

Special Education Services

Description	Initiation (date)	Frequency	Length (time)	Duration (date)	Location	To Support

Related Services

Description	Initiation (date)	Frequency	Length (time)	Duration (date)	Location	To Support

Student:				
DOB:		Age:	Grade:	Gender:

Transportation:

If the student's transit time or needs are different from that of non-disabled peers, please describe and justify these needs. Please, record as a related service if additional provisions are necessary.

_____
_____
_____
_____

Health Plan:

Please describe any medical conditions requiring school health or nurse services. The description should include frequency, and the provider of this service. Be sure to record any related services appropriately.

_____
_____
_____
_____
_____

Does this student require an Emergency Evacuation Plan?
__Yes __No

Accessible Materials:

If this student requires any instructional materials provided in an accessible format, please describe the environments, tasks, tools, and services related to their provision:

_____
_____
_____
_____

Assistive Technology:

Please describe this student's assistive technology needs:

_____
_____
_____
_____

Extended School Year:

Please record extended school year services required in order to provide a free and appropriate education for this student: (Record ESY services under special education and related services if needed.)

_____
_____
_____

Technical Assistance:

Please document the types of supports necessary to provide public agency personnel with the knowledge and skills necessary to implement the student's individualized education program and the general intent of the supports:

_____
_____
_____
_____

Program Modifications:

Please describe any program modifications needed to enable the student to advance appropriately toward attaining the annual goals, be involved in and make progress in the general education curriculum, participate in extracurricular and other nonacademic activities or be educated or participate with other students with disabilities and non-disabled students.

_____
_____
_____
_____

Student:				
DOB:		Age:	Grade:	Gender:

Progress Reporting:
Please describe when periodic reports on the progress the student is making toward meeting the annual goals will be provided:

Least Restrictive Environment and Program:

School of Legal Settlement: _____
School of Service: _____
Additional information regarding school of service:

(For Transition IEPs) Course of Study focused on improving academic and functional achievement of the student in order to support the attainment of post-secondary goals:

LRE Placement Category based Federal Program Types:

School Age (6-21) - Student **will be** Age 6+ as of next December 1st	
50	Regular class 80% or more (In a regular classroom for 80% or more of the day)
51	Resource Room (In a regular class for 40% to 79% of the day)
52	Separate Class (In a regular class for less than 40% of the day)
53	Separate day school facility
54	Residential Facility
55	Correctional Facility
56	Parentally placed in private school
57	Homebound/hospital

Preschool Age (3-5) - Student **will not** be 6+ as of the next December 1st	
30	Regular Early Childhood class 80% of the time
31	Regular Early Childhood 40-79% of the time
32	Regular Early Childhood 40% or less of the time
33	Separate Class
34	Separate School
35	Residential Facility
36	Service Provider Location
37	Home

Additional Descriptors:

Any potentially harmful effects of the services on the student or on the quality of services needed:

Reasons for placement determination including reasons for rejecting other options:

Student: _____
DOB: _____ Age: _____ Grade: _____ Gender: _____

Considerations:

Please consider the student's participation in general education and record any supplementary aids and services that are determined by the case conference committee to be appropriate and necessary in order to afford the student equal opportunity for participation with non-disabled students.

Student will be able to participate in all educational programs and activities available to non-disabled students.
___ Yes ___ No
(If No, please state the exceptions and describe the reasoning for these exceptions:

_____
_____
_____
_____

Student will be able to participate in all non-educational and extracurricular activities available to non-disabled students.
___ Yes ___ No
(If No, please state the exceptions and describe the reasoning for these exceptions:

_____
_____
_____
_____

Student will participate in the general physical education program available to non-disabled students.
___ Yes ___ No
(If No, please state the exceptions and describe the reasoning for these exceptions:

_____
_____
_____
_____

Student will be educated in the school he or she would attend if not disabled.
___ Yes ___ No
(If No, please state the exceptions and describe the reasoning for these exceptions:

_____
_____
_____
_____

The length of the instructional day will be the same as the instructional day for non-disabled peers.
___ Yes ___ No
(If No, please state the exceptions and describe the reasoning for these exceptions:

_____
_____
_____
_____

Participants:

The following individuals participated in the case conference committee meeting. Those individuals identified as Teacher of Record, General Education Teacher, Public Agency Rep and Instructional Strategist attended the entire meeting unless parental excusal was obtained before the meeting.

Position	Name	Additional Title
_____	_____	_____
_____	_____	_____
_____	_____	_____

Page **12** of **13**

Figure 21.3. IEP Accommodations and Transition. From www.sped.sbcsc.k12.in.us/ PDF%20Files/Blank%20Transition%20IEP.pdf

22
Tabesh

Key Topics

Assessment; Assistive Technology; Collaboration; Content Area Instruction; Inclusion; Language Development; Multilingual; Psychosocial

Tabesh is an 11-year-old male currently in fifth grade. He and his family are refugees from Afghanistan, where his father was killed when Tabesh was 2 years old. At that time, Tabesh had not started talking yet, so his mother suspected he might have hearing issues and took him to a hospital clinic for testing. Results indicated a *moderate* to *severe sensorineural hearing level*. Tabesh's mother speaks Dari at home, uses *listening and spoken language* (LSL) to communicate with him, and he utilizes *binaural digital hearing aids*.

By the time Tabesh was 3 years old his mother applied for emigration to Canada so he would have more educational options than were available in the refugee camp where they were living in Afghanistan. After a wait of nearly four years, Tabesh and his two brothers, one older and one younger, immigrated to Toronto, Canada, with their mother when he was 7 years old. Tabesh was then able to begin consistent schooling in a kindergarten *small group resource classroom* for *d/Deaf* and *hard of hearing* (d/Dhh) students in a neighborhood public school with a *teacher of the d/Deaf and hard of hearing* (TODHH).

His *Individual Education Program* (IEP) *team* struggled to assess his *first language* (L1; Dari) to determine his foundation for acquiring a *second language* (L2; English), as no one in the school district knew Dari and the system did not have access to assessments in the family's *home language*. By second grade Tabesh had acquired *basic interpersonal communicative skills* (BICS; Cummins, 2000) in English to use within social settings, but he continued to struggle with *cognitive/academic language proficiency* (CALP; Cummins, 2000). From second through fourth grade Tabesh increased his BICS and CALP and made significant progress in his resource setting. At the end of fourth grade his IEP team completed the *Placement and Readiness Checklists (PARC): General Education Inclusion Readiness Checklist* (Johnson, 2011). Based on the results, his progress, and discussions among the team, it was determined that Tabesh would transition to a general education classroom for fifth grade science, math, and social studies and with his TODHH in the resource classroom for his daily language arts and reading time to increase his language and vocabulary skills.

Tabesh's public elementary school, along with many other regions on Canada (McIntosh et al., 2011), implemented an evidence-based assessment and *intervention* framework, often referred to as *Response to Intervention* (RTI; framework of a service delivery model and with eligibility decision-making in place of traditional models of assessment; McIntosh et al., 2011). This service delivery model pinpointed areas where he and other students with general and special needs in his science, math, and social studies classrooms needed supplemental instruction (see Appendix C for instructional strategies related to language and literacy acquisition and development). Screening and ongoing school-wide assessments were used by the educational team (i.e., TODHH, general education teacher, *school psychologist, educational assistants*) to make data-based decisions and monitor his progress in his new setting. Encompassing the foundations of *Universal Design for Learning* (UDL; design of school buildings, infrastructure, curriculum, personnel, and classroom environments to provide accessibility to the most diverse possible range of learners; Rose & Gravel, 2010), RTI is a proactive approach to assessment and intervention at multiple levels (or tiers).

In his science, math, and social studies classes, Tabesh's teachers used tier 1 interventions (i.e., everyone receives the same instruction and core curriculum) utilizing *accommodations* (e.g., *preferential seating*, *DM/FM system*, pre-teaching vocabulary, visuals to connect concepts; Luckner & Pierce, 2013). When the educational team met for the first time in Tabesh's fifth grade year (they met three times per year to review student progress), his progress on vocabulary and comprehension of core concepts in science and social studies was minimal and stagnated for two weeks. The team determined he needed further assistance and should receive targeted, intense instruction with tier 2 interventions (i.e., explicit vocabulary instruction, *pre/re-teaching vocabulary* and core concepts, and building background knowledge of core concepts; Luckner & Pierce, 2013). The TODHH would work closely with his general education teacher to provide this intervention to not only Tabesh but also other students in his class who were struggling with similar issues. Bi-weekly monitoring of scores on curriculum-based measurements (i.e., content-based vocabulary checklist) and data collected from language samples (i.e., frequency count and correct use of targeted vocabulary) documented Tabesh's increase in his expressive and receptive knowledge. Considering his progress, the team decided to continue with the tier 2 interventions and that individualized tier 3 interventions would not be necessary for Tabesh at this time. They will continue to review his progress bi-weekly and determine the most effective delivery model for Tabesh's academic success in this inclusive environment.

However, the team also discussed Tabesh's social-emotional development and his general education teacher noted his anxiety in the classroom (e.g., it is overwhelming for him to follow some conversations and activities). They decided to begin including activities that will increase his confidence (e.g., list of scenarios from the general education setting for the TODHH to role-play with him in the resource setting), and he will be assigned a "buddy" in the general education classroom that he could check in with if he misses information in class. Both these activities will scaffold his *self-advocacy* skills to increase his ability to let his teacher and his classmates know when he needs further clarification in the general education setting. To address his anxiety, the school counselor will observe him in class and meet with him weekly for two months.

The TODHH also investigated avenues for increasing Tabesh's *audiological access* in order to document if this is related to his stress level in the classroom. The TODHH will discuss with the educational team the importance of consistent use of his FM/DM system by him, his classmates, and his teachers and refer Tabesh to an *audiologist* for his annual testing because it has been a year and half since his last visit. Inconsistent visits had been an ongoing issue for Tabesh and his family because his mother is working full-time and the family does not have a vehicle. The team will monitor the benefits of these supports to decrease stressors and increase language acquisition.

Discussion Questions

1. BICS can take one to two years to develop, and CALP can take five to seven years to develop during second language acquisition (Cummins, 2000). How do these time frames align with Tabesh's language acquisition journey? Why is it vital that all members of the educational team understand these dual language acquisition concepts?
2. How can data collected in an RTI framework be used to write and determine progress on IEP goals and objectives?
3. How will the team's suggested strategies and activities decrease Tabesh's anxiety in the classroom? How might the role-play assist Tabesh in reducing anxiety and increasing language acquisition at the same time?
4. How are UDL concepts incorporated into the RTI framework?

Activities

1. Investigate RTI in your school district and what tools are available for collecting and analyzing data to assist an IEP team in instructional planning, instructional implementation, and progress monitoring.

2. Two examples of self-advocacy activities were identified that Tabesh's teachers could potentially utilize to help him reduce anxiety and increase confidence in the classroom. Provide one to two additional strategies that Tabesh's team could use and include citations of your references and links to resources.

3. Conduct a literature review of two to three articles on dual language acquisition within and outside the field of students who are d/Dhh. Provide a 500-word summary of what we know in the field about students who are acquiring multiple languages across modalities.

4. Research and list resources and services in your community that would help ensure a student's and his/her family's needs (e.g., transportation to audiology appointment) are being met.

ADDITIONAL RESOURCES

Progress Monitoring:
  Education Resources for Teachers of the Deaf and Hard of Hearing, University of Minnesota http://www.cehd.umn.edu/DHH-Resources/Webinars/default.html
  DIBELS https://dibels.uoregon.edu
  AIMS Web http://AIMSweb.com
  Easy CBM http://www.easycbm.com
  Curriculum-based Measures http://interventioncentral.org
Response to Intervention:
  RTI for success http://www.rti4success.org/
  IRIS Center at Vanderbilt University https://iris.peabody.vanderbilt.edu/
  Research Institute on Progress Monitoring www.progressmonitoring.org
Universal Design for Learning:
  Pepnet2 Fast Facts about Universal Design http://www.pepnet.org/sites/default/files/Universal%20Design%20Learning-%20launch.pdf
  National Center on Universal Design for Learning http://www.udlcenter.org/
  CAST http://www.cast.org/our-work/about-udl.html#.WMSwfhLytUd
Inclusion:
  Placement and Readiness Checklists (PARC, 2011) http://www.handsandvoices.org/pdf/PARC_2011_ReadinessChecklists.pdf
    General Education Inclusion Readiness Checklist
    Interpreter/Transliterated Education Readiness Checklist
    Captioning/Transcribing Readiness Checklist
    Instructional Communication Access Checklist

Supporting Document

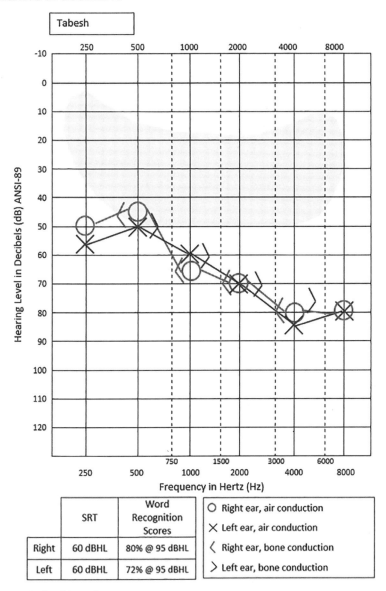

Figure 22.1. Tabesh's audiogram.

23
Aiden

Key Topics

Accommodations; Culture; Inclusion; Psychosocial

Aiden is 11 years old and beginning sixth grade at a local public middle school that houses grades 6–8. Aiden has a *severe* to *profound unilateral sensorineural hearing level* in the left ear and typical hearing in his right ear. Aiden's hearing status was confirmed at 6 months of age. All other family members have typical hearing. Aiden uses a *hearing aid* at home and school. With the use of the hearing aid, he has access to speech sounds. Aiden uses spoken language as his primary *mode of communication*. An audiological evaluation determined that Aiden's *speech perception* skills are above 80% yet deteriorate with noise, as measured by the *Pediatric AzBio Sentence Lists* (BabyBio; Spahr et al., 2014).

During the latter part of fifth grade, Aiden began to exhibit social and emotional struggles when at school. He grew his hair to cover his hearing aid, and he became frustrated that he couldn't always understand conversations in the cafeteria or on the playground. There were other environments where the sound level quickly escalated and made it difficult for Aiden to distinguish a speaker's message (e.g., during school assemblies or group activities in the classroom). In addition, toward the end of the day, Aiden often experienced *listening fatigue*. When Aiden became frustrated, he would shut down and withdraw from the conversation, resulting in lack of engagement. In elementary school, these issues didn't seem to irritate Aiden because his itinerant *teacher of the d/Deaf and hard of hearing* (TODHH) often advocated for him by insisting that speakers utilize his *assistive listening device* (ALD), such as a *DM system* designed to reduce the *signal-to-noise ratio*. In middle school, the expectations were greater and the classroom environments changed frequently, moving from class to class as the periods progressed throughout the day. Although the ALD was an *Individual Education Program* (IEP) *accommodation*, Aiden was uncomfortable carrying it from class to class and asking the other kids to use it.

During the transition from elementary to middle school, it became obvious that Aiden was struggling with his identity as a *hard of hearing* adolescent. He often questioned his parents about his *hearing loss* because he was not exposed to other individuals with different levels of hearing. As a hard of hearing individual, Aiden felt uncertain about whether he belonged to the hearing versus hard of hearing world. His parents noticed that he didn't speak about having interactions with friends at school. Since the beginning of the school year, Aiden's teachers observed him becoming increasingly withdrawn from class discussions and peer interactions.

His itinerant TODHH suggested that the members of his IEP team hold a meeting to help Aiden during his difficulty transitioning to middle school. Although she was working with Aiden on *auditory-verbal* training to help Aiden manage the noise distractions and listening skills, she felt it was crucial to add *self-advocacy* goals that would help Aiden develop his social and emotional skills during his middle school years. In addition, she wanted the team to reassess his goals and accommodations to make sure they aligned with his needs in the middle school environment.

Accommodations that were already present in Aiden's IEP included sitting near the front of the classroom, sitting on the left side of the classroom to access information with his right ear (better ear), use of *closed captioning* for all videos, and continuous use of the ALD. Aiden attended the *IEP meeting* to participate and be aware of his new goals. When the *IEP team* met, the following self-advocacy goals were added:

- Aiden will meet with his TODHH to discuss three strengths and three challenges to be incorporated into his IEP at least three months prior to his next IEP meeting.
- Aiden will meet with a mentor who is hard of hearing on a bi-weekly basis to generate a strategy or strategies to resolve issues Aiden is experiencing at school. Aiden will implement at least two strategies with 100% success as measured by a teacher observation checklist.
- Aiden will request the use of the ALD by his teachers, substitute teachers, assembly speakers, or peers 80% of the time.
- Aiden will implement two *auditory verbal* strategies to manage noise and improve listening with 90% accuracy as measured by the TODHH observation checklist and the *Pediatric AzBio Sentence Lists* test (administered by his *audiologist* each quarter).

The IEP team included the following accommodations for his transition to middle school:

- Copy of notes/note taker
- Allow extra time to process information
- Repeat information when requested or signaled
- Use of closed captioning during videos
- Use of *Communication Access Real-time Translation* (CART) in large meetings such as assemblies
- Tutoring, as needed

Due to Aiden's social and emotional challenges, the team also agreed visits to the school counselor at least every other week would be helpful. Aiden would be required to work with the counselor on developing his social-emotional skills.

Discussion Questions

1. How might the TODHH assist Aiden in identifying a hard of hearing mentor?
2. What are the potential strategies that Aiden's mentor might suggest using in different settings?
3. As an educator, what additional training might you need to prepare you to recognize and work with students who have social/emotional issues, including challenges with self-identity?
4. How and when should an itinerant TODHH intervene when dealing with the social and emotional issues of their students? Why are boundaries between the TODHH and student important, especially for itinerant TODHHs who have worked with students for multiple years?

Activities

1. Prepare an activity for the class that could help improve Aiden's self-esteem and *self-identity*. This activity will be presented by both Aiden and the TODHH. Suggestions can be found in the Additional Resources. Make sure to include at least two of the advocacy items listed below.
   Advocacy items:
   ✓ Turn-taking/not talking over each other
   ✓ Clear line of sight to see the speaker
   ✓ Teacher faces student when presenting materials
   ✓ Share with teacher/peers how a hearing aid works
   ✓ Reduce external noises when possible (animal tanks, fan, AC, door to outside areas) or ask to be seated in another location
2. As a TODHH, help Aiden develop a presentation that will reduce misunderstandings and stigmatisms about hearing loss as well as help hearing students and staff better understand why the ALD is crucial for Aiden to communicate throughout the day.
3. Develop a teacher observation checklist that will help measure Aiden's use of the strategies suggested by his mentor. Provide the setting in which Aiden's teacher will use this checklist.
4. Use the success for kids with hearing loss resource (http://successforkidswithhearingloss.com/self-advocacy/) to identify two to three age-appropriate instructional strategies

that address Aiden's social skills and self-advocacy. How would these strategies assist in Aiden's social and emotional development?

5. Does your state have standards that address self-advocacy? If so, what standards can be used to help Aiden during his middle school years? If not, identify a state that does, and discuss what standards you would use and why? (See Additional Resources for assistance.)

6. Use the *Listening Inventory for Education-Revised* (LIFE-R) http://successforkid swithhearingloss.com/life-r/ with a student. How can this inventory help students advocate for themselves and their needs identified?

Additional Resources

Auditory-Verbal Mentoring Program http://www.auditory-verbal-mentoring.com/

Expanded Core Curriculum for the Deaf, State of Iowa https://www.gadoe.org/ Curriculum-Instruction-and-Assessment/Special-Education-Services/Documents/ Eligibility%20Areas/DHH/ECC-DHH%20revised%20January%202013.pdf

IEP Checklist http://www.handsandvoices.org/pdf/IEP_Checklist.pdf

Self-Advocacy for the Deaf http://successforkidswithhearingloss.com/self-advocacy/

Special Standards State of Florida http://www.cpalms.org/Public/PreviewIdea/ Preview/2259

Uhler, K., Warner-Czyz, A., Gifford, R., & PMSTB Working Groups. (2017). Pediatric Minimum Speech Test Battery. *Journal of American Academy of Audiology, 28,* 232–247.

Supporting Document

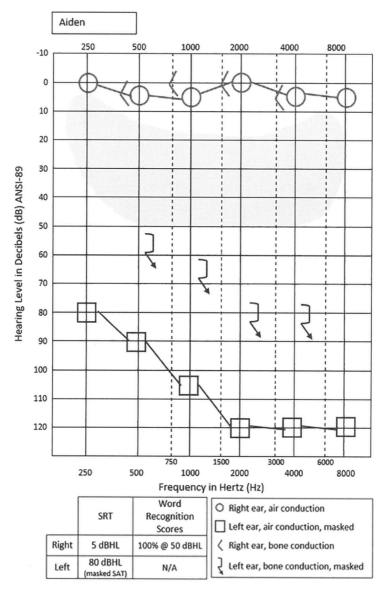

Figure 23.1. Aiden's audiogram.

24
Marcus

Key Topics

Content Area Instruction; Deaf with a Disability; Inclusion; Language Development; Literacy

Marcus is 12 years old and currently enrolled in sixth grade at a local charter school, a publically funded independent school. When Marcus was born prematurely at 33 weeks, he passed his newborn *hearing screening* using *otoacoustic emissions* (OAE) testing. However, at around 2 years of age, Marcus' mothers became concerned because his speech didn't seem consistent with that of his peers in his playgroup. After meeting with the pediatrician, Marcus was referred for audiological testing. The results were as follows: an additional OAE (normal, indicating Marcus' outer hair cells work properly), *auditory brainstem response* (ABR; abnormal, indicating sound did not consistently travel to his brain), *acoustic immittance tests of tympanometry* and *acoustic reflex* (normal, no fluid in the ear), *play audiometry* (varied), and speech recognition testing (varied). The tests were conducted over the course of 12 months, typically spaced four months apart because some of the test results were inconclusive and contradictory (normal one session, abnormal the next). The results of the tests showed that Marcus' left ear had a *mild* to *moderate hearing level* with his right ear identified with variable hearing. There were times when he responded to sound and other times he did not.

Because of these results, the *audiologist* identified Marcus with *Auditory Neuropathy Syndrome Disorder* (ANSD), which indicates a dysfunction in the transmission of sound from the inner ear to the brain. Marcus was fitted with *hearing aids* by the time he was 3 years old. Since then, he has used a hearing aid regularly in the left ear, yet consistently tries to remove the aid from the right ear. When Marcus is unaided, he seems confused at times. Marcus' parents have been actively involved in his *audiological management* and communication needs.

Directly after Marcus received his hearing aids, he began school in an *inclusive* preschool with intensive services. *Intervention* consisted of regular visits to the audiologist, *Speech Language Pathologist* (SLP) services two times a week, and visits once a week from the *teacher of the d/Deaf and hard of hearing* (TODHH). Despite these thorough intervention services, Marcus did not consistently produce spoken language or respond to simple directions. When Marcus did attempt to communicate using spoken language it was often unintelligible. The audiologist recommended that Marcus receive a *cochlear implant* (CI) in his right ear. During the summer before he turned 4, his parents followed this recommendation and Marcus received the CI.

Marcus' greatest challenges have been with *phonological awareness*, thus impacting his language development as well as his literacy acquisition. He was consistently a year and a half behind his hearing peers. By the fourth grade, the TODHH determined he showed deficits in *decoding*, which were due to weaknesses in phonological awareness. The *Comprehensive Test of Phonological and Print Processing* (C-TOPP; Wagner, Torgeson, Rashotte, & Pearson, 2013; see Appendix B) and a diagnostic decoding survey were used to determine his phonological awareness score and decoding levels. The TODHH has been working with Marcus from fourth to sixth grade. Over the past three years, she has worked with him on phonological instruction to help increase his language and literacy skills (see Appendix C for instructional strategies related to language and literacy acquisition and development).

Discussion Questions

1. What are the five areas of reading as described by the National Reading Panel? Why is phonological awareness critical to developing literacy?
2. Because ANSD varies greatly from one child to the next, describe what might be the possible challenges with identifying a child as having ANSD.
3. What are other types of formal and informal assessments that can be used to determine Marcus' current levels and growth in reading?
4. Consider the fact that the TODHH had been working with Marcus for three years. How might you use Marcus' comprehensive progress reports to determine the timeline of growth of his language and literacy skills?

Activities

1. Make a presentation for parents and teachers that defines ANSD, the symptoms, and possible strategies teachers can use to address the challenges these learners face.
2. Create three *Individualized Education Program* (IEP) goals to promote Marcus' language and literacy skills.
3. What other types of assessments can be used to determine Marcus' current levels and growth in reading?
4. Make a list of pros and cons of *d/Deaf* and *hard of hearing* (d/Dhh) students being placed in general education settings versus *deaf education program* settings.

ADDITIONAL RESOURCES

A detailed overview of ANSD and its effects *https://www.nidcd.nih.gov/health/auditory-neuropathy*

A free survey for assessing students decoding skills https://www.reallygreatreading .com/diagnostic-decoding-surveys-beginning-and-advanced

SUPPORTING DOCUMENT

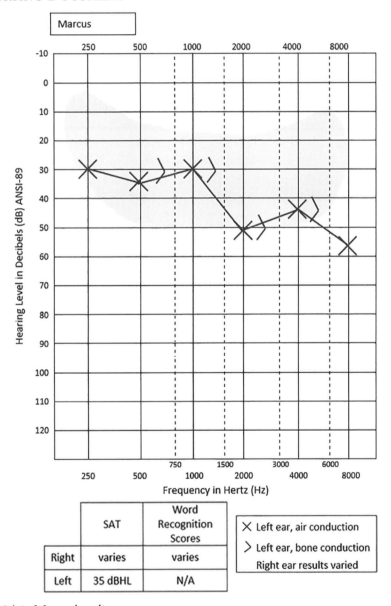

Figure 24.1. Marcus' audiogram.

25
Marley

Key Topics

Accommodations; Content Area Instruction; IEP/IFSP/504; Literacy; Modality; Placement

Marley is a 12-year-old student who is transitioning from her local elementary school in a rural area, where she was the only *d/Deaf* or *hard of hearing* (d/Dhh) student at her school, to sixth grade at a *school for the deaf*. Based on *Universal Newborn Hearing Screening* (UNHS) results, Marley was referred to an *audiologist* and identified with a *moderate* to *severe sensorineural hearing level* in her right ear and a moderate hearing level in her left ear. The *audiologist* recommended *behind-the-ear hearing aids* for both ears. Her family also was referred to the state's *early intervention* program for in-home services. Marley is the oldest child of three siblings, and her mother was young and single when Marley was born. Due to her inexperience and other priorities, Marley's mom did not consistently follow through with early intervention services. After three no-show appointments, early intervention services were discontinued per state policy. Additionally, Marley's mother frequently moved among residences in town, eventually resulting in her signing guardianship over to her maternal grandparents when Marley began first grade. While living with her mother, Marley's hearing aid use was inconsistent and she did not attend preschool.

When she began kindergarten, Marley's language and listening skills were severely delayed. She attended kindergarten within the general education class at her local school. Her *Individual Education Program* (IEP) *team* discussed Marley's *accommodations* and decided to provide daily tutoring sessions for *sign language*, *educational interpreting* services, weekly sessions with a *Speech Language Pathologist* (SLP), and one-on-one instruction from a *teacher of the d/Deaf and hard of hearing* (TODHH). However, like many *educational interpreters*, Marley's interpreter was under-qualified in both *sign language* skills and instructional strategies for language instruction (Schick, Williams, & Kupermintz, 2006). The interpreter used a form of *Signed English* to accompany spoken language during instruction; however, Marley had limited *uptake* to both modes due to her lack of language foundation. Additionally, the large student *caseload* of the *itinerant* TODHH and the school system's limited funding were barriers to more intensive language instruction for Marley. While she made progress in both spoken and sign language, she remained delayed in comparison to her peers. These language deficits negatively affected her achievement in literacy and content areas. For instance, based on the *Basic Reading Inventory* (BRI) (Johns, 2017; see Appendix B), Marley's instructional *sight word* vocabulary and reading comprehension were at the second grade reading level.

During the summer between fifth and sixth grade, Marley attended a three-day summer camp at the state residential school for the deaf at the recommendation of the TODHH. While her grandparents were concerned about the distance between home and the school for the deaf, they agreed to let her attend. This was a life-changing event for Marley. For the first time, she met other d/Deaf students and communicated directly with her peers, although at a basic level due to her limited sign skills at the time. When she returned home, she convinced her grandparents to let her try sixth grade at the school for the deaf. Her IEP team convened with administrators and teachers from the school for the deaf via online conferencing. They discussed Marley's needs and accommodations as she transitioned from her public school placement to the school for the deaf, which utilized a *bilingual/bicultural environment* and used *American Sign Language* (ASL) for instruction.

First, the ASL teacher conducted a receptive assessment with Marley to determine her understanding of information presented in ASL using the *American Sign Language Receptive Skills Test* (ASL-RST; Enns, Zimmer, Boudreault, Rabu, & Broszeit, 2013; see Appendix B), which measures a student's comprehension across nine categories. Marley's overall score was in the low end of the average range (i.e., nearly one *standard deviation* below the mean score of 100). She scored lowest in determining the difference between nouns and verbs, *size-and-shape-specifiers* (SASSes; i.e., *classifier* handshapes that show what objects look like), *role shift*, and *conditionals*. The IEP team decided Marley would receive daily two-hour sessions of ASL instruction from the school's certified ASL teacher with a few other students who were acquiring ASL. This would also provide an opportunity for Marley to practice appropriate social skills within a visual environment in a *small group* setting. For example, Marley is learning how to direct her visual attention to the signer, when it is an appropriate time for her to take a turn signing, and so on.

The school for the deaf also enculturates students to the Deaf community by providing Deaf role models, discussing the rules and norms of *Deaf culture*, how to use visual communication, sign language etiquette, and so forth. Because the residential school received many students who attended their local elementary schools but transitioned to the school for the deaf to meet their instructional needs in middle and high school (Musselman & Akamatsu, 1999), the school provides instruction based on ability levels to meet student needs. The IEP team decided Marley would begin sixth grade in the smaller and lower-level sixth grade class to receive more intense and individualized instruction (see Appendix C for instructional strategies related to language and literacy acquisition and development).

DISCUSSION QUESTIONS

1. The BRI (Johns, 2017) provides grade-level *sight word* lists and reading passages to assess a student's frustration, instruction, and independent reading levels. First, a teacher administers the grade-level sight word lists to determine each level for a student. Next, a teacher administers a reading passage at the student's instructional reading level, as determined by the word lists. The teacher asks the student to look over the passage then read it aloud as s/he conducts a *miscue analysis* (i.e., identifies strategies and errors a student makes when reading aloud). Then the teacher asks the student to engage in a *retell* of the passage, and finally, asks the student the included 5 to 10 comprehension questions about the passage. As her TODHH, how would you use an assessment battery such as the BRI to monitor Marley's vocabulary and reading comprehension progress across time?

2. As her TODHH, how could you collaborate with the ASL teacher to embed Marley's language learning from ASL class into your literacy or *content area* instruction?

3. Based on Marley's local elementary school experiences, how could you as an educator work with parents/guardians of your current/future students and school administrators to advocate for qualified educational interpreters?

4. The ASL-RST (Enns et al., 2013) measures a student's comprehension of ASL across nine categories. Briefly summarize how this assessment is administered, the information an educator can obtain from it, and how this information can inform individualized instruction.

ACTIVITIES

1. Interview an educational interpreter either in-person or via online conferencing or email. Here are some questions you might ask:
   a. How did you get into the interpreting field?
   b. What qualifications are required for an interpreting position?
   c. What type of ongoing professional development do you participate in?
   d. How do you promote collaboration with parents?
   e. How do you engage in professional learning communities and support systems?
   f. What different skills have you found that you need when working with different students?
   g. Do you provide tutoring services or language instruction with students?

2. Investigate the various distances from cities within your state to the residential school for the deaf. How might the travel time affect Marley? Brainstorm the positive and negative implications of travel time on the social-emotional development of d/Dhh children.

3. Discuss within small groups (see Guardino & Cannon, 2016; Jackson, Ammerman, & Trautwein, 2015):

   a. What are some barriers to educational services Marley might experience in the rural community?

   b. Does your state/province have early intervention service policies regarding family no-shows to appointments? What are ways professionals can support parents to prevent this consequence to the student?

   c. What are some alternative methods to service provision for *Individualized Family Service Plan* (IFSP)- or IEP-mandated services (e.g., tele-practice; Ouellette & Costello, n.d.; The Center for Speech and Hearing, n.d.)?

   d. Marley received 30-minute weekly sessions with an SLP during her local elementary school experience. Is this sufficient to develop speech and/or language skills that are caused by a limited language in the first five years of life?

ADDITIONAL RESOURCES

An overview of a residential school for the deaf and their approach to a bilingual philosophy https://www.youtube.com/watch?v=bn8DreFE_OY

Laurent Clerc National Deaf Education Center https://www.gallaudet.edu/gallaudet-interpreting-service/for-clients/additional-information/working-with-interpreters

National Consortium of Interpreter Education Centers http://www.interpretereducation.org/

Registry of Interpreters for the Deaf, Inc. http://rid.org/

Supporting Document

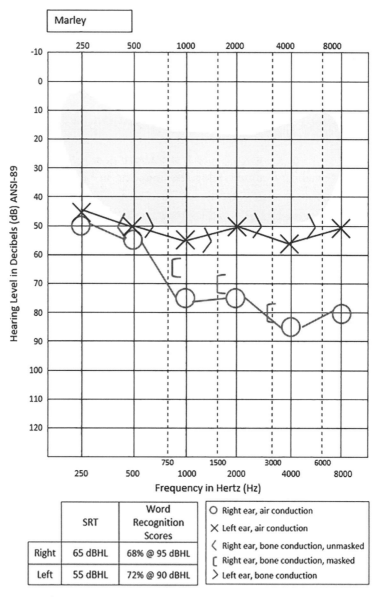

Figure 25.1. Marley's audiogram.

26
Layla

KEY TOPICS

Assessment; IEP/IFSP/504; Language Development; Literacy

Layla is a 13-year-old female with a *moderate* to *severe hearing level* entering the seventh grade this fall. Layla's *sensorineural hearing loss* was first identified at birth via the *Universal Newborn Hearing Screening* (UNHS), and she was fitted with *binaural digital hearing aids* at 3 months of age. She has continued to wear *hearing aids* and now uses an *assistive listening device* (ALD) designed to reduce *signal-to-noise ratio* in all of her classrooms and for her extracurricular activities (e.g., she is on the school soccer team). Her parents and extended family all have typical hearing. Layla has two older brothers (15 and 17 years old) who are also avid soccer players, and they practice with Layla regularly.

Layla communicates with her family via listening and spoken English. She sometimes struggles to keep up with the conversations occurring on the soccer field as well as during group activities within the general education classroom. Layla has also exhibited issues with comprehending grammatical features in her reading and writing. One area, for example, is comprehension and production of the past progressive tense (e.g., "The dogs were eating"; "While Kim was working at school, her friends were playing in the park"), which describes or gives emphasis to a specific event in the past. This impacts her reading comprehension, especially with fiction books, and she does not use this tense in her written assignments in class. Layla's *teacher of the d/Deaf and hard of hearing* (TODHH; Ms. Landon) has recently administered an informal grammar assessment (*Comprehension of Written Grammar* [CWG]; Cannon & Hubley, 2014; Easterbrooks, 2010; see Appendix B), and the results indicated specific grammar structures she struggled to comprehend when reading passages (see Table 26.1). Ms. Landon also administered the *Basic Reading Inventory* (BRI; Johns, 2017; see Appendix B), and Layla's results indicated a reading level of approximately fifth grade. Layla receives instruction from Ms. Landon two times per week to increase her literacy and language development by working on her *Individualized Education Program* (IEP) goals and objectives (see Appendix C for instructional strategies related to language and literacy acquisition and development).

Ms. Landon focus is on the goals to increase Layla's comprehension of written grammar in order to improve her reading level. To monitor her progress and the effectiveness of instruction, Ms. Landon devised short, informal assessments she will administer as "warm ups" at the beginning of each individual 30-minute session over the course of the six weeks (see Figure 26.2 for example). In order to increase her comprehension of grammar, Ms. Landon will *scaffold* the skills for Layla by developmentally sequencing the lessons to build upon each other (see Figure 26.3 for an outline of a scaffolded unit plan). Ms. Landon knows how important it is to increase Layla's skills across multiple contexts (e.g., *through-the-air* communication, texts, writing, etc.). As her *itinerant* TODHH she has limited time with Layla and needs to use it as efficiently as possible. Ms. Landon utilized a novel Layla was reading in her general education language arts class to practice grammatical structures (e.g., past progressive) with Layla by asking her questions that included the structures; providing opportunities for Layla to use the structures by identifying novel passages that contain them and discussing the meaning and asking Layla to use the structures within her written answers to chapter questions. Ms. Landon then used the data from each session and charted it on a graph (see Figure 26.4). Layla showed progress across the six-week period as Ms. Landon focused on explicit instruction of grammar skills over the course of 12 lessons (twice a week) to increase her overall receptive and expressive skills.

DISCUSSION QUESTIONS

1. How can interactive progress monitoring tools (applications and software) be utilized to reduce the data collection workload on itinerant TODHH?

2. How could you use Ms. Landon's process of incorporating assessment to monitor goals and progress across content areas (i.e., social studies, science) into instruction in a cyclical way? What does this do to improve efficiency and intentionality of instruction?

3. Why is it so vital for an itinerant TODHH to have efficient lessons that focus on goals and build upon each other? Why are sequential lessons that scaffold skills so important? How is scaffolding beneficial to *d/Deaf* and *hard of hearing* (d/Dhh) students who require additional support across *content areas*?

4. How would you collaborate with the general education teacher to continue to increase Layla's skills and ensure they transfer to her work in the general education setting?

ACTIVITIES

1. Select a goal or objective from a familiar IEP and develop your own informal assessment model to monitor progress based on the case study.
2. Develop a unit plan outline based on the example provided in the Supporting Documents for another grammar issue (select from the list of grammar structures in Table 26.1) or another language or literacy skill using scaffolded instruction.
3. Research the interaction between vocabulary knowledge (semantic) and grammar structure knowledge (syntax) in both receptive and expressive skills with d/Dhh students. Write a one-page explanation of how the interactive relationship between these two elements of language might contribute to gaps in literacy skills for d/Dhh students.

ADDITIONAL RESOURCES

Luckner, J. & Pierce, C. (2013). Response to intervention and students who are deaf and hard of hearing. *Deafness and Education International, 15*(4), 222–240.

Progress Monitoring http://www.progressmonitoring.net

Response to Intervention http://www.rti4success.org/essential-components-rti/progress-monitoring

Universal Newborn Hearing Screening https://report.nih.gov/nihfactsheets/ViewFactSheet.aspx?csid=104

Supporting Documents

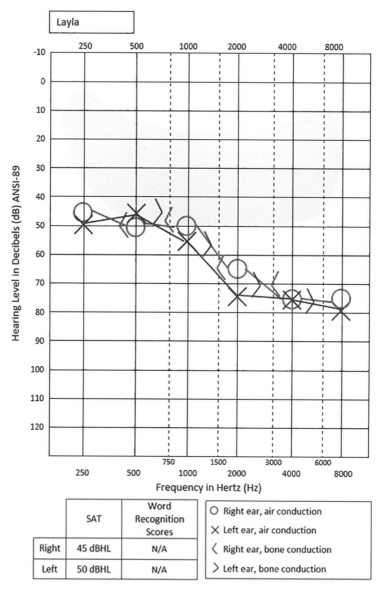

Figure 26.1. Layla's audiogram.

Table 26.1. Assessment Results of Comprehension of Written GrammarInformal Assessment.

Name: Layla

School: ABC Middle School

Grammatical Structure	1st	2nd	3rd	4th
1. Imperative				
2. NP + Vi				
3. NP + Vi + Adv-p				
4. NP + Vi + Adv-a			X	
5. NP(S) + Vt + NP(D.O.)				
6. NP + be + Adj	X	X		
7. NP + be + Adv-p				
8. NP + be + Adv-a				
9. NP + be + NP				
10. NP + be + (for+N)				
11. is + ing				
12. are + ing				
13. was + ing	X	X	X	
14. were + ing	X	X	X	
15. Vh + tense (agreement)	X	X	X	X
16. Vh (idiomatic)				
17. modal will				
18. comparative		X	X	
19. superlative				
20. possessive 's				
21. reversible passive	X	X		
22. non-reversible passive				
23. for/to complement				
24. adverbial clause				
25. NP complement				
26. perfect tense	X	X		X

Warm Up - Informal Assessment Example (can be completed using paper/pencil, a whiteboard, or interactive tablet/computer game)
Put the verbs in the past progressive form:

1. When I texted my friends, they (play) | were playing | Angry Birds.

2. Yesterday at eight I (prepare) [ ] breakfast.

3. The dogs (play) [ ] in the backyard when it suddenly began to rain.

4. While Kim (work) [ ] in her office, her colleagues (eat) [ ] their lunch.

5. Most of the day we (swim) [ ] in the pool.

Figure 26.2. Warm-up example.

Unit Goal: To increase comprehension and production of the past progressive tense
            in reading and writing
Lesson 1:   What is past progressive tense?
Lesson 2:   Auxiliary "be" and past progressive tense
Lesson 3:   Main verbs and past progressive tense
Lesson 4:   -ing: What does it mean and why should I care?
Lesson 5:   Past progressive tense singular
Lesson 6:   Positive sentences and past progressive tense
Lesson 7:   Negative sentences and past progressive tense
Lesson 8:   Past progressive tense plural
Lesson 9:   Subjects and pronouns in past progressive tense sentences
Lesson 10: Was/Were: A review
Lesson 11: Question sentences and past progressive tense
Lesson 12: Bringing it all together: Tense and comprehension

Figure 26.3. Scaffolded unit plan outline example.

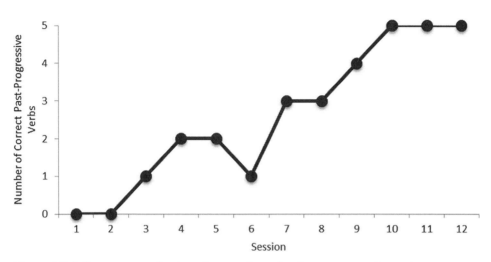

Figure 26.4. Progress monitoring chart and graph of past progressive verb tense.

27
Yolanda

Key Topics

Assessment; Culture; IEP/IFSP/504; Language Development; Modality; Multilingual; Placement; Psychosocial; Transition

Yolanda is a 14-year-old female who is *deaf* and was born to hearing parents in a small town in southwest Mexico. Her mother reported that Yolanda's birth was typical with no complications. At the time, Mexico did not have *Universal Newborn Hearing Screening* (UNHS) services at the hospital where Yolanda was born. Yolanda's parents became concerned when she was not using spoken language at 16 months of age because her four older siblings all used spoken language around 12 months of age. Yolanda's parents became increasingly worried when she did not speak by the time she was 2 years old. At this time they took her to a physician who referred them to an *audiologist*. The audiologist performed a hearing evaluation and diagnosed Yolanda with a *profound bilateral sensorineural hearing loss*. Yolanda was provided with *hearing aids* at the time yet constantly struggled to keep the aids in her ears. After a few months, Yolanda didn't seem to greatly benefit from the use of the hearing aids and ceased wearing them on a regular basis.

Yolanda's parents used *home signs*, gestures, and some *Mexican Sign Language* (lengua de señas Mexicana; LSM) they learned from a few local deaf people. They occasionally attended a church that provided a *sign language interpreter*. Yolanda's siblings picked up some LSM and used it with Yolanda in the home. *Early intervention* services were not available in Yolanda's hometown. When Yolanda turned 5 years old, she attended a school for students with disabilities. However, she had inconsistent access to LSM because the school struggled to find educators who knew *sign language*, given the predominant educational philosophy of *listening and spoken language* (LSL) throughout Mexico (Faurot, Dellinger, Eatough, & Parkhurst, 1999). In first and second grades she learned basic LSM and *Signed Spanish* (i.e., LSM signs in spoken Spanish word order), some *sight words* (Spanish and English), and basic math operations. When she was 9 years old her family moved to the southwest region of the United States.

For the next five years, they moved around the southern United States, living with family members and saving money to settle into their own home. This resulted in a disjointed educational experience for Yolanda and inconsistent opportunities to form friendships and peer bonds. While she was determined eligible for special education services, she attended multiple schools during this time frame and received educational services from varied professionals, including *teachers of the d/Deaf and hard of hearing* (TODHHs). When Yolanda was 14 years old, her parents bought a house in a suburb of a major metropolitan city in the southeast. Yolanda was first enrolled in the local suburban middle school where two TODHHs taught a handful of *d/Deaf* and *hard of hearing* (d/Dhh) students in both separate classes and general education settings. Yolanda's new TODHH, Mr. Baker, worked with her parents, a Spanish interpreter, and the *school psychologist* to assess Yolanda's language and literacy skills (read her *Individualized Education Program* [IEP] in the Supporting Documents, Figure 27.3, for more assessment information).

Assessments revealed that Yolanda had a typical IQ. She knew signs (LSM) for many vocabulary items and sight words (English and Spanish); however, Mr. Baker was challenged in determining their accuracy due to the extensive differences between LSM and *American Sign Language* (ASL; Faurot et al., 1999). Yolanda used many initialized signs, as is common in LSM, incorporating the first letter of the (Spanish) word within the sign (e.g., equipo "E" for TEAM; Faurot et al., 1999). The Spanish interpreter assisted Mr. Baker with the spoken Spanish terms for words and referred to an online LSM video dictionary to assist with translating Yolanda's LSM signs.

Mr. Baker also observed Yolanda's interaction and communication with her mother and noticed that their communication was limited to basic vocabulary and syntax. Yolanda and her mother used the same signs repeatedly, combined with gesturing and pointing, and were unable to engage in discussions above a functional level. The limited vocabulary and syntax utilized between Yolanda and her mother indicated she did not have a complete *first language* (L1) in order to discuss complex concepts with her mother (e.g., puberty, interpersonal friendships, intimate relationships, etc.).

After Mr. Baker completed the assessments, he established an IEP meeting with Yolanda's parents, Yolanda, the school psychologist, a district level administrator, a Spanish interpreter, an ASL interpreter, a *Speech Language Pathologist* (SLP), and the second TODHH (Ms. Hodson). The *IEP team* discussed Yolanda's present levels of performance, her assessment results, goals and objectives, and placement options for educational services. The IEP team all recommended that the parents consider placing Yolanda at the day *school for the deaf* in a large metropolitan area as opposed to the *deaf education program* at her local school where Mr. Baker worked. In the local school most of the students who are d/Dhh use ASL via an *educational interpreter* or in the *resource* classroom with one of the TODHH. As a result of Yolanda's language needs, she will be isolated in the *resource* classroom for all of her classes until her ASL skills increase to a level where she is able to use an ASL interpreter in the *inclusion* setting.

In contrast, the day school for the deaf will meet Yolanda's need to be immersed in a language-rich environment where she can receive constant exposure to ASL. This recommendation was also based on the need for Yolanda to form friendships and have Deaf role models to increase her social skills and confidence levels.

Yolanda and her parents visited the school for the deaf following the IEP meeting. Her parents were hesitant to send her on a daily 45-minute bus ride to and from school, but they were pleased with the language environment in the school and saw how readily Yolanda adapted to students' conversations with her. Yolanda also appeared to begin social interaction with students in the hallways and classrooms during their visit, and they felt the supportive and social nature of the school would increase her language and social skills (see Appendix C for instructional strategies related to language and literacy acquisition and development). Therefore, the IEP team decided that Yolanda would transfer to the day school for the deaf. The team agreed that Yolanda must acquire a *first language* (L1; ASL) before she could learn a *second language* (L2; English). Based on the assessment data, Yolanda currently has a limited sign-based L1 (LSM), a limited L2 (Spanish), and an emerging L3 (ASL) and L4 (English).

DISCUSSION QUESTIONS

1. You are a teacher at the day school and Yolanda is transferring into your class. She has limited knowledge in any print-based language. Where will you begin? What materials/curriculum will you use to meet the attached IEP goals and objectives?

2. What type of psychosocial issues do you think Yolanda and her family are experiencing during this transition time? How might her IEP team help Yolanda and her family address these issues?

3. Consider Yolanda's unique communication needs. What are the critical issues to address during her transition to a new school? Why is a language-rich environment so important for Yolanda at this stage?

4. How will Yolanda's cultural background influence her language acquisition? What are the benefits of exposure to two cultures and multiple languages?

ACTIVITIES

1. Imagine you are the TODHH at the school for the deaf who will be Yolanda's case manager for her next academic school year. Develop language, literacy (reading and writing), and math goals and objectives using the criteria for "SMART goals and objectives" (see Supporting Documents, Figure 27.2) create at least two new SMART goals for each content area.

2. Again pretend that Yolanda is transferring into your class. She has limited knowledge in any print-based language. Where will you begin? What materials/curriculum will you use to meet the sample IEP goals and objectives (see Supporting Documents, Figure 27.3)?

3. Yolanda will transition to high school but has very little school experience. Develop a specialized *transition plan* for Yolanda. What factors need to be considered when Yolanda transitions into high school?

4. Making friends and connections will likely increase Yolanda's communication skills more quickly and increase her self-confidence. Brainstorm a plan to address Yolanda's social skills.

Additional Resources

Gallaudet University's Laurent Clerc National Deaf Education Center published an entire issue on Deaf *English Language Learners* (ELLs), with a focus on communication, language, and literacy. The concepts presented in this issue of *Odyssey* are helpful to better understanding this unique population. http://www.gallaudet.edu/Documents/Clerc/Odyssey-2000-v1i2-full.pdf

Pepnet2 offers numerous services for older youth, including transition and advocacy information. Many of their resources are translated for families who are *culturally and linguistically diverse.* http://www.pepnet.org/resources/deaf

Mexican Sign Language (lengua de señas Mexicana; LSM) http://aulex.org/lsm/

Supporting Documents

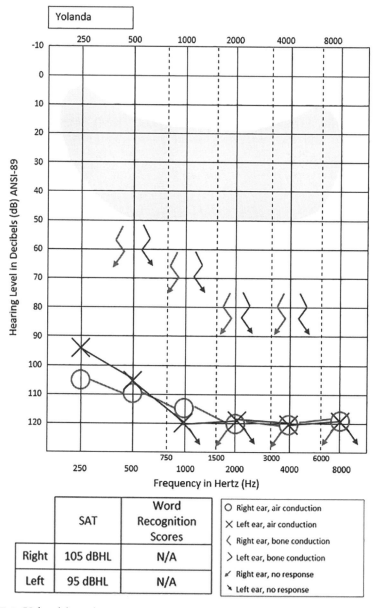

Figure 27.1. Yolanda's audiogram.

- S.M.A.R.T. Guidelines
  - **S**pecific: written in clear, concise language focused on a particular skill
  - **M**easurable: written in a manner that allows measurement of a particular skill
  - **A**chievable & **A**ction-oriented: written in terms of what the student will do and realistic for the time frame of the IEP
  - **R**elevant & **R**ealistic: written so that the skill is achievable and meaningful as well as focused on positive changes
  - **T**ime-related: notes the time period they should be accomplished in
- Three parts must be included to make sure your goals and objectives are S.M.A.R.T.:
  - The target behavior
    - John will complete 10–12 addition or subtraction problems….
    - Sara will put away her materials, get out her visual schedule, and point to a symbol of the next activity….
    - Michael will construct paragraphs that consist of at least one opening, two middle, and one ending or transition sentence….
  - The context in which the target behavior should occur
    - …when provided with a worksheet in math class….
    - …when informed that an activity will end….
    - …when presented with an open-ended question in English or social studies class….
  - The criterion for mastery…
    - with at least 80% mastery on curriculum-based assessment.
    - 4 out of 5 times as measured by teacher probe and checklist.
    - in 8 out of 10 attempts as measured by writing samples and homework assignments.
- Six questions to see if your goals and objectives are S.M.A.R.T.:
  1. *Who?*
     Relates to the student
  2. *Does what?*
     Observable behavior describing what the student will do to complete the goal or objective/benchmark
  3. *When?*
     Relates to the specific point in the time when something will have been learned or completed
  4. *Given what? (conditions)*
     Describes the "givens" that will need to be in place for the goal or objective/benchmark to be completed.

5. *How much?*
   Mastery (performance accuracy)
   Criteria; how many times behavior observed
6. *How will it be measured ?*
   Describes performance data
   Progress Monitoring through informal assessment

- (Who?) will (Do What?) (When?) (Given what?) (How much?) (Measured How?)
  ○ John will complete 10–12 addition or subtraction problem when provided with a worksheet in math class with at least 80% mastery on curriculum-based assessment.
  ○ Sara will put away her materials, get out her visual schedule, and point to a symbol of the next activity when informed that an activity will end four out of five times as measured by teacher probe and checklist.
  ○ Michael will construct paragraphs that consist of at least one opening, two middle, and one ending or transition sentence when presented with an open-ended question in English or social studies class in 8 out of 10 attempts as measured by writing samples and homework assignments.

Figure 27.2. S.M.A.R.T. guidelines for goals and objectives.

NAME: Yolanda Lopez
SCHOOL: School for the Deaf   GRADE: 8
BIRTHDATE: 3/20/98   AGE: 14
ADDRESS: 789 5th Ave., Smalltown, US
PHONE #:   555-555-5555
PARENT / GUARDIAN: Rosa Lopez (mother) & Mark Lopez (father)

WHAT IS THE STUDENT CURRENTLY ABLE TO DO?

Record information from assessment data, including standardized tests, criterion-referenced measures, class assignments, and observations. Indicate if the student is "at," "above," or "below" the relevant grade level for academics and functional life skills.

Strengths: Yolanda's strengths include her eagerness to learn and her positive attitude. Yolanda exhibits the desire to communicate with those around her and is a social young girl who wants to get to know her new classmates and teachers. Yolanda's base knowledge of Spanish and MSL vocabulary is a strength that can be used to build her new languages: ASL (L3) and English (L4). Yolanda's parents speak Spanish and English and are eager to learn ASL to better communicate with their daughter.

Weaknesses:

Yolanda's weaknesses include her inconsistent school history and the fact that she is exposed to four languages in her existing and new environments. Her limited knowledge of spoken or printed Spanish and limited MSL skills prevent her use of a solid language foundation from which to build English and ASL. Although her knowledge of MSL will benefit her language development in another language, especially based on her CDI scores, her teachers are unable to capitalize on the use of MSL during instruction because they have no knowledge of the language. Additionally, Yolanda's limited exposure to math instruction has resulted in her low assessment scores and classroom performance. Yolanda needs to increase her communication skills in ASL and her knowledge of English print.

The following are summaries of recent assessments Yolanda completed with her TODHH:

Reading:

BRI: Below Pre-Primer level in English; able to produce a few signs to accompany a picture story but no inclusion of narrative structure.

Math:

Brigance (Brigance Comprehensive Inventory of Basic Skills): Number Sense: The results indicate that Yolanda is at a second grade instructional level on her computation and knowledge of number concepts.

Problem Solving: Below K level (although English print knowledge is needed to complete this subset of the assessment)

Language:

Receptive One Word Picture Vocabulary Test: Yolanda was not able to complete this assessment, as she only knew the signs for two words tested and therefore her score was invalid.

CDI (Words and Gestures and Words and Sentences): The MacArthur Communicative Development Inventory: Words and Sentences (16–30 months). This inventory was given to Yolanda's parents to complete regarding her communication abilities at home, although this is not a measure of Yolanda's abilities in English or ASL, it is a measure of her overall language and communication skills in her L1 and L2. Her CDI scores indicated that she was in the 90th percentile for 2;6 (years; months). This information suggests that Yolanda has a basis for language but that her communication skills are significantly delayed and she needs to improve her conversation and vocabulary skills to increase her language skills.

WHAT DO WE WANT THE STUDENT TO BE ABLE TO DO?

Brainstorm ideas about what the student should be able to do. Record these goals on a separate sheet of paper and sort them into educational areas (subject area, reading, writing, mathematics, behavior, social/emotional, physical, etc.).

The IEP team's current goals for Yolanda include increasing her English and ASL vocabulary and her conversational skills. The team believes that these goals will allow Yolanda to assimilate into her new environment, build peer relationships, and have access to academic subjects presented in English. These are the major concerns of the team at this time, due to the fact that building a language foundation is the most important goal for Yolanda.

REVIEW DATE:

WHAT CHANGES DO WE NEED TO MAKE?

Based on the assessment data, evaluate the success of the IEP. Suggestions/revisions may involve changing the goals or the support plan.

The team feels that Yolanda's educational placement should change. Due to the overall agreement that increasing her language skills is the first priority, the team discussed what school environment would promote this goal. Yolanda currently receives all instruction in a resource classroom. She currently cannot use an interpreter because she lacks sufficient ASL skills to comprehend instruction and to adequately express herself. At this time, she communicates best with her TODHH. The TODHH in this setting has three students throughout the day in his class who communicate using ASL when the other students use speech to communicate. Therefore, Yolanda's exposure to peer and adult language models throughout the day are limited in the current setting. The team agreed that the local day school for the deaf would be a more suitable placement for Yolanda at this time so that she would be immersed in an ASL environment to increase her conversation skills and build the necessary foundations for language.

WHO WAS INVOLVED IN PLANNING THE I.E.P.?

TEAM MEMBERS:	NAME	SIGNATURE	
		REVIEW	
			(INITIAL)

1. **Student (if appropriate)** <u>Yolanda Lopez</u>   _____   _____
2. **Parent / Guardian** <u>Rosa Lopez</u>   _____   _____
     <u>Mark Lopez</u>   _____   _____
3. **TODHH** <u>Mr. Baker</u>   _____   _____
4. **TODHH** <u>Ms. Hodson</u>   _____   _____
5. **Administrator** <u>Ms. Brownwood</u>   _____
6. **Support Personnel** <u>Ms. Carter (Spanish Interpreter)</u>
     <u>Ms. Perry (SLP)</u>   _____   _____
     <u>Mrs. Landon (ASL Interpreter)</u>

Goals	Objective(s)
1. Yolanda will increase the appropriate use of classroom discourse skills to 80% accuracy as measured by observations, teacher/SLP-made probes, and written work.	**1.** Retell a story giving the appropriate story order using gestures and ASL. **2.** Answer literal comprehension questions about a text that was read to her in relation to the character(s), setting, and/or major events in the story, including the beginning, middle, and end. **3.** Answer interpretive comprehension questions about a text that was read to her such as: "What do you think will happen next in the story? Why? How did the characters feel about one another? What lesson could be learned from this story?"
2. Yolanda will increase semantic skills (word meaning) in the area(s) of ASL and English vocabulary to 80% accuracy as measured by teacher/SLP-made probes, pre/post tests, language sampling, story retelling, and/or written work.	**1.** Identify/state basic personal information (first and last name, age, date of birth, grade, and school). **2.** Engage in conversation with peers and teachers by asking and answering wh- and yes/no questions. **3.** Understand and use words to describe, categorize, classify, and compare during conversation and written work.

3. Yolanda will increase her receptive and expressive question skills by 85% of the time as measured by observations, teacher/SLP-made probes, pre/post-test, language samples, story retelling, and/or written work.	**1.** Nod "yes" or "no" when asked simple yes/no questions. **2.** Answer the following types of simple yes/no questions: "Do you want --?" "Is your name (name) here?" "Do you want/have/see/etc.…?" "Are you (adjective)?" "Can you (verb)?" "Can I have it?" "Are you ready?" "Have you finished?" **3.** Ask a yes/no question to gain information from peers and adults.
4. Yolanda will correctly use language for a variety of functions/intents (statements, questions) to 85% of occurrences as measured by observations, teacher-made checklists, and vocabulary pre/post test.	**1.** Use statements to identify/label objects, actions, and events. **2.** Use statements to describe objects, actions, and events. **3.** Use statements to compare objects, actions, and events.

Strategies / Methods / Techniques	By Whom	Ongoing Assessment / Evaluation
• **Goal 1, Obj. 1–3:** **Guided Reading strategies, Shared Reading Project strategies, story retells, modeling**	**TOD**	Date: Pre/Post Assessment Work Samples Anecdotal Data Progress Monitoring
• **Goal 2, Obj. 1–4:** **Label objects and repeated use of visuals, themed vocabulary units that relate to prior knowledge and personal experiences, Johnson's Conversational Model, modeling**	**TOD**	Date: Pre/Post Assessment Work Samples Anecdotal Data Progress Monitoring
• **Goal 3, Obj. 1–3 & Goal 4, Obj. 1–3:** **Scaffolding, dialogue journals (using pictures/drawings and writing), scripts, scenarios, reduction sequence for questioning and conversation breakdowns**	**TOD**	Date: Pre/Post Assessment Work Samples Anecdotal Data Progress Monitoring

ADAPTATIONS & ACCOMMODATIONS

Accessibility:	Assignments & Homework:
o access to all areas of school	o alternate assignments or format
o fire exits & routes	o length &/or number (decrease)
o furniture & storage	o partner or group assignments
o health & personal care	o time allowed (increase)
o parking lot, roads, & walkways	o other: _____
o play areas & equipment	
o showers, restrooms, & fountains	**Teaching Strategies:**
o transportation to/from school	o advance organizers/key visuals
other: _____	o alternate content/skills
	o demonstrate/model processes/ product
Behavior Management:	o feedback immediate/frequent
o consequences (clear/consistent)	o practice guided/independent
o expectations/rules (clear/consistent)	o multisensory (oral/experiential/ written)
o home-school program	o memory (reduce/teach strategies)
o outside agency support	o pace quick/slow
o reinforcement (class/group/ individual)	o short sessions/lessons
o routines established & followed	o teach key concepts/vocabulary
o school counseling program	o other: _____
o student contract/goal setting	
o teach/assignments at skill level	**Equipment & Specialized Materials:**
o teach & reinforce social skills	o augmentative communication device
o other: _____	o braille machine/materials
	o calculator (large keys/reg./voice)
Organizational & Study Strategies:	o camera (digital/video)
o visual strategies (chart, blackboard)	o computer processor
o class/individual visual schedule/ timetable	o computer printer/peripherals
o concrete measures of time (timer/ watch)	o hearing aids/personal or class FM system
o color-coded binders, etc.	o headphones/listening center
o organized classroom set-up	o fine/gross motor equipment

o routines for use of materials	o standing frame/walker
o student planner/home-school book	o adapted switches/ handles, etc.
o teach organizational/study skills explicitly	o tape recorder
o other: _____	o wheelchair (reg./electric)
	o reference books
Reading, Writing & Notetaking:	o spell checker/grammar checker
o alternate formats of notetaking: carbon	o other: _____
o copy/outline/photocopy/taped notes	
o alternate formats reading: braille/ enlarged print/rebus/tapes/videos	
o alternate formats writing: computer/ printing/typewriter/word process	**Following Directions:**
o alternate materials/texts: easier reading level/parallel unit	o Provide only one or two directions at a time
o notetaker, reader &/or scribe (parent/ peer/staff/volunteer)	o Restate directions in clear simple language
o other: _____	o Stand close to the student and gain eye contact before giving directions
	o Provide visual support for directions (on students desk, or on board)
Increasing Written Output:	
o Allow for a scribe, or a tape to record responses	**Testing & Evaluation:**
o Establish the process for revision (first draft, sharing, revising, second draft, sharing, revising; third draft, polishing; final, publishing)	o alternate setting/time
o Have the student write ideas on post-it notes and then rearrange them to make an outline	o alternate test/format
o Teach keyboarding skills	o time (increase/short sessions)
o Use an outline and two column notes for paragraph and essay writing	o open book/take home exams
o Use graphic organizers	o oral (reader/scribe/tape)
	o rewriting permitted

	o recognize and give credit for class participation
	o review the grading process before the test
	o provide examples of criteria for each letter grade
	o allow student to retake test
	o teach relaxation strategies
	o provide sample items at the beginning of the test
	o provide visual graphic cues as the test directions change
	o repeat directions to the student once you have given them to the class
	o use take-home tests for practice
	o other: _____

Figure 27.3. Sample IEP for Yolanda.

28

Steven

Collaboration; Content Area Instruction; Inclusion; Modality; Transition

Steven is 14 years of age. Based on family history, he was identified with a *moderate to severe bilateral reverse slope sensorineural hearing loss*. The *etiology* is genetic, as his father and grandfather have the same type of hearing loss. A reverse slope loss means that Steven has limited access to *low frequency* sounds, such as the vowels of English, and has near-typical hearing access to the *high frequency* sounds of English, such as /s/, /f/, and /th/. This is the opposite of most people with sensorineural hearing levels who tend to have access to *low frequency* sounds but not *high frequency* sounds. Steven had typical hearing at birth, but his *hearing level* declined until he was about 5 years of age, when it stabilized. Because his family was aware of the possibility that Steven would have this type of hearing condition, they acquired *audiograms* for him every six months to monitor his hearing. Steven uses *digital behind-the-ear wide-band hearing aids*, which means he has access to sounds up to 16,000 *hertz* (Hz). His hearing aids are tailored to his individual needs so that the *lower frequencies* are amplified significantly and the *higher frequencies* are only slightly amplified. Steven uses *listening and spoken language* (LSL) to communicate. During conversations he uses *speechreading* skills to compensate for missing some of the low frequency vowel sounds. Therefore, it is imperative that the speaker is facing Steven when speaking. Steven has a difficult time hearing conversations using the phone and prefers to text, email, or use online video-conferencing such as Skype in place of using the phone. He also does not hear low frequency environmental sounds, such as engines and machines, but has learned to adapt to his environment by using his vision and tactile skills.

Steven attended a church-run day care. His parents decided to enroll him in a private elementary school where he received instruction in small grade-level classes. Because he was in a private school, he did not receive services from an *Individual Education Program* (IEP), which applies only to public schools or when the public school decides to place a student in a private school setting. His speech development resembled that of a typically hearing child, so he did not receive speech therapy services. Steven was successful in this placement with the use of his hearing aids and sitting in front of the class to maximize his ability to use *speechreading* during instruction.

Because his private school included only kindergarten to fifth grade, Steven transitioned to his local public middle school. His family was concerned that Steven would miss instructional information within the larger class sizes typical of public schools. While Steven has a documented moderate to severe hearing level based on his audiogram, his hearing level does not adversely affect his educational achievement, as he is on-level with his same-grade peers. Because of this, he is not eligible for an IEP. However, his family acknowledged that Steven had been successful in his educational attainment at the elementary level due to his previous small class sizes and that he will need supports in place to be successful in this new educational setting. As a result, the school has established a meeting focused on the *Section 504* of the *Rehabilitation Act of 1973* eligibility, in place of an IEP, and a *Section 504 plan* for *accommodations* to meet Steven's needs for educational access.

Steven and his general education teachers, *teacher of the d/Deaf and hard of hearing* (TODHH), principal, and parents attended the meeting. While the TODHH will not be providing services to Steven under the Section 504 plan, she is joining the meeting to offer insight on accommodations. Steven's parents explained that he received *preferential seating* and used hearing aids during elementary school. They expressed their concerns about the larger, noisier instructional environments at the middle school and their concerns that Steven might miss information. Steven's father also noted that at times it may seem as though Steven has "selective hearing" or is inattentive but that these characteristics are related to his particular hearing level. In addition to preferential seating so that Steven could utilize *speechreading*, the TODHH suggested accommodations such as teacher use of an *FM/DM system* to reduce distance and reduce *signal-to-noise* ratio by minimizing background noises in class, use of *closed captioning* on all videos, identification of the speaker in class, teacher use of Steven's name when directing questions to him, and proposed that Steven *self-advocate* by alerting the teacher when he misses information.

After this meeting Steven's accommodations were shared with his general education teachers across each year of middle school. His teachers collaborated among themselves to discuss how they implemented these accommodations across diverse classes. They also turned to the TODHH when needed for specific questions about use of the FM/DM system and closed captions. His general education teachers maintained contact with Steven's parents to ensure Steven was successful in middle school. Steven also practiced alerting teachers when he missed information.

Now Steven is preparing to transition to high school. His parents are concerned about the instructional content and strategies his teachers will use within large class sizes with higher-level content, such as Steven's Advanced Placement classes and higher-level science and math classes. They fear that the teachers will use lecture-style presentations and that Steven will miss vital information. They also are concerned about Steven's access to information presented in large social situations such as within the lunch room and auditorium. Steven's Section 504 plan team is meeting to discuss his parents' concerns and accommodations that may benefit him in this new educational setting. The TODHH suggested that Steven maintain the previous accommodations from middle school and mentioned that the following teacher-initiated accommodations might benefit him in high school: copies of notes from a peer note-taker; copies of class PowerPoint presentations and lists of content terminology in advance of lessons; writing assignments on the board; provision of wait time for Steven to view visual materials before teachers present auditory information; use of materials from the Described and Captioned Media Program (https://dcmp.org/); and intentional groupings such as *pair and share* within instruction (see Appendix C for effective instructional strategies). During middle school, Steven practiced asking for clarification but said that he feels awkward when he has to ask for repetition continuously in front of his peers. The TODHH suggested that Steven use an agreed upon signal with his teachers to indicate that he needs information repeated, such as wiggling his fingers atop his desk. Steven's team agreed upon these accommodations, and his general education teachers were provided with copies of his accommodations and signed that they received and understood them.

Discussion Questions

1. How can Steven and his teachers monitor and evaluate the effectiveness of his accommodations in high school?
2. (a) What platforms (e.g., online technology, forms, etc.) might Steven's teachers use for intentional collaboration? (b) How will the teachers' professional and personal dispositions affect their collaborative success?
3. (a) What are the differences between a Section 504 plan and an IEP? (b) Why did Steven receive educational services via a Section 504 plan during middle school?
4. While Steven's transition from a private elementary to a public middle and high school was relatively seamless, how might teachers promote smooth transitions between educational settings for other students?

Activities

1. Find a copy of a familiar sounds audiogram with a *speech banana/string bean* indicated on it (this is an audiogram that shows where the sounds of the English language fall by *decibel* and *frequency*). Based on Steven's reverse slope hearing loss, which speech sounds do you think he does and does not have access to? How might

this affect his comprehension of spoken language? As a TODHH, what instructional strategies might you use to ensure Steven has maximum access to speech sounds?

2. Here is a way to simulate Steven's access to spoken language. First, write out a sentence. Next, remove all of the vowels, leaving blanks. Now show it to someone and ask them to fill in the blanks and read the sentence correctly. Next, write the sentence again but remove all of the consonants, leaving blanks for each one. Again ask someone to read the sentence. What did you notice between the removal of vowels and the removal of consonants?

3. Compare and contrast the legal requirements of the *Individuals with Disabilities Education Improvement Act* (IDEIA) and *Section 504 of the Rehabilitation Act of 1973* by completing the questions in Table 28.1.

4. Describe how you would use resources from the Described and Captioned Media Program (https://dcmp.org/) to present a unit on Shakespeare's *Hamlet* or DNA replication to meet the needs of a student like Steven.

5. If a student has an IEP or a Section 504 plan, you'll likely hear the terms "accommodation" and "modification" from the IEP or Section 504 teams. While they may be similar, they serve different purposes. Accommodations change how a student learns the material. A modification changes what a student is taught or expected to learn. Research examples to help explain the differences between them.

Table 28.1

Questions	IDEIA	Section 504
What is the purpose of each law?		
How is a disability defined?		
Who receives services?		
What kinds of services are provided?		
How are public and private schools treated differently?		
How do these laws overlap?		
How is due process (e.g., fair treatment of parents or school system) defined for each law?		

Additional Resources

Center for Hearing Loss Help overview of reverse slope hearing loss
    http://hearinglosshelp.com/blog/
    the-bizarre-world-of-extreme-reverse-slope-hearing-loss/#what

Supporting Documents

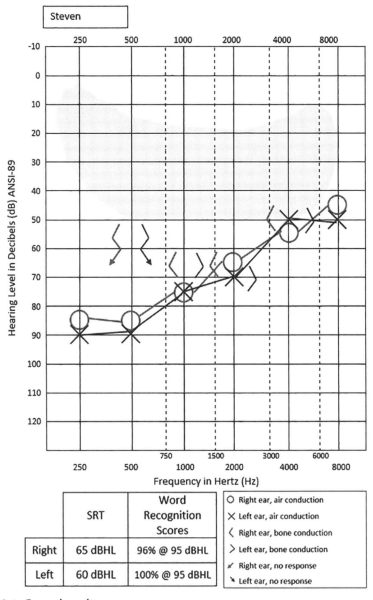

Figure 28.1. Steven's audiogram.

29
Emily

Accommodations; Deaf with a Disability; IEP/IFSP/504; Inclusion; Parent Involvement; Psychosocial

Emily is 16 years old and currently enrolled in the 10th grade in a public high school in an *inclusive* setting. She was born with a *mild* to *moderate bilateral sensorineural hearing level* and has consistently worn her *hearing aids* since she was 6 months old. Emily's *early intervention* services were highly effective and helped her reach developmental milestones within the average range of her hearing peers. Therefore, Emily has been enrolled in *inclusive* settings since the age of 3 years, with weekly services from the *Speech Language Pathologist* (SLP). Her academic performance was on grade-level through the kindergarten and first grade, therefore she didn't qualify for services from a *teacher of the d/Deaf and hard of hearing* (TODHH) at that time. She uses *listening and spoken language* (LSL) as her *mode of communication*.

In second grade, Emily's teacher noticed that Emily seemed to struggle comprehending *high-frequency* word meanings, consistently reversed her letters b/d, and regularly transposed words such as dam/mad and rat/tar. The school district was using the *Response to Intervention* (RTI) framework and the teacher provided *small group* instruction (tier 2), yet these struggles didn't resolve themselves. The *RTI team* then decided to begin one-on-one instruction (tier 3); however, by the end of the second grade Emily did not make adequate progress. The RTI team then referred Emily to a *school psychologist* to see if she was eligible to receive services for a possible *learning disability* (LD). Emily's diagnostic evaluation indicated that she had an LD and would greatly benefit from various reading and writing strategies designed to assist students with LDs (see Appendix C for instructional strategies related to language and literacy acquisition and development).

From the third through eighth grade, Emily remained in an inclusive setting for all subject areas except language arts. During language arts (450 minutes per week), she went to the *resource* classroom and received instruction from a special educator who was *highly qualified* in LDs. The district did not have TODHH available to serve Emily. Her *Individualized Education Program* (IEP) *team* agreed a TODHH wasn't necessary given Emily's primary disability was her LD. Overall, Emily greatly bene-fited from the educational arrangement and specialized instruction and made ade-quate progress in elementary and middle school.

The transition to high school posed new challenges for Emily. Because Emily was on grade level, her IEP team decided to reduce her services from 450 minutes a week to 270, so she would now only going to a *study skills* class three times a week for assis-tance with her language arts coursework. The special educator teaching the study skills class was not highly qualified in LDs. During the study skills class, the teacher would assist students with varying exceptionalities with their various assignments from other classes. With this new academic arrangement, Emily was not adjusting well to the demands of high school. Not only did Emily lack the previous support she had from a teacher who understood and specialized in LD, but her services also had been signifi-cantly reduced from what she had during her elementary years.

On a regular basis, her teachers noted that Emily seemed frustrated. Emily shared with her teachers and parents that she was falling behind in her coursework. Emily's parents were very concerned, as this was the first time that Emily seemed overwhelmed with school and was performing at a level they considered less than her ability. Her parents were hoping that the ninth grade was just a "tough transition" year and they would see her doing better during the 10th grade, although this was not the case. By the end of the ninth grade, both Emily's parents and her teacher decided to hold an IEP meeting to discuss *accommodations* that might help Emily be more successful in the high school environment.

At the IEP meeting, Emily's parents stated that she was on grade level when she completed eighth grade. They firmly believed that the special educator was unable to assist Emily in a way that the previous special educator did because she did not have special training nor a degree specializing in LDs. The team discussed ways in which the teacher could mirror some of the accommodations Emily had in elementary school that seemed to have greatly helped Emily. Emily shared that she enjoyed when her elementary special education teacher would use the iPad to help her review high fre-quency words by pairing the vocabulary with pictures. She also stated that her teacher often showed her examples prior to Emily doing assignments on her own. Other accommodations helpful to students with an LD that were discussed by the team included: practice and review; *modeling, prompting, shaping*; slower pace; and incorpo-rating technology (Soukup & Feinstein, 2007). The special educator expressed con-cern that she was unable to control the instruction delivered by the general education teachers and she was doing her best to (1) advocate for Emily by sharing her accom-modations with the teachers, and (2) assist her during the study skills class. The special educator stated she was willing to co-teach with the general education language arts teacher, but should she engage in such collaboration, she wouldn't have enough time to serve all the students on her *caseload*. Emily was worried because she felt she didn't have the same guidance, support, and instruction that she had in elementary school. The parents were unsatisfied with the current academic arrangement and demanded to have a *parent advocate* at a follow-up IEP meeting. The parents were worried about losing more time and watching Emily fall further behind now that she was entering the 10th grade.

Prior to the follow-up IEP meeting, Emily and her parents met with a parent advocate and discussed the details of Emily's case. A parent advocate is a volunteer who understands students with disabilities and the IEP process. The advocate typically has experience with various cases involving children and adolescents with special needs and can help parents during the IEP meeting to advocate for what they feel is the most appropriate *Free and Appropriate Public Education* (FAPE) in the *Least Restrictive Environment* (LRE). The parents shared with the advocate that they were certain that a teacher with a degree specializing in LD must provide services to Emily or she would continue to regress.

The follow-up IEP meeting was contentious. The parents pointed out that the special educator was not highly qualified in LD. The administrator suggested that the special educator would pursue a certification in LD, but this would not resolve the parent's immediate concerns. In summary, Emily's parents refused to sign the IEP with the notion that they would settle the need for Emily to have a teacher who specialized in LD through *due process*. In conclusion, the administrator and the parent advocate suggested that the two parties enter into *voluntary mediation* to resolve their differences.

DISCUSSION QUESTIONS

1. How might having a teacher not qualified in LD contribute to Emily's difficulty in high school? What other factors could be contributing to her academic struggles?
2. Why did Emily not receive services from a TODHH? What expertise and insight could a TODHH offer to assist the IEP team?
3. What is due process, and how could it have been avoided with this case study? Outline or create a visual map of due process, from mediation through the Supreme Court.
4. Emily isn't receiving any accommodations for her hearing status/level. What other accommodations could be added to the IEP to help assist with the academic rigor of high school (e.g., *Communication Access Real-time Translation* [CART], class notes, etc.)?
5. Who is part of the RTI team, and what are their roles?

ACTIVITIES

1. Using the article cited within the case study by Soukup and Feinstein (2007), as well as other resources, describe how to use the following accommodations with students who are *d/Deaf* or *hard of hearing* (d/Dhh) and have an LD: practice and review; *modeling, prompting, shaping*; slower pace; positive feedback and reinforcement, and incorporating technology.

2. Explore where parents in your region can locate a parent advocate. Provide at least two different resources for parent advocates. Cite the name and contact information of the organization or company, the cost if applicable, and the time frame to scheduling an appointment. This may require that you call the organization. Only one of your two resources can be virtual (online).

3. Create a brochure for general education teachers about students who are d/Dhh and have an LD. On this brochure include (1) the definitions of *deafness* and LD, (2) the different ways an LD manifests itself, (3) possible ways to assess if a student has an LD, and most importantly, (4) strategies educators use with students who are d/Dhh and have an LD. Provide at least two citations from peer-reviewed journals and three resources for recipients of the brochure to use for additional information.

4. Investigate who is part of the RTI team at your local school and what the team member's roles and responsibilities are on the team.

5. If a student has an IEP or a Section 504 plan, you'll likely hear the terms "accommodation" and "modification" from the IEP or Section 504 plan team. While they may be similar, they serve different purposes. Accommodations change how a student learns the material. A modification changes what a student is taught or expected to learn. Research examples and further explain the differences between accommodations and modifications.

ADDITIONAL RESOURCES

Federal government defines IDEA http://idea.ed.gov/

Hands & Voices addresses students who are d/Dhh with disabilities http://handsandvoices.org/articles/deafhh-plus/V14-4_supporting.htm

Response to Intervention Action Network: A program of the National Center for Learning Disabilities http://www.rtinetwork.org/learn/what/whatisrti

Wrights Law is a resource for parents and professionals who advocate for children with disabilities as defined by U.S. federal laws http://www.wrightslaw.com/info/iep.index.htm

Supporting Document

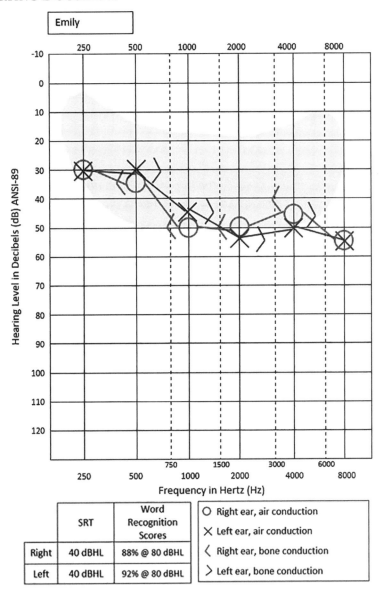

Figure 29.1. Emily's audiogram.

30
Wyatt

Key Topics

Accommodations; Assessment; Collaboration; Content Area Instruction; Deaf of Deaf; IEP/IFSP/504; Inclusion; Language Development; Literacy; Placement; Transition

Wyatt is currently 16 years of age and has two *Deaf* parents and one hearing sibling. Wyatt has a *severe* to *profound sensorineural bilateral hearing level*. He wears *binaural hearing aids* at school and has been learning and using *American Sign Language* (ASL) since birth. Wyatt's mother, Rachel, has a severe bilateral hearing level since birth, with a hearing twin sister. Craig, Wyatt's father, is from a family that traces deafness in their family back at least six generations. Wyatt's hearing level was identified at birth. Rachel and Craig requested *early intervention* services in the home when Wyatt was 3 months of age. He uttered his first words *through-the-air* at 4 months, with a vocabulary of 10 signs at 6 months of age, 25 signs at 8 months, 50 by 12–18 months, 125 by 18–24 months, and 250 by 24–36 months. From a *language sample analysis* by the *early interventionist* (EI), Wyatt's expressive skills appeared to be at the simple sentence level at 3 years of age. His use of multiword-signed utterances mirrored that of typical language development in hearing children (Easterbrooks & Baker, 2002). Wyatt also exhibited early visual interactions such as *deictic gazing, mutual gaze, joint reference*, as well as facial expressions to communicate language and gestures and signs to communicate intent (Easterbrooks & Baker, 2002).

His parents understood the importance of language and literacy activities on Wyatt's development and incorporated components of the *Shared Reading Project* (Schleper, 1995) into their daily ASL storytelling time. Exposure to ASL and English print allowed Wyatt to become bilingual while enrolled in a clustered preschool program for *d/Deaf* and *hard of hearing* (d/Dhh) children housed at an elementary school about 30 minutes from his family's home in a suburban area of the Midwest. His parents began to serve as mentors and personal contacts in their local Hands & Voices chapter and early intervention program. This allowed them to make connections with other families in the area to provide further socialization and language opportunities for their son with other d/Dhh peers.

Because the *school for the deaf* in their state closed in the late 1980s, this was not a placement option for Wyatt; therefore, he attended an *inclusive* preschool program. He received services from a *teacher of the d/Deaf and hard of hearing* (TODHH) and an ASL *interpreter*. Wyatt was familiar with using an interpreter, but explicit focus on how to use one in the classroom was very important for his future placement. In elementary school, Wyatt was in general education classes for the majority of the day with two ASL interpreters. An *itinerant* TODHH visited the school three times per week to monitor Wyatt's academic progress and collaborate on evidence-based *interventions* with the general education teacher and special education coordinator, and with the interpreters at the school on any issues (see Appendix C for instructional strategies related to language and literacy acquisition and development).

Wyatt made typical progress from kindergarten through sixth grade with the supports described. Wyatt's parents continued to utilize community and family resources to provide *Deaf culture* and socialization activities for Wyatt, and they encouraged him to participate in local activities at his school and in the hearing community. It was important to Wyatt's parents that he interacts with all people in his community because in their experience it is vital that deaf people to become bilingual in ASL and English not as a choice but as a necessity (Grosjean, 2008). Many of Wyatt's friends and teachers at school developed ASL skills over the course of his time there, which created a supportive communication environment.

Wyatt moved to his local middle school and struggled at first to keep up with the pace of moving to different classrooms for each period with various teachers. He joined a study skills class provided by the *Learning Support Specialist* in the school during one of his elective periods. Explicit instruction of strategies to help organize and synthesize information from the general education classroom was very beneficial for Wyatt throughout seventh and eighth grades. Wyatt's receptive ASL skills were assessed during this time to determine his progress and begin to plan for the courses he would take in high school. His TODHH administered the *American Sign Language Receptive Skills Test* (ASL-RST; Enns et al., 2013; see Appendix B) and *Individual Education Program* (IEP) goals were developed to increase his *classifier* production based on the results. The teacher and team were concerned about Wyatt's transition to high school and how best to support his processing of information, especially because he struggled slightly when transitioning to middle school. Therefore, upon entering high school, his teachers, interpreters, and parents gathered for a team meeting to discuss what that transition would look like for Wyatt. The special education coordinator and an administrator from the middle school were also present to provide information about the scheduling, classes, and services available. During this *transition meeting* it was determined that a *study skills* class would be added to Wyatt's schedule each semester for added support and *Communication Access Realtime Translation* (CART) would be used along with his interpreter. This allowed Wyatt many benefits during his high school classes.

Now during Wyatt's junior year he continues to excel in his academic courses, receiving services from an itinerant TODHH and interpreters in his college prep courses. His IEP team is preparing to incorporate his *transition plan* for his junior and senior year in high school and to make goals for post-secondary placements. Wyatt has expressed an interest in applying to the *National Technical Institute for the Deaf* (NTID) and *Gallaudet University*. His future goals are to become a social worker for families and children who are d/Dhh.

Discussion Questions

1. What factors led to Wyatt's typical language development and academic progress throughout his schooling?
2. How does the shortage of schools for the deaf change Wyatt's educational placement options? How would his experiences have differed if there were a school for the deaf in his area?
3. What factors need to be considered in selecting Wyatt's post-secondary institution?
4. What transition services are available for him in selecting an institution and receiving accommodations and adaptions? What accommodations and adaptations should be suggested for Wyatt by his IEP team?
5. What is CART? What are the benefits of beginning CART with Wyatt in high school? How do CART services connect to bilingualism?

Activities

1. Review the technology connections below and role-play the team meeting by developing an updated transition plan for Wyatt with the rationale for decisions on the template provided.
2. Research the post-secondary choices and determine which one would have the best major for Wyatt's future goals.
3. Research the post-secondary choices to determine what accommodations and adaptions are available.
4. Research two peer-reviewed journal articles that study CART services for students who are d/Dhh or have other disabilities. Summarize these articles and provide an analysis based on facts from the articles of how CART could potentially benefit Wyatt.
5. Research bilingual-bimodal (bi-bi) language acquisition in ASL and English, and explain the benefits of teaching d/Dhh children using the bi-bi approach in an educational setting.

Additional Resources

ASL assessment http://www.signlang-assessment.info/index.php/american-sign
-language-receptive-skills-test.html

Post-secondary university options:
http://www.gallaudet.edu/
http://www.ntid.rit.edu/

Shared Reading Project http://www3.gallaudet.edu/clerc-center/our-resources/
shared-reading-project.html

School for the Deaf programs http://www.deafed.net/PageText.
asp?hdnPageId=105#AK

Transition:

- http://raisingandeducatingdeafchildren.org/
transition-planning-for-secondary-age-deaf-and-hard-of-hearing-students
- http://www.gadoe.org/Curriculum-Instruction-and-Assessment/Special-Education
-Services/Documents/Transition/Transition%20Plan%20Directions.pdf
- Sample transition plan (http://www.gadoe.org/curriculum-instruction-and
-assessment/special-education-services/pages/sample-special-education-forms.aspx

Supporting Documents

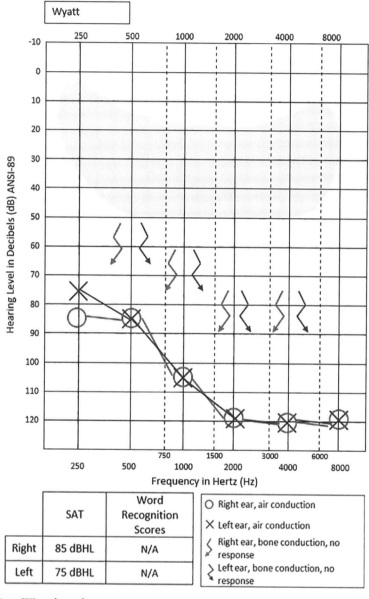

Figure 30.1. Wyatt's audiogram.

Name: Wyatt	**Projected date of Graduation:** Currently entering freshman year	**Date of Initial Transition Program Development:** <u>Freshman year</u> **Update:**

Preferences, Strengths, Interests and Course of Study based on Present Levels of Performance and Age-Appropriate Transition Assessments (Areas for consideration include course of study, post-secondary education, vocational training, employment, continuing education, adult services, and community participation): Wyatt's present levels of performance are on grade level with his hearing peers. Observation of Wyatt in his middle school setting were conducted by his Itinerant Teacher of the Deaf and the high school Learning Support Specialist, along with a short follow-up interview to determine Wyatt's goals for high school and develop his transition plan with his IEP team. From the interview it was determined that Wyatt is interested in pursuing a university degree and would like to attend college-prep courses in high school. He is not yet sure what area of study he would like to pursue. The IEP team determined that this is an attainable goal for Wyatt if provided sufficient accommodations because his reading scores are on grade level. The team made the following accommodations and placement recommendations: study skills class with a high school Learning Support Specialist, continued use of ASL interpreters, continued support from an Itinerant teacher of the Deaf, and introducing the use of CART and a FM system to provide captioning of conversations during class (this may enable Wyatt to view the transcripts after class for review), as well as provide support in following conversations or text during group class discussions.

Desired Measurable Post-Secondary/Outcome Completion Goals (These goals are to be achieved after graduation and there must be a completion goal for Education/Training and Employment.)

Education/Training - Wyatt will complete courses in order to pursue a college-prep high school diploma in order to continue on to a post-secondary degree.

Employment – Wyatt will pursue part-time employment during high school and college to gain skills and determine his area of interest for his college major and future employment.

Independent Living (as appropriate) -

Based on age-appropriate transition assessments, in the spaces below, include measurable Transition IEP Goals and Transition Activities/Services appropriate for the child's post-secondary preferences, strengths, and needs. Note: There must be at least a measurable Transition IEP Goal to help the child reach each of the desired Measurable Post-Secondary/Outcome Completion Goals.

Education/Training (Goals based on academics, functional academics, life-centered competencies or career/technical or agricultural training needs and job training.)			
Transition IEP Goal(s)	**Transition Activities/ Services**	**Person/Agency Involved**	**Date of Completion/ Achieved Outcome**
Wyatt will continue to improve his study skills and use of accommodations to maintain a B average in his college-prep course work during the transition to his freshman year in high school.	Teacher of the DHH – bi-weekly checks from an itinerant teacher for Wyatt and his teachers on his progress and to assist in concept development and maintain assistive technology equipment Learning Support Specialist – small group classroom for study skills class equivalent to elective credit Accommodations – ASL interpreters, CART, FM system, Hearing Aids, extended time on tests as needed, copy of teacher lecture/notes, maintain updated calendar/agenda (for communication of assignments, topics, and due dates for enhanced communication between the TOD, LSS, General Ed teachers, Wyatt, and his parents)	Teacher of the DHH Learning Support Specialist General Education Teachers ASL interpreters CART providers Audiologist Student (Wyatt) Parents	End of this school year

Development of Employment (Goals based on occupational awareness, employment-related knowledge and skills, and specific career pathway knowledge and skills.)			
Transition IEP Goal(s)	**Transition Activities/ Services**	**Person/ Agency Involved**	**Date of Completion/ Achieved Outcome**
Wyatt will discover his interests regarding current and future employment during his freshman year of high school in preparation for acquiring a part-time job in high school and to select a career pathway for post-secondary work.	Career survey – Wyatt will complete a questionnaire/ survey during study skills class in order to determine his interests and strengths related to employment goals. Employment application – Wyatt will complete a mock employment application for a position of interest based on the results of the career survey to learn the requirements of the position and how to advocate for any needed accommodations.	Teacher of the DHH Learning Support Specialist Career Guidance Counselor Student (Wyatt) Parents	End of this school year
Community Participation (Goals based on knowledge and demonstration of skills needed to participate in the community [e.g., tax forms, voter registration, building permits, social interactions, consumer activities, accessing and using various transportation modes.])			
Transition IEP Goal(s)	**Transition Activities/ Services**	**Person/ Agency Involved**	**Date of Completion/ Achieved Outcome**

Adult Living Skills & Post School Options (Goals based on skills for self-determination, interpersonal interactions, communication, health/fitness, and the knowledge needed to successfully participate in Adult Lifestyles and other Post-School Activities [e.g. skills needed to manage a household, maintain a budget and other responsibilities of an adult.])			
Transition IEP Goal(s)	**Transition Activities/ Services**	**Person/ Agency Involved**	**Date of Completion/ Achieved Outcome**

Related Services (Goals based on Related Services that may be required now to help a child benefit from regular and special education and transition services [e.g., speech/language, occupational therapy, counseling, vocational rehabilitation training, or the planning for related services that the individual may need access to as an adult.])			
Transition IEP Goal(s)	**Transition Activities/ Services**	**Person/Agency Involved**	**Date of Completion/ Achieved Outcome**

Daily Living Skills (Goals based on adaptive behaviors related to personal care and well-being to decrease dependence on others.)			
Transition IEP Goal(s)	**Transition Activities/ Services**	**Person/Agency Involved**	**Date of Completion/ Achieved Outcome**

TRANSFER OF RIGHTS

of his/her rights,
if any, that will

(Required by age 17): _____ was informed on _____ transfer at age 18.
                              Name   Date

RIGHTS WERE
TRANSFERRED

(Required by age 18): _____ was informed on _____ of his/her rights.
                              Name   Date

Figure 30.2. Wyatt's transition plan.

Transition Service Plan

Name:	Projected date of Graduation:	Date of Initial Transition Program Development: _____ Update: _____

Preferences, Strengths, Interests and Course of Study based on Present Levels of Performance and Age Appropriate Transition Assessments (Areas for consideration include course of study, post-secondary education, vocational training, employment, continuing education, adult services and community participation)

Desired Measurable Post-Secondary/Outcome Completion Goals (These goals are to be achieved *after* graduation and there must be a completion goal for Education/Training and Employment)

Education/Training -

Employment -

Independent Living (as appropriate) -

Based on age appropriate transition assessments, in the spaces below, include measurable Transition IEP Goals and Transition Activities/Services appropriate for the child's post-secondary preferences, strengths and needs. Note: There must be at least a measurable Transition IEP Goal to help the child reach each of the desired Measurable Post-Secondary/Outcome Completion Goals.

Education/Training (Goals based on academics, functional academics, life centered competencies or career/technical or agricultural training needs and job training.)

Transition IEP Goal(s)	Transition Activities/Services	Person/Agency Involved	Date of Completion/ Achieved Outcome

Development of Employment (Goals based on occupational awareness, employment related knowledge and skills and specific career pathway knowledge and skills.)

Transition IEP Goal(s)	Transition Activities/Services	Person/Agency Involved	Date of Completion/ Achieved Outcome

Transition Service Plan

Community Participation (Goals based on knowledge and demonstration of skills needed to participate in the community (e.g., tax forms, voter registration, building permits, social interactions, consumer activities, accessing and using various transportation modes.))

Transition IEP Goal(s)	Transition Activities/Services	Person/Agency Involved	Date of Completion/ Achieved Outcome

Adult Living Skills & Post School Options (Goals based on skills for self-determination, interpersonal interactions, communication, health /fitness and the knowledge needed to successfully participate in Adult Lifestyles and other Post School Activities (e.g. skills needed to manage a household, maintain a budget and other responsibilities of an adult.)

Transition IEP Goal(s)	Transition Activities/Services	Person/Agency Involved	Date of Completion/ Achieved Outcome

Related Services (Goals based on Related Services that may be required now to help a child benefit from regular and special education and transition services (e.g., speech/language, occupational therapy, counseling, vocational rehabilitation training or the planning for related services that the individual may need access to as an adult.)

Transition IEP Goal(s)	Transition Activities/Services	Person/Agency Involved	Date of Completion/ Achieved Outcome

Daily Living Skills (Goals based on adaptive behaviors related to personal care and well-being to decrease dependence on others.)

Transition IEP Goal(s)	Transition Activities/Services	Person/Agency Involved	Date of Completion/ Achieved Outcome

TRANSFER OF RIGHTS (Required by age 17): _____ was informed on _____ of his/her rights, if any, that will transfer at age 18.
Name   Date

RIGHTS WERE TRANSFERRED (Required by age 18): _____ was informed on _____ of his/her rights.
Name   Date

Figure 30.3. A blank transition plan.

31
Jordan

KEY TOPICS

Assistive Technology; Content Area Instruction; Deaf with a Disability; Parent Involvement; Placement; Psychosocial; Transition

Jordan is a 17-year-old male with a *mild* to *moderate sensorineural hearing level* who wears *binaural hearing aids* and is currently in 11th grade in a general education high school in the Midwest United States. Jordan's mother has a mild hearing level with unknown origin and Jordan received *hearing screening* when he was born because of his multiple risk factors, including his family history. Jordan's mother has struggled with substance abuse since Jordan was a young child. Jordan's father is not and has never been present in his life. Jordan received intermittent *early intervention* services because he and his mother moved frequently. This pattern was repeated once he began elementary school, so several different *teachers of the d/Deaf and hard of hearing* (TODHHs) in the multiple school districts worked with Jordan and his mother throughout his elementary and middle school years.

In middle school, Jordan increasingly became frustrated and occasionally acted out both before and after school (e.g., he came to school with a black eye from fighting boys in his neighborhood; he was caught shoplifting at a local store; he was caught breaking windows in a nearby abandoned building). These behaviors had a negative impact on his friendships and schooling. He was frequently absent from school, and although he utilized his *accommodations* (*FM/DM system*, copy of teacher's notes, etc.) and hearing aids, he was still making slow academic progress. In eighth grade Jordan began acting out during school as well (e.g., violent outbursts in and outside of class; refusal to complete work; refusal to work with others; refusal to use hearing aids during school). His *Individual Education Program* (IEP) *team* referred him for evaluation by a *school psychologist*. His behaviors were interfering with his academic progress, which was already delayed due to inconsistent schooling and his moderate hearing level. The *school psychologist* determined Jordan was eligible for services to support his *emotional behavior disorder* (EBD), and a behavior specialist began working with his general education teacher and his *itinerant* TODHH who saw him once a week. The team began using *positive behavior and intervention supports* (PBIS) with Jordan, including proactive steps to encourage the use of his hearing aids, systemic methods to calm frustration (e.g., counting backwards from 10; *mindfulness exercises*; appointments with the school counselor to discuss the source of his frustration; enrollment in the Big Brother mentor program, etc.).

Although supports were put in place by his previous *IEP team*, Jordan's frustration escalated in high school when he again moved to a new district and had a new set of teachers and a new IEP team. He also lost contact with his Big Brother mentor whom he had grown close with during their visits. He began having trouble focusing in class and had multiple misunderstandings with classmates, partly due to the noisy school environment and the fact that he refused to wear his hearing aids. After repeated bullying incidents over the past two years from two classmates in his P.E. class who were teasing him about his speech, Jordan became extremely upset. He punched the school lockers, causing property damage, and injuring his hand. The school administrator recommended suspending Jordan from school for 14 days, but since he receives special education services this recommendation cannot be followed without a *manifestation determination* meeting.

His TODHH called a *manifestation determination review* with the IEP team (general education teachers, special education teacher, *behavior interventionist*, TODHH, Jordan, parent, school administrator, district administrator). The team attempted to have three meetings, but Jordan's mother never responded to their meeting notifications (email, certified mail, phone) and did not attend. Since the *manifestation determination* must take place within 10 days of the incident, the team proceeded at the third meeting without his mother present. The team determined that Jordan's conduct may be related to his EBD, but in order to make an *evidence-based decision* they needed more information. They decided the *behavior interventionist* would complete a *Functional Behavior Analysis* (FBA; see Supporting Documents and Additional Resources) to determine the source of Jordan's behaviors and then use this information to develop a *Behavior Intervention Plan* (BIP; see Supporting Documents and Additional Resources) to reinforce problem-solving skills he learned from PBIS in middle school. The BIP will also help the team determine PBIS that will help Jordan respond to stressful situations without violent outbursts. These techniques may help reduce his negative behaviors and increase the likelihood of his success at school. The special education teacher offered to work with the behavior interventionist to complete the FBA and BIP and consult with the school psychologist and counselor as they develop a plan for Jordan's emotional and behavior issues.

Jordan's TODHH also suggested the team consider adding *Communication Access Real-Time Translation* (CART) to his accommodations (peer note taker, recordings of lessons, and teacher summary notes for lecture classes), which produces a real-time printed transcription of information. Jordan could also utilize CART to assist him in focusing in his core courses (science, social studies, math, and language arts) during his senior year. His TODHH shared with the team that he thinks this might reduce some of Jordan's frustration and behavioral incidents because he would have more complete access during lectures and activities. These supports may also help reduce Jordan's frustration as senior year will be yet another transition to new classes for him. The special education teacher and behavior interventionist caution the team not to make changes to Jordan's accommodations until the results of the BIP are complete so that *evidence-based decisions* can be made about the reasons for his behavior.

DISCUSSION QUESTIONS

1. Review Figures 31.2 and 31.3 in the Supporting Documents, and provide as much information as possible, based on details in the case study, to develop the outline of a FBA and a BIP for Jordan.
2. What other steps could the IEP team take to involve Jordan's mother in mitigating his academic and behavior deficits? What responsibilities do teachers have to report parent neglect, and what are your local reporting agencies?
3. How does Jordan's struggle with focus in the classroom affect his ability to learn content in his science, social studies, and math courses? What role does motivation play in helping Jordan remain engaged with *content area* instruction?
4. What academic or extracurricular activities might assist Jordan in building his confidence, engagement, and interaction with peers? How could positive peer relationships buffer the potential negative impact of bullying?
5. As stated in the case study, Jordan and his mother frequently move and apparently do not have a stable home life. Jordan's personal and academic needs are clearly interfering with his ability to learn and adjust in school. How might adding a social worker or counselor to the IEP team better support (or benefit) Jordan and his mother?

ACTIVITIES

1. CART can be utilized in different formats (e.g., remotely with a laptop; projected on a screen with active stenographer in the room). Explore the additional resources regarding the different ways CART can be used and what formats are most appropriate for various settings (i.e., high school vs. post-secondary). Explore new technologies that provide text-based accommodations and consider how these might support students who are *d/Deaf* and *hard of hearing* (d/DHH).
2. Every state has one parent training and information center and community parent resource center. Find one for your state, and list the state regulations related to

meeting notifications for IEPs. Obtain a copy of the procedural safeguards to demonstrate your understanding of the regulations in your region.

3. Explore the resources provided, and others, regarding PBIS. Determine if these supports are used in your local district. If they are, find training or resources and compile a summary of the information to present to your class. If they are not being used, design a proposal for your district supervisor about why PBIS should be implemented to increase achievement and positive behavior.

ADDITIONAL RESOURCES

Communication Access Realtime Translation (CART) https://www.nad.org/resources/technology/captioning-for-access/communication-access-realtime-translation/

Child abuse and neglect information with links to local information https://www.childwelfare.gov/pubPDFs/define.pdf

Functional Behavior Assessment Guide and Step-by-Step provided a case study: Shippen, M. E., Simpson, R. G., & Crites, S. A. (2003). A practical guide to functional behavioral assessment. *Teaching Exceptional Children, 35*(5), 36–44. https://www2.bc.edu/alec-peck/FBA-TEC-2003.pdf

Positive Behavioral Interventions and Supports http://www.pbis.org/

Manifestation Determination http://www.parentcenterhub.org/repository/manifestation/

Supporting Documents

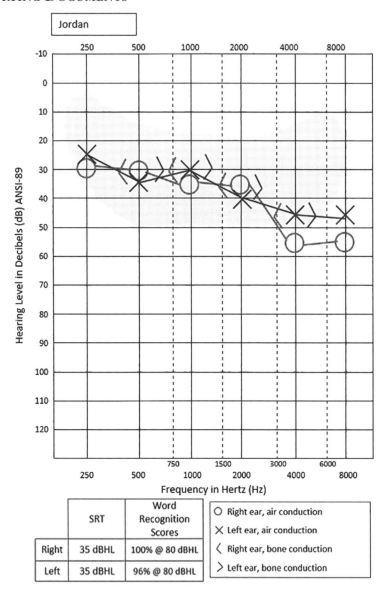

Figure 31.1. Jordan's audiogram.

1. Identify the behaviors that need to change.
2. Determine where the behaviors do and do not occur.
3. Collect data on the student's performance from as many sources as possible.
4. Develop a hypothesis about why the behaviors are occurring.
5. Identify alternative behavior to replace the behavior that needs to change.
6. Test the hypothesis.
7. Evaluate the success of interventions.

Figure 31.2. Steps for a Functional Behavioral Assessment (FBA).

1. Target behaviors
2. Measurable goals
3. Intervention description and method
4. When to start and how frequent the intervention will take place
5. Method of evaluation
6. Responsibility for each part of intervention and evaluation
7. Data from evaluation

Figure 31.3. Steps for a Behavior Intervention Plan (BIP).

32
Anthony

Key Topics

Accommodations; Audiological Management; Modality; Transition

Anthony is 18 years of age. He was identified with a *profound bilateral sensorineural hearing level* at 6 months of age and received a *cochlear implant* (CI) at 1 year of age. His family is very involved in his *audiological management* and his educational services. Each year his CI *mapping* is updated to meet his listening needs. He and his family participated in *early intervention* services until then he transitioned to his local *inclusive* preschool program. At 5 years of age he transitioned to a private school that used a *listening and spoken language* (LSL) philosophy and stayed through fifth grade because he benefitted from the *small group* instruction and the *audiological access*. The school's philosophy included the development of rigorous LSL skills within an environment that maximized *auditory access*. His teachers were certified *Listening and Spoken Language Specialists* (LSLS) and taught in small classes of five to eight students so that each student received individualized instruction. Each classroom had a *sound-field system*, and teachers used *FM systems* to ensure optimal auditory access for each student. His parents also attended training sessions to maximize communication access and interactions at home. Anthony was successful with this communication approach. Although he occasionally missed some words within instruction and conversation, he developed an awareness of when he missed information and the ability to ask for repetition of information when needed.

When he transitioned to the local public middle school, he was the only *deaf* student at his school. He received educational services in the general education classroom with his typically hearing peers. His *accommodations* included *preferential seating* at the front of the classroom to ensure visual access to instruction; teacher use of an *FM/DM system* in each class; a copy of the teacher's notes, and *closed captions* on any videos shown in class. This placement was a drastic change from his instruction within a small class size in an ideal auditory environment at his previous school, and Anthony found he was missing chunks of instructional information even with these accommodations. His grades declined due to the missing information. His *Individual Education Program* (IEP) *team* decided to add *sign language* support via an *educational interpreter*

within his *content area* classes to ensure Anthony had access to all instructional information. He also received a daily *study skills* course during which the *interpreter* and the
general education teachers collaborated to preview the content-related vocabulary in
sign language. This approach proved successful for Anthony's three years in middle
school. However, he began to feel isolated without deaf peers and no one but the
interpreter with whom he could use sign language. His parents did not learn sign language because conversation in the home environment remained accessible for Anthony.
Like many adolescent deaf students, Anthony sought peers who were similar to him.
After consideration among Anthony, his family, and his IEP team, he decided to
attend a school with deaf peers.

For ninth grade Anthony transitioned to the state residential *school for the deaf*,
which was a *bilingual/bicultural environment* of instruction and conversation was in
sign language with access to English via print. Instead of individual accommodations,
all instruction was provided in small grade-level groups with consistent visual support
and provision of closed captions for all videos. At first Anthony felt overwhelmed with
the level of sign language used by his peers and their consistent questions about his
English-like sign skills. He also felt awkward abandoning the use of spoken English
within this environment. However, he continued to use his CI and quickly learned
how to match his communication style to his communication partners and frequently
paired sign language with spoken language as he formed his own deaf identity. Anthony
rapidly assimilated to this environment with deaf peers and role models.

When he was 14 years old he had his initial *transition meeting* with his IEP team to
discuss possible pathways after high school. His team consisted of his parents, a few
teachers, the school principal, the *vocational rehabilitation* (VR) counselor, and the
school *Speech Language Pathologist* (SLP). Anthony completed an interest inventory to
identify potential college and career pathways. Based on his results, he decided he
would like to pursue an acting career with the National Theatre of the Deaf. During
this meeting, his team decided upon transition goals that included enrollment in a
sequence of *American Sign Language* (ASL) courses across his subsequent years in high
school; attending *Deaf cultural* events to further develop his fluency in ASL; joining
the school's traveling theater group; researching possible universities that offered theater as a major; contacting those universities via relay service and email to request
program information; and using a video phone to interview deaf thespians.

Now Anthony is a senior, and it is time for his final IEP meeting to solidify his
transition plans after high school. He is using the self-empowered *ASPIRE model*
(http://www.gaspdg.org/aspire) to present the results of his previous transition goals
to his IEP team. Anthony will discuss his current interests, his desires, his strengths,
and areas he needs to develop to be successful in college and with his future career.
This meeting also serves as a platform for Anthony to fine-tune his advocacy skills for
when he meets with the VR counselor.

Discussion Questions

1. Discuss the social aspects of this case. What are the effects of the significant shifts in communication mode, the shift from neighborhood to residential school, and the effects on peer and familial relationships?
2. What supports might the IEP team have put into place upon Anthony's transition from the LSL program to his neighborhood school? What opportunities to support his social (and extracurricular) development might have been missed?
3. Based on Anthony's interest to become an actor, as an IEP team member, provide additional resources he might pursue related to deaf actors and deaf theater (e.g., the Deaf Professional Arts Network)?
4. What are some of the challenges with using an FM/DM system in a local middle school and a residential high school setting? What are some ways to alleviate these challenges?

Activities

1. Investigate your local VR services. Who is/are the VR counselors? Who is involved in the VR process? What services are offered? As a *teacher of the d/Deaf and hard of hearing* (TODHH), how would you invite the VR team to participate in your *IEP meetings*?
2. Find an interest inventory related to the transition from secondary school to employment/education. How would you use this survey with a student? Based on possible answers from the inventory, develop measurable transition goals (e.g., "Sally will enroll in a local financial management course and provide a paragraph summary of how she will independently manage her money" or "Sammy will visit three universities and provide a *graphic organizer* that includes a list of pros and cons for attendance at each university").
3. Search "Quickbook of Transition Assessments" and download the pdf file. Identify a student with whom you have worked or whom you know. Select the appropriate grade level from the Quickbook of Transition Assessments. Discuss with a peer how you might utilize the Parent and Student/Teacher versions of the Suggested Transition Activities as a TODHH.
4. Investigate the supports available to assist students who transition from local neighborhood programs to state residential programs (e.g., *Alexander Graham Bell Association* Leadership Opportunities for Teens [LOFT], National Association of the Deaf Youth Leadership, etc.).

Additional Resources

A Transition Guide https://www2.ed.gov/about/offices/list/osers/transition/products/postsecondary-transition-guide-2017.pdf

National Collaborative on Workforce and Disability http://www.ncwd-youth.info/
    innovative-strategies/practice-briefs/using-career-interest-inventories-to-inform
    -career-planning
National Technical Assistance Center on Transition http://transitionta.org/
Pepnet 2 Deaf and Hard of Hearing http://www.pepnet.org/

Supporting Document

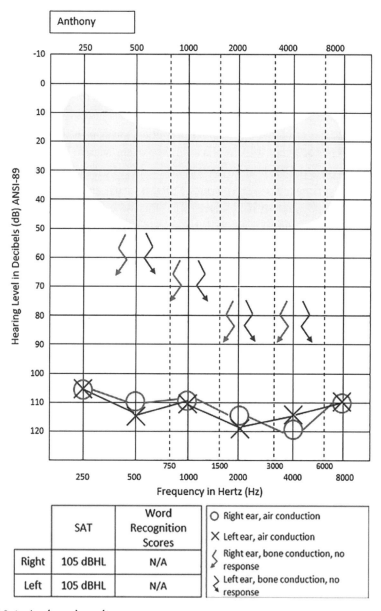

Figure 32.1. Anthony's audiogram.

33
Merritt

KEY TOPICS

Collaboration; Deaf of Deaf; IEP/IFSP/504; Psychosocial; SES; Transition

Merritt is 18 years old and a confident young male in his senior year of high school. He was born with a *profound bilateral sensorineural hearing level*. Both of his parents are also *Deaf*. He has attended a residential *school for the deaf* in the southeast region of the United States as a day student since kindergarten. Merritt has never used *assistive listening devices* (ALDs). His family is immersed in the *Deaf community* and *Deaf culture*, and their primary *mode of communication* is visual and his *first language* (L1) is *American Sign Language* (ASL). Merritt's parents have always been supportive of him, helping him succeed in school and thrive in extracurricular activities.

Because this is Merritt's senior year, he has many important decisions to make regarding his future academic and athletic careers. Merritt is the Most Valuable Player (MVP) of the high school football team and has maintained a 3.0 GPA throughout his high school years. His success, in part, is due to his father's role as the assistant football coach, and his mother's academic support as a middle-school teacher. During his junior year of high school, Merritt was approached by various college recruiters because of his impressive skills as a football player. Merritt also has been seriously involved with his girlfriend for the past three years and hopes to continue the relationship after high school. While many aspects of his life are favorable, his transition from high school to college will require him to make some significant decisions that will affect his future. Merritt is considering the following:

(1) Which university should he attend?
(2) How will he pay for college?
(3) What *accommodations* and supports will he need to be successful in the university setting?
(4) How will he decide a major based on his career interests?
(5) Will he be able to maintain his relationship in college?

During the summer prior to his senior year, he received news that he had been accepted to *Gallaudet University*, the *National Technical Institute for the Deaf* (NTID), and an in-state public university. Gallaudet is a university where students, staff, and faculty utilize ASL and English in a *bilingual/bicultural environment*. NTID is a technological college for students who are deaf, housed within the Rochester Institute of Technology (RIT) offering multiple instructional approaches to maximize communication access. In contrast, the in-state public university tends to have few deaf students, but their *Disability Resource Center* (DRC) would ensure Merritt would have accommodations to fully access instruction. Gallaudet and NTID are both out-of-state universities and did not offer full scholarships for his attendance. However, Gallaudet offered him a position on the football team and a partial scholarship. NTID does not have a football team. The in-state university offered Merritt a full scholarship if he agrees to play football and maintains a GPA of 2.5 or better. Merritt's girlfriend is planning to attend NTID as a software engineering major. Merritt is having a difficult time weighing his options but realizes that paying for school will be a challenge if he decides to attend college out-of-state.

In order to assist Merritt in his decision-making, his parents requested a follow-up *transition meeting*. The parents wanted more information regarding the available accommodations Merritt may need to support his academic success should he choose the in-state university. Members of the transition team included: *vocational rehabilitation* (VR) representative, Merritt's parents, Merritt, the school counselor, and his *teacher of the d/Deaf and hard of hearing* (TODHH).

Discussion Questions

1. Given that Merritt has been at an ASL/English bilingual/bicultural environment academically throughout his K–12 career, compare and contrast how his university experience may differ based upon the three universities he has to choose from.

2. Discuss the role of each member of the transition team. What expertise do they bring to the team? How will their unique perspectives help Merritt answer the five questions outlined in the case study?

3. What are the key elements of a transition plan meeting?

4. Will Merritt's accommodations vary based upon the university he chooses?

5. Discuss the implications of a deaf student attending a university where the majority of students use sign language versus not.

ACTIVITIES

1. Make a list of the accommodations that students who are d/Deaf are likely to need in college. Create a flyer with explicit steps that these students will need to take to assure that these accommodations are in place when he begins college. Hint: Contact a local university of college and speak with their DRC.
2. Many people benefit from learning new material in a visual format. Create a *graphic organizer* to help Merritt work through three of the five decisions he will have to make.
3. Explore the PepNet 2.0 or National Deaf Center websites in the Additional Resources. Of the resources you find within the website, identify two different links you could use to assist Merritt during his transition from high school to college. Describe why you believe each of these links would be helpful.
4. Research the VR resources in your county or state for students who are *d/Deaf* and *hard of hearing* (d/Dhh). Provide a link and contact information for one or two resources. Contact them (via email or phone). Ask them how they could possibly assist you with a student such as Merritt.
5. Identify scholarships that are specifically available for students who are d/Dhh.

ADDITIONAL RESOURCES

National Technical Assistance Center on Transition hosts resources helpful to navigating the transition process with students with disabilities. Search for the *Age Appropriate Transition Assessment Toolkit 4.0.* http://transitionta.org/transition planning

PepNet 2.0 is not an updated resource yet contains a wealth of information on post-secondary and career transition for teenagers and adults who are d/Dhh. http://www.pepnet.org/

Post-secondary Transition Guide (2017) https://www2.ed.gov/about/offices/list/osers/transition/products/postsecondary-transition-guide-2017.pdf

The National Deaf Center is the newest federally funded project for postsecondary outcomes for people who are d/Dhh. http://www.nationaldeafcenter.org/

Supporting Document

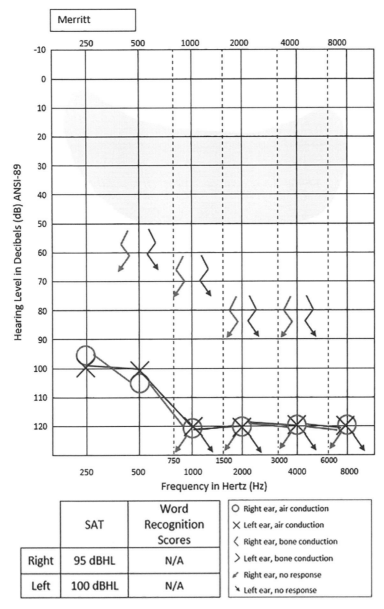

Figure 33.1. Merritt's audiogram.

34
Rolando

Accommodations; Culture; Deaf with a Disability; Multilingual; Psychosocial; SES; Transition

Rolando is a 19-year-old male with a *moderate conductive hearing level* and *Down syndrome*. He has a moderate *intellectual disability*. Rolando was born in a large metropolitan city in Portugal where his parents and two older sisters lived. Although his Down syndrome was identified at birth, Rolando's hearing level was identified after experiencing repeated *otitis media with effusion* (commonly referred to as "glue ear"). This condition is common among children with Down syndrome who may have narrower *eustachian tubes* that do not allow proper drainage of fluid and result in repeated ear infections. These infections led to permanent *middle ear* damage for Rolando by the time he was 4 1/2 years old. He began wearing *binaural hearing aids* when he was 5 years old that increased his hearing to a *mild* to *moderate level*. Rolando also began wearing eyeglasses for *near-sightedness* by the time he was 6 years old.

Rolando's *home language* is Portuguese, and he is significantly younger than his two sisters who are both married with children of their own. Rolando is nonverbal and utilizes his *Augmentative Alternative Communication* (AAC) applications on his tablet to communicate. The applications allow him to tap pictures, symbols, and/or text to express his thoughts.

In the Portugal school system Rolando was *mainstreamed* with his typically developing peers in an *inclusive* environment for the majority of his school day, and he also participated in a small group *resource* classroom with other students with *developmental* and *intellectual disabilities*. A special education teacher taught Rolando when he was in the resource classroom and collaborated with his general education classroom teacher and a full-time *educational assistant* who worked with him throughout the school day. His parents felt the educational services were very inclusive for Rolando, but they lacked vocational training or preparation of life skills for him beyond school.

Due to their older ages, Rolando's parents were particularly worried about his future and who would support his needs as an adult. Six years ago, when Rolando was in sixth grade his father lost his employment and the family was forced to leave their home of over 25 years due to financial constraints. His parents had younger cousins in the northeastern region of the United States who had been living there 24 years and who have an adult daughter with *cerebral palsy* (CP). The cousins offered financial and emotional support to the family and hoped their experience with their daughter could help Rolando's parents navigate the U.S. education and immigration system. His parents also wanted Rolando to get to know his extended family better, since his parents and cousins agreed he could stay with them if his parents' health began to decline. This significant change in their home lives will provide an emotional support system for the parents and psychosocial support for Rolando who will have a role model in the home. The family applied for visas and moved Rolando, his mother, and father to the United States, and his two sisters stayed behind in Portugal with their young children.

Upon arriving in the United States when Rolando was 13 years old, his parents brought his eligibility paperwork from Portugal, which was accepted by the district and an *Individualized Education Program* (IEP) team reviewed the U.S. special education system so his parents could understand their rights, with the help of their cousins as supports and advocates. Rolando was determined to be eligible for services from a special education teacher for his moderate intellectual disability and from a *teacher of the d/Deaf and hard of hearing* (TODHH) and a *Speech Language Pathologist* (SLP) for his moderate hearing level and language delays. He was then enrolled in his local public school where he attended *small group*, *self-contained* classes with a special education resource teacher who primarily worked with students with developmental disabilities and had taught two previous *d/Deaf and hard of hearing* (d/Dhh) students. In addition, his TODHH collaborated with his special education resource teacher to provide the best communication and language access for Rolando. In his small group class Rolando used his AAC tablet to work on a *life skills curriculum* via software in preparation for job training, and he also participated in school-wide activities throughout the day.

His special education teacher was involved with the local Special Olympics, and several of her students participated so she invited Rolando to do the same. When he was 14 years old Rolando became involved in the sport of bowling, which gave him confidence and an opportunity to meet and become friends with many other students with special needs who participated on his team. Group conversations were sometimes a challenge because of the noise level in the bowling alley. When Rolando was 16 years old, his TODHH and his resource teacher worked together to set up a *Community-Based Instruction* (CBI) placement that incorporated his interest in bowling. As a result, Rolando began working at a bowling alley cleaning bowling balls, lanes, and shoes three times a week.

Now that Rolando is 19 years old and his family has lived in the United States for six years, his parents have permanent residency status and hope their cousins and teachers can help them determine Rolando's eligibility for Social Security Income, Medicaid, and/or vocational rehabilitation (VR) services to provide him with the best options for his future. Because his parents are now at retirement age and are not working in the United States, they understand that Rolando can continue to receive special education services until he is 22 years old but are concerned about what he will do after this time. Rolando's cousin with CP works part-time at a dry cleaner, and his parents would like to learn more about vocational services in their area to determine if Rolando could secure part or full-time employment upon completing school. Rolando's *IEP team* developed an initial draft of a *transition plan* (see Supporting Document) to meet his parents' requests and his future needs.

DISCUSSION QUESTIONS

1. Who should Rolando's teachers collaborate with to gain answers to his parent's questions about financial and social benefits (i.e., Medicaid, Social Security Income for disabilities, VR)?
2. Why was Rolando placed in a small group class for the majority of his school day in the United States when he was previously mainstreamed in Portugal?
3. Why is it so important to involve kids in extracurricular activities, particularly those with special needs?
4. What are two or three transition goals that could be added to Rolando's initial transition plan for after high school (see Supporting Document)?
5. What do you know about AAC applications? The applications allow Rolando to tap pictures, symbols, and/or text to express his thoughts and to communicate. How might this device increase his social interaction, school performance, and self-esteem?

ACTIVITIES

1. Investigate supportive work environments for CBI training in your local area. What are places in your community that hire students with special needs?
2. Investigate AAC devices using the included resources. How are students assessed to determine if they might benefit from AACs? What kinds of AACs might be challenging for some d/Dhh students and why?
3. Review the nonprofit organization Special Olympics.
   a. Who established the organization?
   b. Who participates? What are eligibility requirements?
   c. What sports are included?
   d. What benefits come from participation?

e. What are criticisms of the Special Olympics?

f. How do Special Olympics differ from Deaflympics?

g. As a TODHH, how might you play a role in Special Olympics or Deaflympics?

4. Investigate the VR services available in your state or province, and update the transition plan in Figure 34.2 to include goals and outcomes for working with these agencies to determine the best outcomes for Rolando.

5. Research different types of educational placements and determine which placement is the most appropriate for Rolando. Provide valid reasons why you feel the placement is the most appropriate for him.

ADDITIONAL RESOURCES

Augmentative and Alternative Communication information
American Speech-Language Hearing Association
http://www.asha.org/public/speech/disorders/AAC/
http://www.asha.org/slp/clinical/aac/

Down Syndrome and deafness
Down Syndrome Education online https://www.down-syndrome.org/updates/222/
National Down Syndrome Society http://www.ndss.org/Down-Syndrome/What-Is-Down-Syndrome/
Down Syndrome Association http://www.ndcs.org.uk/document.rm?id=2299

Transition and post-secondary information
Pepnet2 transition info http://www.pepnet.org/resources/education-and-training/transitions
National Down Syndrome Society http://www.ndss.org/Resources/Transition-and-Beyond/Life-After-High-School/

SUPPORTING DOCUMENTS

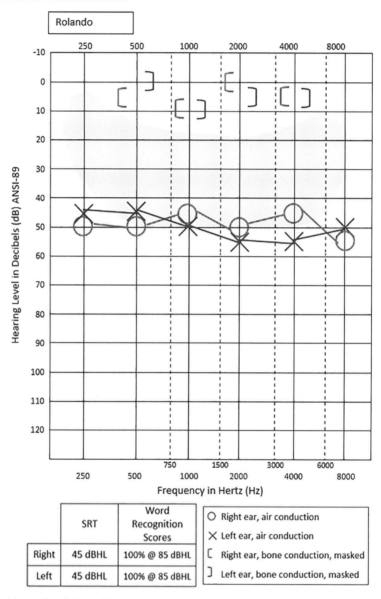

Figure 34.1. Rolando's audiogram.

Course of Study and Current Level of Performance Matched with Preferences, Strengths, and Interests
Rolando is a 19-year-old high school student working toward a special education diploma. He is currently participating in a resource classroom focused on a life skills curriculum, and he completes CBI at a bowling alley due to his love of the sport and participating in the Special Olympics. Rolando is very friendly and uses his AAC device to communicate. Rolando's parents want him to have full- or part-time employment as an adult.
Post-Secondary Goals and Desired Outcomes
Education/Training: Rolando will obtain his high school diploma and seek an employment training program with the help of rehabilitation services.
Employment: Upon graduation from high school, Rolando will obtain employment at a facility that will provide appropriate accommodations for his delays and hearing level and where public transportation is accessible.
Independent Living: Rolando will independently go to and from work and follow his own work schedule to arrive promptly.
Transition Goal(s)
1. Rolando will work on his independent living skills within the resource room setting and CBI placement to increase his ability to navigate transportation and maintain a routine and schedule.
Activities: 1. Rolando will practice navigating public transportation and independently follow a visual schedule regarding his CBI work in preparation for new employment. 2. Rolando will ask his CBI work placement location if they would be interested in hiring him for paid, part-time work after high school considering his experience.
Person/Agency Involved
a. Rolando, special education resource teacher, parents, TODHH, SLP, VR counselor.

Figure 34.2. Transition plan.

35
Sunny

KEY TOPICS

Deaf with a Disability; Placement; Transition

Sunny is a 20-year-old student who was identified with a *moderate bilateral hearing level* when she was 3 years of age and will soon transition from school to work. She is an only child of a single mom and has no siblings. When Sunny was young her mother was concerned that Sunny did not always respond to communication and seemed to have difficulty paying attention at times. After a visit to the *audiologist*, Sunny was identified with a moderate *hearing level* at 3 years of age and fitted with *bilateral hearing aids*. Her mother works full-time to support the two of them. She completed a community introductory course in *sign language* and has always used spoken language paired with the signs she knows when communicating with Sunny. She wanted to continue sign language classes but had difficulty balancing all of her responsibilities with the class schedule. Sunny uses spoken language with sign support for communication and instruction.

Sunny attended a preschool program for children with varying special needs and made gradual language gains, although she was delayed compared to her hearing peers. Sunny attended the majority of her elementary years in separate classes at her local school with a *teacher of the d/Deaf and hard of hearing* (TODHH), where she received *small group* classroom instruction in language, literacy, and *content areas* and joined her grade-level peers for elective courses (e.g., art) with an *educational interpreter*. Despite these services, Sunny remained delayed in her language and literacy development during her early elementary years. After additional assessments, Sunny was diagnosed with a mild *intellectual disability* (i.e., *deaf with a disability*). She continued with her separate class instruction but also received one-on-one language instruction from the TODHH. When her *Individual Education Program* (IEP) *team* met at the end of Sunny's fifth grade year, they decided Sunny might benefit from a language-rich environment in which those around her used sign language. Her IEP team decided that a residential *school for the deaf* might provide Sunny with more exposure to sign language from peers and increase her language skills. Additionally, students at the school for the deaf were permitted to attend school until their 22nd birthday; this extended time would provide opportunities for Sunny to develop her language and independent living skills.

The IEP team held a *transition meeting* with her mother and educators from both her previous school and the school for the deaf. The team decided that Sunny would receive instruction in a special education class at the school for the deaf and non-academic classes with her grade-level peers (e.g., elective and *American Sign Language* [ASL] classes). Sunny quickly made friends at the school for the deaf and became involved in extracurricular activities, such as the Prom Planning Committee and Future Farmers of America.

When she turned 14 years old, the IEP team held a transition meeting and addressed Sunny's post-secondary desires. Sunny completed an occupational interest inventory and decided she enjoyed the culinary arts. Sunny and the IEP team made decisions regarding Sunny's goals related to her future employment and independent living skills.

First, they aligned available classes to meet Sunny's needs. She continued in her small group classroom for language and literacy instruction, her ASL class, and also enrolled in a home economics class. She also assisted with management of the produce grown in the school's greenhouse for two years. When she was 16 years old she joined the *Community-Based Instruction* (CBI) program available in town. She completed two years of a half-day internship with a local restaurant preparing food and cleaning the kitchen. Now she is 20 years old and transitioning from school to employment and independent living. Sunny is currently reading at a second grade level and recognizes many functional words in print. She wants to find a restaurant to work at and become responsible for managing the city bus route from the school to her work place. Sunny and the IEP team developed objectives to address her future goals (see Sunny's *transition plan*, Supporting Documents).

DISCUSSION QUESTIONS

1. What type of supports might Sunny need during this transition?
2. Given that Sunny is *deaf* with a mild *intellectual disability*, how might this have affected her educational and social development? Should the professionals or parent have any differing expectations for her educational and social outcomes? Why or why not?
3. Describe other independent living skills Sunny may need for her post-secondary life.
4. Some students have only one parent or guardian at home who must juggle many responsibilities when providing for his or her family. What are some barriers parents may face? As an educator, how can you help parents overcome these barriers?

Activities

1. Add two to three additional goals and related details to Sunny's transition plan.
2. Via your school library, access the *American Annals of the Deaf*, volume 160, issue 4. Summarize how information from these articles pertains to Sunny and other students who are *deaf with disabilities*. Provide explicit citations from the articles related to aspects of Sunny's case study.
3. Identify two or three community agencies and their provided resources and materials that can assist Sunny in transitioning from school to independent life.
4. What are some *self-advocacy* skills Sunny might need as she transitions to the work force and independent living? Develop an activity to help Sunny with her self-advocacy skills.
5. Design an activity to help Sunny understand what "*accommodations*" and "*modifications*" mean in terms of the academic world and social/work worlds. Research and list possible accommodations and modifications Sunny would need for her future job.

Additional Resources

Pepnet 2, *Deaf and hard of hearing.* http://www.pepnet.org

Project10 Transition Education Network, University of South Florida St. Petersburg. http://project10.info/DetailPage.php?MainPageID=158

Supporting Documents

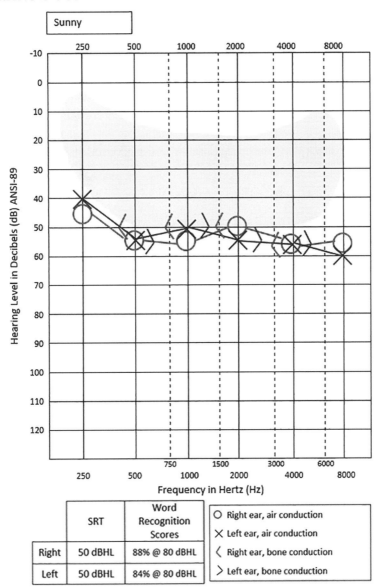

	SRT	Word Recognition Scores
Right	50 dBHL	88% @ 80 dBHL
Left	50 dBHL	84% @ 80 dBHL

- O Right ear, air conduction
- X Left ear, air conduction
- ⟨ Right ear, bone conduction
- ⟩ Left ear, bone conduction

Figure 35.1. Sunny's audiogram.

TRANSITION SERVICE PLAN

Preferences, strengths, interests, and course of study based on Present Levels of Academic Achievement and Functional Performance (PLAAFP) and Age-Appropriate Transition Assessments:

Sunny is currently a freshman at the Bestever School for the Deaf. Sunny recently completed the Conover Interest Inventory and decided she wants to work in the field of culinary arts (i.e., food preparation at a restaurant) after high school graduation. Sunny currently participates in the school's Teachers as Advisors class each Friday to discuss her transition plan and goals. Sunny wants to live independently and support herself by working in a restaurant.

Date of Transition Assessment: 8/6/2015

Name of Assessment: Conover Interest Inventory, Teachers as Advisors student/teacher interview

These goals will be supported by participation in the following course of study: Culinary Arts

1. Education/Training Sunny will identify safe food handling procedures.		
Transition IEP Goals	**Transition Activities/Services**	**Person/Agency Involved**
Sunny will identify five different tasks relevant to safe food preparation within a restaurant setting. **Evaluation Method:** Informational evaluation via TAA interview **Criteria for Mastery:** 80% accuracy in identification of five different safe food preparation tasks **Expected Completion Date:** 12/15/15	1. Sunny will intern at a local restaurant in food preparation. 2. Sunny will create a graphic organizer to list these five different tasks.	TAA teacher, student, parent, restaurant manager

2. Employment/Training Sunny will complete an internship of 8 hours per week at a local restaurant.		
Transition IEP Goals	**Transition Activities/ Services**	**Person/Agency Involved**
Sunny will identify three possible local restaurants for future employment. **Evaluation Method:** Informational evaluation via TAA interview **Criteria for Mastery:** 100% accuracy in identification of three possible restaurants **Expected Completion Date:** 12/15/15	1. Sunny will visit the local community with her TAA and identify potential restaurants for future employment. 2. Sunny will create a graphic organizer to compare and contrast the three different restaurants.	TAA teacher, student, parent, restaurant manager

Figure 35.2. Transition plan for Sunny.

Appendix A
Case Study Scope and Sequence Matrix

The following table shows the comprehensive list of case studies. The cells marked with an X indicate the "key topics" addressed in the scope of that student's case study. All case studies contain elements that require the reader to conduct inquiry-based learning by brainstorm strategies needed for academic, behavior social, and/or emotional success.

Case Study #	Student	Page (s)	Age year; month	Accommodations	Assessment	Assistive Technology	Audiological Management	Collaboration	Content Area Instruction	Culture	Deaf of Deaf	Deaf with a Disability	Early Intervention	IEP/IFSP/504	Inclusion	Language Development	Literacy	Modality	Multilingual	Parent Involvement	Placement	Psychosocial	SES	Transition
1	Anwar	1–5	:4			X	X						X	X		X				X				
2	Jackie	6–10	1;6		X			X		X	X					X	X			X				
3	Liam	11–17	2		X	X	X	X					X			X				X				
4	Dashawn	18–24	3		X			X					X	X	X					X	X			
5	Celeste	25–29	3	X	X							X	X	X				X			X			X
6	Spencer	30–34	3		X		X				X													
7	Isabella	35–38	4					X		X			X		X		X		X	X		X	X	
8	Faith	39–42	4		X	X	X							X	X	X	X			X		X	X	
9	Drake	43–47	5	X			X	X		X		X	X	X	X		X			X	X			X
10	Bianca	48–52	5		X							X		X					X					X
11	Ava	53–57	6		X	X	X	X							X									
12	Dwayne	58–61	6					X							X									
13	Olivia	62–65	7						X	X							X				X	X		
14	Santiago	66–71	7		X				X	X						X	X		X				X	

#	Name	Pages	n																				
15	Xavier	72–75	7		X	X		X					X	X	X		X	X	X		X		
16	Sam	76–79	8	X	X					X	X	X	X	X	X	X	X	X	X		X		
17	Dylan	80–83	8					X	X			X	X	X		X			X	X			
18	Megumi	84–88	9	X		X				X	X	X	X	X	X	X	X	X		X	X		X
19	Susanna	89–98	9		X		X				X								X				
20	Rosie	99–102	9	X	X		X	X	X		X	X	X	X									
21	Jayden	103–112	10	X	X			X	X	X			X			X	X		X	X			
22	Tabesh	113–117	11		X	X	X	X			X	X	X	X	X	X	X		X	X			
23	Aiden	118–122	11	X					X		X									X			
24	Marcus	123–125	12					X	X	X		X	X	X	X	X							
25	Marley	126–130	12	X				X	X		X	X	X	X		X			X				
26	Layla	131–137	13		X	X					X	X	X										
27	Yolanda	138–151	14	X			X			X	X	X	X	X	X		X	X	X	X			
28	Steven	152–156	14				X	X			X		X	X		X							
29	Emily	157–161	16		X				X	X	X	X	X		X		X	X		X			
30	Wyatt	162–173	16	X	X		X	X	X	X	X	X	X	X	X			X	X				
31	Jordan	174–179	17			X	X	X	X								X		X	X			
32	Anthony	180–183	18	X						X	X					X				X	X		
33	Merritt	184–187	18			X	X	X		X	X	X										X	X
34	Rolando	188–193	19	X				X	X	X							X					X	X
35	Sunny	194–200	20					X	X								X		X			X	X

Appendix B
Comprehensive List of Assessments

Articulation
Arizona Articulation Proficiency Scale-3rd Ed. (Arizona-3; Fudala, 2000)
Auditory Development/Speech Perception
Auditory Perception Test for the Hearing Impaired-3rd Ed. (APT/HI-R-3; Allen, 2015)
Auditory Speech Language (AuSpLan; McClatchie & Therres, 2003)
Early Speech Perception Test (ESP; Moog & Geers, 1990)
Word Associations for Syllable Perception (WASP; Koch, 1999)
Auditory Functioning
Functional Auditory Performance Indicators (Stredler-Brown & Johnson, 2001)
Ling Six Sound Test (Ling, 1989)
Cognition
Differential Ability Scales-II (DAS-II; Elliott, 2007)
Theory of Mind (Wellman & Liu, 2004)
Conversational Proficiency
Sign Language Proficiency Interview (SLPI; Newell, Caccamise, Boardman, & Holcomb, 1983)
Starting with Assessment Toolkit Kendall P-levels (French, 1999)
Decoding
Decoding Skills Test (DST; Richardson & DiBenedetto, 1985)
Woodcock Johnson Tests of Achievement-3rd Ed. (Woodcock, McGrew, & Mather, 2001)
Phonological Awareness
Test of Phonological Awareness Skills (TOPAS; Newcomer & Barenbaum, 2003)
The Comprehensive Test of Phonological Processing (CTOPP-2; Wagner, Torgesen, Rashotte, & Pearson, 2013)

| **Expressive Language** |
| Clinical Evaluation of Language Functions-5th Edition (CELF-5) (Wiig, Semel, & Secord, 2013) |
| The Cottage Acquisition Scales for Listening, Language and Speech (CASLLS; Wilkes, 1999) |
| The Checklist of Emerging ASL Skills (see Easterbrooks & Baker, 2002) |
| The Listening Comprehension Test (Bowers, Huisingh, & LoGiudice, 2006) |
| The Teacher Assessment of Spoken Language (TASL; Moog & Biedenstein, 1998) |
| **Expressive Vocabulary** |
| Comprehensive Receptive and Expressive Vocabulary Test, 2nd Ed. (CREVT-2; Wallace & Hammill, 2001) |
| Expressive One Word Picture Vocabulary Test (EOWPVT; Brownell, 2000b) |
| **Fingerspelling** |
| Phonological Awareness Test for Deaf and Hard of Hearing (PAT-DHH) (Schwartz, Schick, Whitney, & Coady, 2011) |
| **Motivation** |
| The Elementary Reading Attitude Survey (ERAS; McKenna & Kear, 1990) |
| The Motivation for Reading Questionnaire (MRQ; Wigfield & Guthrie, 1995) |
| **Reading Comprehension** |
| The Gray Silent Reading Test (GSRT; Wiederholt & Blalock, 2000) |
| The Johns' Basic Reading Inventory (BRI; Johns, 2008) |
| The Test of Reading Comprehension, 4th Ed. (TORC-4; Brown, Hammill, & Wiederholt, 2008) |
| The Woodcock Reading Mastery Test-Revised (WRMT-R; Woodcock, 1987) |
| **Reading Fluency** |
| AIMSWEB (Pearson, 2014) |
| Maze tests (L. S. Fuchs, D. Fuchs, D., Hosp, & Jenkins, 2001) |
| Running Records for Classroom Teachers (Clay, 2000) |
| Test of Silent Word Reading Fluency (Rose, McAnally, Barkmeier, Vernig, & Long, 2006; Pro-Ed, Inc.) |
| The Signed Reading Fluency Rubric for Deaf Children (Easterbrooks & Huston, 2008) |

The Test of Silent Contextual Reading Fluency (TOSCRF; Hammill, Wiederholt & Allen, 2006)
The Test of Silent Word Reading Fluency (TOSWRF; Mather, Hammill, Allen, & Roberts, 2004)
Reading Vocabulary
Adapted Dolch Words and Bridge Lists (Fairview Learning, n.d.)
Basic Reading Inventory (BRI; Johns, 2017)
Receptive Language
ACCESS for ELLs 2.0 (WIDA, 2014)
American Sign Language Proficiency Interview (ASLPI; Gallaudet University, 2014)
American Sign Language Receptive Skills Test (ASL-RST; Enns, Zimmer, Boudreault, Rabu, & Broszeit, 2013)
American Sign Language Receptive Test (RT-ASL; Schick & Hoffmeister, 2001)
Comprehension of Spoken Language (CASL; Carrow-Woolfolk, 1999)
Comprehension of Written Grammar (CWG; Easterbrooks, 2010)
The Rhode Island Test of Language Structure (RITLS; Engen & Engen, 1983)
Test for Auditory Comprehension of Language-3 (TACL-3; Carrow-Woolfolk, 1999)
Receptive Vocabulary
MacArthur Communicative Development Inventories (CDI; Fenson et al., 2006)
MacArthur Communicative Development Inventory for American Sign Language (ASL-CDI; Anderson & Reilly, 2002)
Peabody Picture Vocabulary Test, 4th Ed. (PPVT-4 ; Dunn & Dunn, 2007)
Receptive One Word Picture Vocabulary Test (ROWPVT; Brownell, 2000a)
Visual Communication and Sign Language Checklist (Simms, Baker, & Clark, 2013)
School-Readiness
Preschool Language Scale (PLS-5; Zimmerman, Steiner, & Pond, 2011)
Writing Vocabulary
Oral and Written Language Scales (OWLS; Carrow-Woolfolk, 1996)

REFERENCES

Allen, S. G. (2015). *Auditory Perception Test for the Hearing Impaired-3rd Ed. (APT/HI-R-3)*. San Diego, CA: Plural Publishing.

Anderson, D., & Reilly, J. S. (2002). The MacArthur Communicative Development Inventory: Normative data for American Sign Language. *Journal of Deaf Studies and Deaf Education, 7*(2), 83–106.

Bowers, L., Huisingh, R., & LoGiudice, C. (2006). *The Listening Comprehension Test 2*. Austin, TX: PRO-ED Inc.

Brown, V. L., Hammill, D. D., & Wiederholt, J. L. (2008). *Test of Reading Comprehension, (TCR),* 4th Ed. Austin, TX: PRO-ED.

Brownell, R. (2000a). *Receptive One Word Picture Vocabulary Test, 4th Ed*. San Antonio, TX: Pearson Education, Inc.

Brownell, R. (2000b). *Expressive One Word Picture Vocabulary Test, 4th Ed*. San Antonio, TX: Pearson Education, Inc.

Carrow-Woolfolk, E. (1996). *Oral and Written Language Scales (OWLS)*. Circle Pines, MN: American Guidance Service.

Carrow-Woolfolk, E. (1999). *Test for Auditory Comprehension of Language (TACL)* 3rd Ed. Austin, TX: PRO-ED.

Clay, M. (2000). *Running records for classroom teachers*. Dartmouth, NH: Heinemann.

Dunn, L. M., & Dunn, L. M. (2007). *Peabody Picture Vocabulary Test-4rd Ed. (PPVT-4)*. San Antonio, TX: Pearson.

Easterbrooks, S. R. (2010). Comprehension of written grammar (Unpublished assessment). Department of Educational Psychology and Special Education, Georgia State University, Atlanta.

Easterbrooks, S. R., & Baker, S. (2002). *Language learning in children who are deaf and hard of hearing: Multiple pathways*. Boston, MA: Allyn & Bacon.

Easterbrooks, S. R., & Huston, S. (2008). The signed reading fluency of students who are deaf/hard of hearing. *Journal of Deaf Studies and Deaf Education, 13*, 37–54.

Elliott, C. D. (2007). *Differential Ability Scales-II (DAS-II)*. San Antonio, TX: Pearson Education, Inc.

Engen, E., & Engen, T. (1983). *Rhode Island Test of Language Structure* (*RITLS*). Austin, TX: PRO-ED.

Enns, C. J., Zimmer, K., Boudreault, P., Rabu, S., & Broszeit, C. (2013). *American Sign Language Receptive Skills Test*. Winnipeg, MB: Northern Signs Research, Inc.

Fairview Learning. (n.d.). *Adapted Dolch Words and Bridge Lists*. Retrieved from: http://www.fairviewlearning.com/teaching-tools-materials Last accessed 5/1/17

Fenson, L., Marchman, V., Thal, D., Dale, P., Reznick, S., & Bates, E. (2006). *The MacArthur Communicative Development Inventories: User's guide and technical manual* (2nd ed.). Baltimore, MD: Brookes.

Fenson, L., Dale, P. S., Reznick, J. S., Bates, E., Thal, D. J., & Pethick, S. J. (1994). Variability in early communicative development. *Monographs of the Society for Research in Child Development, 59*(5) (Serial No. 242).

French, M. (1999). *Starting with assessment: A developmental approach to deaf children's literacy.* Washington, DC: Laurent Clerc National Deaf Education Center.

Fuchs, L. S., Fuchs, D., Hosp, M. K., & Jenkins, J. R. (2001). Text fluency as an indicator of reading competence: A theoretical, empirical, and historical analysis. *Scientific Studies of Reading, 5*(3), 239-256.

Fudala, J. B. (2000). *Arizona Articulation Proficiency Scale-3rd Ed. (Arizona-3).* Torrance, CA: WPS.

Gallaudet University (2014). *American Sign Language Proficiency Interview (ASLPI).* Retrieved from: http://www.gallaudet.edu/asldes/aslpi.html

Hammill, D. D., Wiederholt, J. L., & Allen, E. A. (2006). *Test of Silent Contextual Reading Fluency (TSCRF).* Austin, TX: PRO-ED.

Johns, J. (2017). *Basic Reading Inventory: Kindergarten through grade 12 and early literacy assessments (12th edition).* New York, NY: Kendall Hunt.

Koch, M. E. (1999). *Word Associations for Syllable Perception (WASP).* Timonium, MD: York Press.

Ling, D. (1989). *Foundations of spoken language for the hearing-impaired child.* Washington, DC: Alexander Graham Bell Association for the Deaf.

Mather, N., Hammill, D. D., Allen, E. A., & Roberts, R. (2004). *Test of Silent Word Reading Fluency (TOSWRF).* Austin, TX: PRO-ED.

McClatchie, A., & Therres, M. (2003). *AuSpLan: Auditory speech and language - A manual for professionals working with children who have cochlear implants or amplification.* Oakland, CA: Children's Hospital & Research Center.

McKenna, M. C., & Kear, D. J. (1990). Measuring attitude toward reading: A new tool for teachers. *The Reading Teacher, 43,* 626–639.

Moog, J. S., & Biedenstein, J. (1998). *Teacher Assessment of Spoken Language (TASL).* St. Louis, MO: Moog Center for Deaf Education.

Moog, J. S., & Geers, A. E. (1990). *Early speech perception test for profoundly hearing-impaired children.* St. Louis, MO: Central Institute for the Deaf.

Newcomer, P., & Barenbaum, E. (2003). *Test of Phonological Awareness Skills (TOPAS).* Austin, TX: PRO-ED.

Newell, W., Caccamise, F., Boardman, K., & Holcomb, B. R. (1983). Adaptation of the Language Proficiency Interview (LPI) for assessing sign communicative competence. *Sign Language Studies, 41,* 311–352.

Pearson, (2014). *AIMSWEB.* Retrieved from http://www.aimsweb.com. Last accessed 5/1/17.

Richardson, E., & DiBenedetto, B. (1985). *Decoding Skills Test (DST).* Parkton, MD: York Press.

Rose, S., McAnally, P., Barkmeier, L., Virnig, S., & Long, J. (2006). *Technical Report #9: Silent Reading Fluency Test: Reliability, validity, and sensitivity to growth for students who are deaf and hard of hearing at the elementary, middle school, and high school levels.* Research Institute on Progress Monitoring (RIPM), University of Minnesota. Retrieved from http://www.progressmonitoring.org/Techreports/TR9dhhsrftTR.doc.

Schick, B., & Hoffmeister, R. (2001, April). ASL skills in deaf children of deaf parents and of hearing parents. Society for Research in Child Development International Conference, Minneapolis, MN.

Schwartz, L., Schick, B., Whitney, A., Coady, J. (November, 2011). *Fingerspelling as a phonological code for deaf and hard-of-hearing students.* American Speech Language & Hearing Association, San Diego, CA. Retrieved from: http://vl2.gallaudet.edu/research/center-papers/schwartz-schick-whitney-coady-2011/ Last accessed 5/2/17

Simms, L., Baker, S., & Clark, M. D. (2013). *Visual Communication and Sign Language Checklist.* Washington, DC: Gallaudet University. Retrieved from: http://vl2.gallaudet.edu/resources/vcsl/ (Last accessed 3/31/17)

Stredler-Brown, A., & Johnson, D. C. (2001). *Functional auditory performance indicators: An integrated approach to auditory development.* Retrieved from: http://www.tsbvi.edu/attachments/FunctionalAuditoryPerformanceIndicators.pdf Last accessed 5/1/17

Wagner, R., Torgesen, J., Rashotte, C., & Pearson, N. A. (2013). *The Comprehensive Test of Phonological Processing (CTOPP-2).* San Antonio, TX: Pearson Education, Inc.

Wallace, G., & Hammill, D. D. (2001). *Comprehensive Receptive and Expressive Vocabulary Test (CREVT),* 2nd Ed. Austin, TX: PRO-ED.

Wellman, H. M., & Liu, D. (2004). Scaling of Theory of Mind tasks. *Child Development, 75,* 523–541.

WIDA. (2014). *ACCESS for ELLs 2.0.* Retrieved from: https://www.wida.us/assessment/ACCESS20.aspx Last accessed 5/1/17

Wiederholt, J. L., & Blalock, G. (2000). *Gray Silent Reading Test (GSRT).* Austin, TX: PRO-ED.

Wigfield, A., & Guthrie, J. T. (1995). *Dimensions of children's motivations for reading: An initial study* (Research Rep. No. 34). Athens, GA: National Reading Research Center.

Wiig, E. H., Semel, E., & Secord, W. A. (2013). *Clinical Evaluation of Language Functions-5th Edition (CELF-5).* San Antonio, TX: Pearson Education, Inc.

Wilkes, E. (1999). *Cottage Acquisition Scales for Listening, Language and Speech (CASLLS).* San Antonio, TX: Sunshine Cottage School for the Deaf.

Woodcock, R. N. (1987). *Woodcock Reading Mastery Tests-Revised (WRMT-R).* Circle Pines, MN: American Guidance Services.

Woodcock, R. W., McGrew, K. S., & Mather, N. (2001). *Woodcock-Johnson III Test.* Itasaca, IL: Riverside Publishing Company.

Zimmerman, I. L., Steiner, V. G., & Pond, R. E. (2011). *Preschool Language Scale (PLS-5).* San Antonio, TX: Pearson Education, Inc.

Appendix C
Theories and Related Evidence-Based Instructional Practices

THEORY OF COGNITIVE DEVELOPMENT

Jean Piaget

Definition:	Learning occurs through active exploration; learners construct their understanding, which is the basis for language development.
Evidence-Based Practices:	Visual support: pictures, visual organizers, videos, sign models, etc. Active learning.
References:	Bell, 2007; Bos & Anders, 1990; Egan, 1999; Hauser, Lukomski, & Hillman, 2008; Horton, Lovitt, & Bergerund, 1990; Smith, 2002; Stoner & Easterbrooks, 2006

MODEL OF WORKING MEMORY

Alan Baddeley

Definition:	The interaction of three memory components (phonological loop, visuospatial sketchpad, and episodic buffer) describe short-term memory performance.
Evidence-Based Practices:	Explicit/direct instruction, incremental rehearsal.
References:	Andrews, 1988; Banks, Gray, & Fyfe, 1990; Brabham & Villaume, 2001; Burns, 2002; Burns, Dean, & Foley, 2004; Cain, Oakhill, & Lemmon, 2004; Calvert, 1981; Hall, 2002; MacGregor & Thomas, 1988; Mercer, Campbell, Miller, Mercer, & Lane, 2000; Paatsch, Blamey, Sarant, & Bow, 2006; Tucker, 1989; Walker, Munro, & Richards, 1998a, 1998b

Constructivist Theory

Jerome Bruner

Definition:	Learning occurs in an organized progression from enactive to symbolic representation based on existing knowledge.
Evidence-Based Practices:	Active learning.
References:	Brabham & Villaume, 2001; Bruner, 1973; Bruner, Goodnow, & Austin, 1956; Harmon, Wood, Hedrick, Vintinner, & Willeford, 2009; Lederberg, Presbindowski, & Spencer, 2000

Structural Cognitive Modifiability and Mediated Learning Experience

Reuven Feuerstein

Definition:	Learners can adapt to demands of a learning situation via direct and mediated interactive learning experiences.
Evidence-Based Practices:	Explicit/Direct Instruction. Scaffolding (i.e., teacher modeling, mediation, student imitation, teacher scaffolding, and feedback).
References:	Andrews, 1988; Banks, Gray, & Fyfe, 1990; Brabham & Villaume, 2001; Bruner, Goodnow, & Austin, 1956; Cain, Oakhill, & Lemmon, 2004; Calvert, 1981; Feuerstein, Hoffman, & Miller, 1980; Hall, 2002; Kozulin & Presseisen, 1995; MacGregor & Thomas, 1988; Mercer, Campbell, Miller, Mercer, & Lane, 2000; Paatsch, Blamey, Sarant, & Bow, 2006; Strassman, 1997; Vygotsky, 1978; Walker, Munro, & Richards, 1998a, 1998b; Wertsch & Sohmer, 1995

Dual Coding Theory

Allan Paivio

Definition:	Connections between verbal associations and visual images facilitate more efficient memory storage and retrieval.
Evidence-Based Practices:	Visual support. Print support. Communication match. Listening technology monitoring.

References: Bell, 2007; Bos & Anders, 1990; Egan, 1999; Hauser, Lukomski, & Hillman, 2008; Horton, Lovitt, & Bergerund, 1990; Paivio, 1991, 2008; Sadoski & Paivio, 2004; Smith, 2002; Stoner & Easterbrooks, 2006

LINGUISTIC INTERDEPENDENCE HYPOTHESIS

Jim Cummins

Definition: One's first language (L1) knowledge facilitates second language (L2) acquisition; Basic Interpersonal Communication Skills (BICS), and Cognitive Academic Language Proficiency (CALP) levels of language.

Evidence-Based Practices: Bilingual instruction (i.e., ASL and printed English). Conversation. Mediation and scaffolding.

References: Bruner, Goodnow, & Austin, 1956; Easterbrooks & Baker, 2002; Easterbrooks & Beal-Alvarez, 2013; Feuerstein, Hoffman, & Miller, 1980; Hermans, Knoors, Ormel, & Verhoeven, 2008a, 2008b; Huttenlocher et al., 1991; Kozulin & Presseisen, 1995; Lederberg & Everhart, 1998; Lederberg, Schick, & Spencer, 2013; Levy, Rodriguez, & Wubbels, 1993; Mayer & Akamatsu, 2000; Paul, 1996; Paul & Gustafson, 1991; Prinz & Strong, 1998; Reese & Newcombe, 2007; Reeves, Newell, Holcomb, & Stinson, 2000; Saffran, Newport, Aslin, Tunick, & Barrueco, 1997; Spencer, 1993; Strassman, 1997; Vygotsky, 1978; Wertsch & Sohmer, 1995

GENERATIVE GRAMMAR AND UNIVERSAL GRAMMAR

Noam Chomsky

Definition: Learners genetically inherit language (syntactic) rules; language knowledge is innate and universal.

Evidence-Based Practices: Bilingual instruction (i.e., ASL and printed English). Explicit Instruction.

References: Andrews, 1988; Bailes, 2001; Banks, Gray, & Fyfe, 1990; Berke, 2013; Brabham & Villaume, 2001; Cain, Oakhill, & Lemmon, 2004; Calvert, 1981; Crume, 2013; Hall,

2002; Lange, Lane-Outlaw, Lange, & Sherwood, 2013; MacGregor & Thomas, 1988; Mashie, 1995; Mercer, Campbell, Miller, Mercer, & Lane, 2000; Paatsch, Blamey, Sarant, & Bow, 2006; Padden & Ramsey, 1998, 2000; Prinz & Strong, 1998; Strong, 1995; Walker, Munro, & Richards, 1998a, 1998b

CRITICAL PERIOD HYPOTHESIS

Eric Lenneberg

Definition:	Particular developmental skills are acquired within particular time frames, or specialized brain areas adapt for other purposes and are unavailable for initial skills.
Evidence-Based Practices:	Early intervention. Repeated viewings of ASL models. Communication match.
References:	Beal-Alvarez & Easterbrooks, 2013; Cannon, Fredrick, & Easterbrooks, 2010; Easterbrooks & Beal-Alvarez, 2013; Golos, 2010; Golos & Moses, 2011; Guardino, Cannon, & Eberst, 2014; Mueller & Hurtig, 2010

SOCIAL DEVELOPMENT THEORY

Lev Vygotsky

Definition:	Learners' social interactions precede their development and produce consciousness and cognition; Zone of Proximal Development; More Knowledgeable Other (MKO)
Evidence-Based Practices:	Modeling (e.g., "think-aloud," demonstrating). Mediation and scaffolding. Conversation. Communication Match.
References:	Bruner, Goodnow, & Austin, 1956; Easterbrooks & Beal-Alvarez, 2013; Feuerstein, Hoffman, & Miller, 1980; Huttenlocher et al., 1991; Kozulin & Presseisen, 1995; Lederberg & Everhart, 1998; Lederberg, Schick, & Spencer, 2013; Levy, Rodriguez, & Wubbels, 1993; Reeves, Newell, Holcomb, & Stinson, 2000; Spencer, 1993; Strassman, 1997; Vygotsky, 1978; Wertsch & Sohmer, 1995

References

Andrews, J. (1988). Deaf children's acquisition of prereading skills using the reciprocal teaching procedure. *Exceptional Children, 54*(4), 349–355.

Bailes, C. N. (2001). Integrative ASL-English language arts: Bridging paths to literacy. *Sign Language Studies, 1*(2), 147–174.

Banks, J., Gray, C., & Fyfe, R. (1990). The written recall of printed stories by severely deaf children. *British Journal of Educational Psychology, 60*(2), 192–206.

Beal-Alvarez, J. S., & Easterbrooks, S. R. (2013). Increasing children's ASL classifier production: A multi-component intervention. *American Annals of the Deaf, 158*(3), 311–333.

Bell, N. (2007). *Visualizing and verbalizing for language comprehension and thinking.* San Luis Obispo, CA: Gander Publishing.

Berke, M. (2013). Reading books with young deaf children: Strategies for mediating between American Sign Language and English. *Journal of Deaf Studies and Deaf Education, 18*(3), 299–311. doi: 10.1093/deafed/ent001

Bos, C. S., & Anders, P. L. (1990). Effects of interactive vocabulary instruction on the vocabulary learning and reading comprehension of junior-high learning disabled students. *Learning Disability Quarterly, 13,* 31–42.

Brabham, E. G., & Villaume, S. K. (2001). Building walls of words. *The Reading Teacher, 54*(7), 700–702.

Bruner, J. (1973). *Going beyond the information given.* New York, NY: Norton.

Bruner, J., Goodnow, J., & Austin, A. (1956). *A study of thinking.* New York, NY: Wiley.

Burns, M. K. (2002). Utilizing a comprehensive system of assessment to intervention using curriculum-based assessments. *Intervention in School and Clinic, 38,* 8–13.

Burns, M. K., Dean, V. J., & Foley, S. (2004). Preteaching unknown key words with incremental rehearsal to improve reading fluency and comprehension with children identified as reading disabled. *Journal of School Psychology, 42,* 303–314.

Cain, K., Oakhill, J., & Lemmon, K. (2004). Individual differences in the inference of word meanings from context: The influence of reading comprehension, vocabulary knowledge, and memory capacity. *Journal of Educational Psychology, 96*(4), 671–681.

Calvert, D. R. (1981). EPIC (Experimental project in instructional concentration): Report of a study of the influence on intensifying instruction for elementary-school age deaf children. *American Annals of the Deaf, 126*(8), 865–984.

Cannon, J., Fredrick, L., & Easterbrooks, S. (2010). Vocabulary instruction through books read in American Sign Language for English-language learners with hearing loss. *Communication Disorders Quarterly, 31*(2), 98–112.

Crume, P. (2013). Teachers' perceptions of promoting sign language phonological awareness in an ASL/English bilingual program. *Journal of Deaf Studies and Deaf Education, 18*(4), 464–488. doi:10.1093/deafed/ent023

Easterbrooks, S. R., & Baker, S. (2002). *Language learning in children who are deaf and hard of hearing: Multiple pathways.* Boston, MA: Allyn & Bacon.

Easterbrooks, S. R., & Beal-Alvarez, J. S. (2013). *Literacy instruction for students who are deaf and hard of hearing.* New York, NY: Oxford University Press.

Egan, M. (1999). Reflections on effective use of graphic organizers. *Journal of Adolescent and Adult Literacy, 42*(8), 641–645.

Feuerstein, R., Hoffman, M., & Miller, R. (1980). *Instrumental enrichment: An intervention program for cognitive modifiability.* Baltimore, MD: University Park Press.

Golos, D. B. (2010). Deaf children's engagement in an educational video in American Sign Language. *American Annals of the Deaf, 155*(3), 360–368.

Golos, D., & Moses, A. (2011). How Teacher Mediation during Video Viewing Facilitates Literacy Behaviors. *Sign Language Studies, 12*(1), 98–118.

Guardino, C., Cannon, J. E., & Eberst, K. (2014). Building the evidence-base of effective reading strategies to use with Deaf English Language Learners. *Communications Disorders Quarterly, 35*(2), 59–73. doi: 10.1177/1525740113506932

Hall, T. (2002). *Explicit instruction.* Wakefield, MA: National Center on Accessing the General Curriculum. Retrieved from http://www.cast.org/publications/ncac/ncac_explicit.html

Harmon, J. M., Wood, K. D., Hedrick, W. B., Vintinner, J., & Willeford, T. (2009). Interactive word walls: More than just reading the writing on the walls. *Journal of Adolescent & Adult Literacy, 52*(5), 398–408. doi:10.1598/JAAL.52.5.4

Hauser, P., Lukomski, J., & Hillman, T. (2008). Development of deaf and hard-of-hearing students' executive function. In M. Marschark & P. Hauser (Eds.), *Deaf cognition: Foundations and outcomes* (pp. 286–309). Cary, NC: Oxford University Press.

Hermans, D., Knoors, H., Ormel, E., & Verhoeven, L. (2008a). Modeling reading vocabulary learning in deaf children in bilingual education programs. *Journal of Deaf Studies and Deaf Education, 13*(1), 1–20.

Hermans, D., Knoors, H., Ormel, E., & Verhoeven, L. (2008b). The relationship between the reading and signing skills of deaf children in bilingual education programs. *Journal of Deaf Studies and Deaf Education, 13*(4), 518–530.

Horton, S. V., Lovitt, T. C., & Bergerund, D. (1990). The effectiveness of graphic organizers for three classifications of secondary students in content area classes. *Journal of Learning Disabilities, 23*, 12–22.

Huttenlocher, J., Haight, W., Bryk, A., Sletzer, M., & Lyons, T. (1991). Early vocabulary growth: Relation to input and gender. *Developmental Psychology, 27*(23), 236–248.

Kozulin, A., & Presseisen, B. Z. (1995). Mediated learning experience and psychological tools: Vygotsky's and Feuerstein's perspectives in a study of student learning. *Educational Psychologist, 30*(2), 67–75.

Lange, C. M., Lane-Outlaw, S., Lange, W. E., & Sherwood, D. L. (2013). American Sign Language/English bilingual model: A longitudinal study of academic growth. *Journal of Deaf Studies and Deaf Education, 18,* 532–544. doi: 10.1093/deafed/ent027

Lederberg, A. R., & Everhart, V. S. (1998). Communication between deaf children and their hearing mothers: The role of language, gesture, and vocalizations. *Journal of Speech, Language, and Hearing Research, 41,* 887–899.

Lederberg, A. R., Prezbindowski, A. K., & Spencer, P. E. (2000). Word-learning skills of deaf preschoolers: The development of novel mapping and rapid word-learning strategies. *Child Development, 71*(6), 1571–1585.

Lederberg, A. R., Schick, B., & Spencer, P. E. (2013). Language and literacy development of deaf and hard-of-hearing children: Successes and challenges. *Developmental Psychology, 49*(1), 15–30. doi:10.1037/a0029558

Levy, J., Rodriguez, R., & Wubbels, T. (1993). Teacher communication style and instruction. In Fisher, D. (Ed.), *The Study of Learning Environments, Vol. 7.* Perth, Australia: Curtin University of Technology Press.

MacGregor, S. K., & Thomas, L. B. (1988). A computer-mediated text system to develop communication skills for hearing-impaired students. *American Annals of the Deaf, 133*(4), 280–284.

Mashie, S. (1995). *Educating deaf children bilingually.* Washington, D.C.: Pre-College Programs, Gallaudet University.

Mayer, C., & Akatamasu, C. T. (2000). Deaf children creating written texts: Contributions of American Sign Language and signed forms of English. *American Annals of the Deaf, 145*(5), 394–403.

Mercer, C. D., Campbell, K. U., Miller, M. D., Mercer, K. D., & Lane, H. B. (2000). Effects of a reading fluency intervention for middle schoolers with specific learning disabilities. *Learning Disabilities Research, 15*(4), 177–187.

Mueller, V., & Hurtig, R. (2010). Technology-enhanced shared reading with deaf and hard-of-hearing children: The role of a fluent signing narrator. *Journal of Deaf Studies and Deaf Education, 15*(1), 72–101.

Paatsch, L., Blamey, P., Sarant, J., & Bow, C. (2006). The effects of speech production and vocabulary training on different components of spoken-language performance. *Journal of Deaf Studies and Deaf Education, 11*(1), 39–55.

Padden, C., & Ramsey, C. (1998). Reading ability in signing deaf children. *Topics in Language Disorders, 18*(4), 30–46.

Padden, C., & Ramsey, C. (2000). American Sign Language and reading ability in deaf children. In C. Chamberlain, J. P. Morford, & R. I. Mayberry (Eds.), *Language acquisition by eye* (pp. 165–189). Mahwah, NJ: Lawrence Erlbaum.

Paivio, A. (1991). Dual coding theory: Retrospect and current status. *Canadian Journal of Psychology, 45,* 255–287.

Paivio, A. (2008). How children learn and retain information: The dual coding theory. In S. B. Newman (Ed.), *Literacy achievement for young children in poverty.* Baltimore, MD: Paul H. Brookes.

Paul, P. V. (1996). Reading vocabulary knowledge and deafness. *Journal of Deaf Studies and Deaf Education, 1*(1), 3–15.

Paul, P., & Gustafson, G. (1991). Hearing-impaired students' comprehension of high-frequency multimeaning words. *Remedial and Special Education (RASE), 12*(4), 52–62.

Prinz, P. M., & Strong, M. (1998). ASL proficiency and English literacy within a bilingual deaf education model of instruction. *Topics in Language Disorders, 18*(4), 47–60.

Reese, E., & Newcombe, R. (2007). Training mothers in elaborative reminiscing enhances children's autobiographical memory and narrative. *Child Development, 78*(4), 1153–1170.

Reeves, J. B., Newell, W., Holcomb, B. R., & Stinson, M. (2000). The sign language skills classroom observation: A process for describing sign language proficiency in classroom settings. *American Annals of the Deaf, 145*(4), 315–341.

Sadoski, M., & Paivio, A. (2004). A dual coding theoretical model of reading. In R. B. Ruddell & N. J. Unrau (Eds.), *Theoretical models and processes of reading* (5th ed.) (pp. 1329–1362). Newark, DE: International Reading Association.

Saffran, J., Newport, E., Aslin, R., Tunick, R., & Barrueco, S. (1997). Incidental language learning: Listening (and learning) out of the corner of your ear. *Psychological Science, 8*(2), 101–105.

Smith, J. J. (2002). The use of graphic organizers in vocabulary instruction. ERIC. ED463556.

Spencer, P. E. (1993). Communication behaviors of infants with hearing loss and their hearing mothers. *Journal of Speech and Hearing Research, 36*, 311–321.

Stoner, M., & Easterbrooks, S. (2006). Using a visual tool to increase adjectives in the written language of students who are deaf or hard of hearing. *Communication Disorders Quarterly, 27*(2), 95–109.

Strassman, B. (1997). Metacognition and reading in children who are deaf: A review of the research. *Journal of Deaf Studies and Deaf Education, 2*, 140–149.

Strong, M. (1995). A review of bilingual/bicultural programs for deaf children. *American Annals of the Deaf, 140*, 84–94.

Tucker, J. A. (1989*). Basic flashcard technique when vocabulary is the goal.* Unpublished teaching materials, School of Education, University of Chattanooga. Chattanooga, TN: Author.

Vygotsky, L. S. (1978). *Mind and society: The development of higher mental processes.* Cambridge, MA: Harvard University Press.

Walker, L., Munro, J., & Richards, F. (1998a). Teaching inferential reading strategies through pictures. *The Volta Review, 100*(2), 105–120.

Walker, L., Munro, J., & Richards, F. (1998b). Literal and inferential reading comprehension of students who are deaf or hard of hearing. *The Volta Review, 100*(2), 87–103.

Wertsch, J. V., & Sohmer, R. (1995). Vygotsky on learning and development. *Human Development, 38*(6), 332–337.

Appendix D
Bananabeangram

The speech banana is a visual reference used to help nonprofessionals and students conceptualize phonemes critical to speech perception and development. Variations of the speech banana have been used in combination with familiar sounds audiograms to compare an individual's hearing levels to approximate estimations of acoustic properties; allowing a visual representation of what sounds an individual has access to, or not, given their hearing level. However, the placement of these images and sound labels on an audiogram are an estimation, at best (Borders & Gardiner-Walsh, 2017). Recently, Madell (2015) put forth a speech string bean to further emphasize listeners have optimal access to all sounds of speech. The *bananabeangram* combines the traditional speech banana with the newer speech string bean. In this text, the placement of the speech banana is based in part, on the work of Killion and Mueller (2010) and Northern and Downs (2014). In the *bananabeangram*, the string bean lies along the upper edge of the banana. Make a transparency to use as an overlay on the case study audiograms to better determine which speech sounds a child is able to hear when aided, or unable to hear when they are unaided.

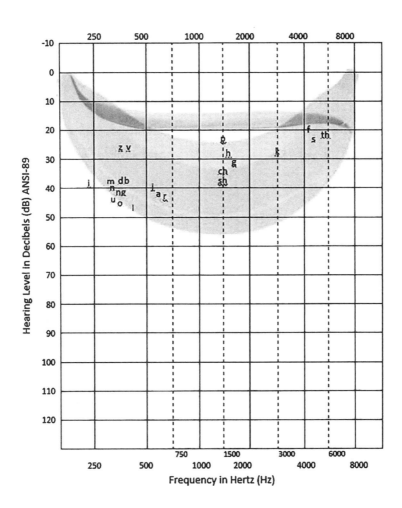

References

Borders, C. & Gardiner-Walsh, S. (March 4, 2017). Rethinking the speech banana. Presentation at the 53rd Annual Conference of the Illinois Teacher of the Deaf and Hard of Hearing (ITDHH).

Killion, M. C., & Mueller, H. G. (2010). Twenty years later: A NEW Count-The-Dots method. *The Hearing Journal, 63*(1), 10. https://doi.org/10.1097/01.HJ.0000366911 .63043.16

Madell, J. (2015). The Speech String Bean. Retrieved from http://hearinghealthmatters .org/hearingandkids/2015/the-speech-string-bean/ on September 25, 2017.

Northern, J. L., & Downs, M. P. (2014). *Hearing in Children, Sixth Edition*. Plural Publishing.

Glossary of Essential Terms

1-3-6 guidelines: The Joint Committee on Infant Hearing position paper calls for infant hearing screening at no later than 1 month of age, confirmation of hearing level at no later than 3 months, and if hearing loss is confirmed, the infant will receive early intervention services as soon as possible but no later than 6 months of age. Eight principles are also outlined in the statement with specific guidelines for family-centered systems with informed choice, access to services, and monitored progress.

Accommodations: supports and services provided to a student to establish equal access to the general education curriculum and which may change how a student learns the material.

Acoustic immittance tests (tympanometry and acoustic reflex): helps identify the part of the ear that may be involved in the hearing loss by evaluating the functional integrity of the eardrum and middle ear anatomy. There are two primary types of acoustic immittance tests: tympanometry and acoustic reflex testing.

Adaptive Physical Education (APE): provided for students with disabilities by professionals with specialized training in developing, implementing, and assessing a physical education instructional program that has been adapted or modified to develop physical, motor, and group sport skills.

Alexander Graham Bell Chapter: an incorporated entity of the national Alexander Graham Bell Association. The current chapters, in 30 U.S. states and the District of Columbia, share a primary goal of increasing awareness of hearing loss and the benefits of early intervention at the state level. Chapter members include parents of children with hearing loss, adults with hearing loss, and the professionals who support them.

Alphabetic knowledge: the ability to name, distinguish letter shapes, and identify the sounds of the English alphabet by pointing to words/letters in a book, saying/signing/singing the alphabet, and connecting letter names and shapes.

American Sign Language (ASL): a visual language with a distinct grammar, separate from English, that conveys meaning via articulations of the hands and arms, and movements of the eyes, face, head, and body; the primary language of Deaf children and adults in the United States and

Canada, particularly those involved in Deaf culture, and a secondary language for hearing children and adults to communicate with Deaf individuals who use ASL.

American Sign Language Receptive Skills Test: a measure of ASL receptive skills in eight grammatical categories, including number/distribution, negation, noun-verb distinction, spatial verbs (action and location), size and shape specifiers and handling classifiers, role shift, and conditionals.

Amplification: the process of increasing the volume of sound, usually through assistive listening devices for those who are deaf or hard of hearing, such as hearing aids, FM/DM systems, sound fields, cochlear implants, etc.

Applied Behavior Analysis (ABA): systematically incorporating interventions and progress monitoring through informal assessment to improve behaviors. This system includes documentation and incremental analysis of progress to ensure the intervention is responsible for the change in behavior.

Articulation: the process by which clear and distinct speech sounds, syllables, and words are formed when the tongue, jaw, teeth, lips, and palate alter the air stream coming from the lungs and through the oral and nasal cavity.

ASPIRE model: Active Student Participation Inspires Real Engagement (ASPIRE); a student-led initiative that allows a student to develop self-determination skills (i.e., problem solving, self-evaluation, choice-making, and decision-making) through active participation in his/her Individual Education Program (IEP) process and shifts the focus of the IEP process from adult-centered to student-centered.

Assistive listening device (ALD): a personal listening device other than a hearing aid that transmits, processes, or amplifies sound.

Assistive technology: refers to all assistive, adaptive, or rehabilitative devices for individuals with disabilities. Assistive technology devices and the services needed to select, locate, and support the user was defined in federal law in the Individuals with Disabilities Education Act of 1990 (Public Law 101-476). Hearing assistive technology, including alerting devices, can be used with or without hearing aids or cochlear implants to reduce stress and fatigue.

Atresia: absence or closure of the external ear (pinna); this means the external ear may be deformed or missing, which affects the trajectory of sound to the middle and inner ear.

Audiogram: a graph that shows the results of a pure-tone hearing test that includes frequency (pitch) in Hertz (Hz) across the X-axis and volume (intensity) in decibels (dB) across the Y-axis; red "O"s indicate the right ear, and blue "X"es indicate the left ear.

Audiological/Auditory access: access to speech sounds and environmental noises in order to communicate effectively.

Audiological management: is the process of providing specialized interventions and education to improve hearing, from identification and diagnosis of hearing loss, fitting of assistive technology and hearing devices, and the instructional services to support communication development.

Audiologist: healthcare professional who is trained to prevent, identify, diagnose, evaluate, and rehabilitate (e.g., provide assistive technology) hearing function for individuals with hearing loss and related issues.

Auditory brainstem response (ABR): utilized in newborn hearing screening and other diagnostic situations, electrodes are placed on the individual's head, sound is presented through earphones, and the brainwave activity is monitored to detect hearing loss.

Auditory habilitation: (also known as auditory or aural rehabilitation) For the pediatric population, audiologic or auditory rehabilitation services are referred to as habilitation as "rehabilitation" refers to the restoration of a lost skill. Auditory habilitation helps children who use hearing aids or cochlear implants and their families learn the strategies and techniques to assist in the development of communication skills through listening.

Auditory Neuropathy Spectrum Disorder (ANSD): Type of hearing loss caused by interference of sound from the inner ear to the brain due to a malformed or absent auditory brainstem.

Auditory skills: those skills relating to how the brain perceives and interprets sound information. Most generally, auditory skills develop in a four-step hierarchy (detection, discrimination, identification, and comprehension), but a wide range of skills (including listening in noise, dichotic listening, etc.) are essential for functional daily listening.

Auditory verbal (AV): practices teaching children to use the hearing provided by a hearing aid or a cochlear implant to understand speech. This parent-centered approach encourages the use of naturalistic conversation and the use of listening and spoken language to communicate. AV practice emphasizes the use of residual hearing to help children learn to listen to, understand, and use spoken language. Children are taught to use hearing and active listening as an integral part of their communication, recreation, socialization, education, and work.

Auditory-Verbal Therapy/Therapist (AVT): a parent-centered approach that emphasizes the use of assistive technology (hearing aids, cochlear implants, FM/DM systems, etc.) and focuses on increasing listening and spoken language.

Augmentative and alternative communication (AAC): a communication method that supplements or replaces the use of speech or sign language and expresses thoughts, needs, wants, and ideas through pictures and symbols on a communication board.

Autism Spectrum Disorder (ASD): neurodevelopmental disorder across a spectrum of degrees (mild to profound) that interferes with an individual's social, educational, and occupational abilities due to issues surrounding communication and interaction with others; individuals present with varying behaviors, including repetitive actions and interests.

Babbling: a stage in child language acquisition and development, typically around 4–9 months, in which an infant utters sounds of his/her spoken language without the production of recognizable words (e.g., ba-ba, maaa); babbling is divided into sub-stages across this time frame.

Bacterial meningitis: the most common form of meningitis, which is an infection of the meninges (membranes) that surround the brain and spinal cord and causes the brain to swell, which interferes with blood flow and can result in paralysis or stroke; caused by a bacterial infection; can result in hearing loss, motor deficits, seizures, and cognitive disabilities.

Basic interpersonal communicative skills (BICS): Surface language skills that children learning a second language use to communicate. BICS involves conversational fluency through gestures, pronunciation, intonation, and vocabulary that are necessary in social interactions. Day-to-day language needed to interact in social situations (e.g., cafeteria, parties, playing sports, etc.). BICs is context-embedded, not cognitively demanding, and doesn't require specialized language but takes approximately six months to two years to acquire.

Basic Reading Inventory (BRI): an assessment program that includes grade-level sight word lists and reading passages, miscue analysis, retell, and comprehension questions to identify a student's frustration, instruction, and independent reading levels.

Behavior Intervention Plan (BIP): a plan of action developed by the Individualized Education Program (IEP) team, including a behavior specialist, based on the functional behavior assessment (FBA) of a student, to understand the function and cause of inappropriate behaviors and replace them with more appropriate behaviors through supports and interventions.

Behavior Interventionist: a professional who is responsible for gathering data on a child's behavior, proposing an intervention, and then tracking that intervention in order to help the child maintain behaviors that allow them to function within their educational setting. Most often these professionals are focused on reducing or replacing disruptive behaviors with positive social-emotional behaviors.

Behavioral observational audiometry (BOA): recommended as developmentally appropriate for children 0–6 months of age, this hearing test includes the parent and infant in a sound booth with sounds at varying frequencies presented to the infant to document quieting, eye widening, being startled, etc.

Behind-the-ear hearing aids: hearing aids that hook over the top of the ear and rest behind the ear with a tube that connects to the earmold worn within the outer ear and ear canal; can be used for all types of hearing losses from mild to profound; most powerful type of hearing aid available.

Bell curve: a way to represent the frequency distribution of measurements that is a true, normal curve, with the majority of measurements within one standard deviation of the average/mean score (e.g., 100) in the center and extremes/outliers (two or more standard deviations above or below the mean; e.g., below 85 or above 115) on either side of the mean that taper. It is called a bell curve because of the bell shape of the curve on a distribution plane.

Bilateral hearing loss: hearing loss in both ears.

Bilingual/bicultural philosophy: an educational philosophy in which ASL is the language of instruction and English is accessed via print as the secondary language. The school and/or classroom emphasizes Deaf culture and involves members of the Deaf community to provide a linguistically and culturally diverse academic environment.

Bimodal device user: simultaneous use of a cochlear implant (CI) on one ear and a hearing aid on the other ear.

Binaural hearing aids: utilizing two hearing aids on both ears.

Bone-anchored hearing aids: hearing aids that transmit sound by direct conduction through bone to the inner ear, bypassing the external auditory canal and middle ear. A prosthesis is surgically embedded into the skull with a small abutment exposed outside the skin.

Braille: a system of written expression that is accessible to individuals with visual impairment with the letters and symbols are represented via a series of raised bumps on paper.

Carrier phrases: phrases or sentences in which the first few words are constant with only the last word changing based on circumstance. The use of carrier phrases can help learners expand their utterances and learn new sentence structures. Examples of carrier phrases include: I want a…; I see a…; May I have a….? Where is the….?

Caseload: the total number of students for which an educator is responsible for providing or monitoring educational services.

Case manager: a person responsible for monitoring a caseload.

Cerebral palsy (CP): a neurological disorder that develops prenatally and affects body movements; muscle control, tone and coordination; reflex; posture and balance; and fine, gross, and oral motor skills. Epilepsy, blindness, deafness, and intellectual disabilities also may be present in individuals with CP.

Chaining: an instructional strategy to assist in mapping ASL to English print by fingerspelling a word, pointing to it in written form, and showing the ASL sign for the word.

CHARGE syndrome: a constellation of congenital malformations and medical conditions. CHARGE is an acronym standing for: coloboma, heart defect, atresia choanae (also known as choanal atresia), retarded growth and development, genital abnormality, and ear abnormality (resulting in hearing loss). CHARGE affects one in every 8,000–10,000 births, though the presentation varies greatly among those affected.

Classifier: a designated handshape in ASL that represents an object or figure (i.e., semantic classifier), provides visual information about the object's characteristics (i.e., size-and-shape-specifier, SASS), or demonstrates a figure's action (i.e., body part classifier).

Clinical Evaluation of Language Fundamentals, Fourth Edition (CELF-4): an individually administered assessment used for the identification, diagnosis, and follow-up evaluation of language and communication disorders in children from ages 5–21 years.

Closed captioning: a printed description of the audio occurring within a video; closed captions are required on devices and videos to provide accessibility.

Cochlea: the spiral cavity of the inner ear that contains hair cells that transport sound to the auditory nerve.

Cochlear implant (CI): an assistive listening device that consists of an array of electrodes and a receiver and that is surgically placed within the organ of the cochlea in the inner ear and under the skin, respectively, that sends and receives electronic impulses from the auditory nerve to the brain; an external transmitter, microphone, and speech processor are worn behind the ear.

Cochlear implant evaluation: an evaluation conducted by a team of professionals to determine candidacy to receive a cochlear implant; the team typically includes a pediatrician (child's primary care physician), an audiologist (audiological exam of hearing level), speech language pathologist (SLP; assesses the speech, language, and listening ability including tests of articulation, receptive and expressive language, and pragmatics), Ear-Nose-Throat doctors (ENT; ear, nose, and throat doctor who will review medical records, including results from MRI or CT scans), and a psychologist and/or social worker (assesses the family's ability to complete the post-surgery follow-up contacts and appointments).

Cochlear implant team: a team involved in a cochlear implant surgery; the surgeon (ENT/otologist/otolaryngologist) and audiologist are the primary members of the team, but depending on the needs of the individual, a developmental pediatrician, speech-language pathologist (SLP), early interventionist, educational specialist, aural rehabilitation specialist, psychologist, and/or social worker may also be team members. The team determines the individual's candidacy to have surgery for a cochlear implant, helps candidates make informed decisions pre-surgery, and provides audiological and educational post-surgery follow-up.

Codeswitching: alternating between two languages to meet the needs of communication partners; also an instructional technique used with students who utilize ASL where the teacher and students alternate between English and ASL in a purposeful manner during instruction to illustrate the differences between the languages and increase vocabulary and reading comprehension.

Cognitive/academic language proficiency (CALP): level of language that students must achieve to complete academic work in the classroom. Basis for all academic content, including reading comprehension, expressive writing skills, and text-embedded vocabulary knowledge. Involves the skills of listening, speaking, reading, and writing about content material. Tasks are context-reduced and cognitively demanding because they include comparing, contrasting, classifying, synthesizing, evaluating, inferring, and other higher-order thinking skills. Takes approximately 5 to 7 years to acquire, or as much as 9–10 years if no previous formal schooling or limited native language.

Communication Access Real-time Translation (CART): a live, word-for-word transcription of speech to text to provide full access to communication in both individual and group settings; may be conducted in-person or remotely.

Communication plan: all children ages 3–21 or until high school graduation will have an individualized communication plan as part of their IEP. The communication plan, resulting from the team's discussion, provides a statement identifying the child's primary communication access as well as social and instructional needs. The plan also indicates that the IEP team will not deny instructional opportunities based on a child's degree of residual hearing, the parents' communication ability, nor the child's experience in that communication modality.

Community-Based Instruction (CBI): for those students who require intensive instruction in functional and daily living skills, the Individualized Education Program (IEP) team can specify they receive CBI in the student's natural environment. The goal is to support students in becoming as independent as possible, in multiple environments, in order to increase overall life satisfaction and learning.

Comprehension of Written Grammar (CWG) test: receptive test of the comprehension of 26 grammatical structures of English print for use with children who are deaf or hard of hearing.

Comprehensive Test of Phonological and Print Processing (C-TOPP): The C-TOPP assesses a student's ability to manipulate phonological information, including removing sounds and adding other sounds to make new words; blending sounds to create words and non-words; identification of initial and final sounds; repetition of words and non-words; and various rapid naming measures (i.e., letters, colors, numbers, and objects).

Conditionals: If-then statements; one action is reliant on something else, such as "If I won the lottery, then I would travel around the world."

Conditioned play audiometry (CPA): designed for children between the ages of 2 and 5, this technique is utilized by an audiologist to assess children's hearing levels through games played within the testing sound booth (e.g., placing balls or blocks in a bag when they hear a tone through the headphones).

Conductive: hearing loss caused by issues in the outer and middle ear, typically obstructing the passage of sound to the eardrum or ossicles. Examples include earwax buildup, infection, perforation of the eardrum, and otitis media with effusion. Conductive hearing loss can occur in conjunction with sensorineural hearing loss and in this case is called a mixed hearing loss.

Congenital: present at birth, possibly due to hereditary or prenatal reasons (i.e., occurred in-utero); such as a congenital hearing loss.

Consultative services: typically provided to students with special needs who do not require daily or weekly assistance to be successful in an inclusive general education environment. During a specified time (e.g., once a month) in the Individualized Education Program (IEP) an educational consultant (either private or district) with specialized training will provide advice and services to the members of the IEP team and/or the student to ensure the student masters his/her goals and objectives.

Content area: a specific area of instruction in the K–12 environment, including reading/English language arts, math, science, and social studies (history, civics).

Cultural broker: someone who can provide the family with cross-cultural background knowledge that will help facilitate communication of complex and highly sensitive subject matter.

Cultural humility: an approach to understanding cultures that recognizes personal bias and beliefs and that views individuals with differing language, religious ideologies, age, gender, sexual orientation, etc. with the goal of understanding and learning from them rather than informing and making assumptions about them.

Culturally and linguistically diverse: a term used by the U.S. Department of Education to describe students who have no or limited English proficiency and come from homes and communities with a language other than English as the home/primary language and varied and diverse cultural backgrounds.

Cytomegalovirus (CMV): a congenital virus transmitted to an infant that causes hearing loss.

Data logging: a feature available on many hearing aids and cochlear implants. When this feature is activated, information about the duration of time the device is on is collected and can be monitored.

d/Dhh: a term that includes all deaf, Deaf, and hard of hearing individuals; all encompassing of any person with a hearing loss.

d/Deaf/deafness: medically (audiologically) defined as a hearing loss, typically within the severe to profound range. Sociological and cultural views on deafness include someone who typically uses a visual means of communication such as ASL and is involved in the Deaf community, although individuals self-define and self-label based on their lived experiences.

Deafblind: a combined loss of both vision and hearing; each loss may occur to various degrees.

Deafblind consultant: a professional with specialized training in working with Deafblind individuals by supporting the family, providing suggestions and recommendations to the Individualized Education Program (IEP) and/or Individualized Family Service Plan (IFSP) team regarding an individual's present levels of performance based on assessment of their hearing and visual needs combined with evidence-based strategies.

Deaf child of Deaf parents: children born with the range of a severe to profound hearing level to parents with similar hearing levels who utilize ASL as their primary language in the home and/or are members of the Deaf community and Deaf culture.

Deaf culture: a culture defined by an agreed upon set of values and beliefs, including use of and preservation of the natural signed language of a country, such as ASL, heritage, literature, traditions, cultural events, theater, social norms (eye contact, shoulder tapping, getting attention), and identity (proud member of the community, self-identification as Deaf/deaf/hard of hearing) shared within the Deaf community.

Deaf education program: a district or private program designed to educate students who are d/Dhh by providing educational specialists, particularly in language development, who can develop individualized assessment and interventions designed to increase students' levels of performance.

Deaf with a disability: d/Dhh individuals who have a disability (i.e., developmental, physical, or cognitive) such as a learning disability, Autism Spectrum Disorder (ASD), Emotional Behavior Disorder, Down syndrome, vision loss, etc.

Decibels (dB): a logarithmic scale used to represent the levels of intensity (loudness) of sound that can be heard by the human ear.

Decoding: the process of translating printed text into meaning by matching letter-sound combinations to create words and activate the meaning of those words for reading comprehension.

Deictic gaze: Use of eye gaze to refer to a person already established in space in a signed language.

Developmental Behavioral Pediatrician (DBP): a doctor that specializes in physical, emotional, behavioral, and social development of children.

Developmental disabilities: physical and/or cognitive delays in developmental milestones that impact functional skills and may require specialized education services and can include children with the following conditions: Attention Deficit Hyperactivity Disorder (ADHD), cerebral palsy, Autism Spectrum Disorder (ASD), Down syndrome, learning disability, intellectual disability, visual impairment, and hearing loss.

Developmental synchrony: young children are most able to obtain certain skills or abilities when the brain is developmentally ready to do so. Acquisition of skills in a synchronous manner is most efficient. Within any given domain of development (e.g., language/speech, motor, self help, feeding, social, emotional, etc.) children acquire skills in a developmental order with certain skills serving as prerequisites to others. The concept of developmental synchrony relates to critical or sensitive periods of neuroplasticity. A remediation approach is necessary when children do not obtain a skill in a synchronous manner.

Dichotic listening: refers to listening to different auditory signals, often speech, presented simultaneously to each ear. Dichotic listening includes two processes: binaural integration and binaural separation. Binaural integration refers to the ability to perceive two different acoustic messages presented to each ear at the same time. Binaural separation refers to the ability to perceive an acoustic message in one ear while ignoring a different acoustic message in the other.

Digital hearing aid: a listening device that does not simply increase the sound wave to amplify, as done by traditional analog hearing aids but breaks the sound waves into discrete units before amplification to provide speech enhancement, reduce background noise, and eliminate feedback.

Disability Resource Center (DRC): also referred to as Access Office, Center of Academic Resources, Access and Diversity, Disability and Access Office, etc.; an office established at a college or university for the purpose of creating an equally accessible and inclusive learning environment for all students and compliance with all laws related to individuals with disabilities.

Down syndrome: a syndrome that occurs due to an extra copy of chromosome 21 and causes low muscle tone, small stature, upward slant to the eyes with varying cognitive and physical delays from mild to severe.

Due process: established by the Individuals with Disabilities Education Improvement Act (IDEIA), due process provides parents and students with the right to participate in the Individual

Education Program (IEP) process, to file an IEP-related complaint, and to resolve any disputes related to a student's IEP through voluntary mediation, due process hearings, and, if needed, the legal system.

Early Hearing Detection and Intervention (EHDI) Act (2007): this updated Act (originally enacted in 2000) enables funding for early hearing detection and intervention programs throughout the United States and has eight goals. The first three goals are commonly referred to as "the 1-3-6 plan" that ensures all infants receive hearing screening prior to 1 month of age, identification of hearing loss should occur by 3 months of age, and early intervention services are provided by 6 months of age. The remaining five goals include a family-centered approach, access to technology, monitoring of communication and hearing level, appropriate early intervention programs, and information should be shared across service providers at all levels.

Early intervention: family-centered intervention services from birth to three years of age that include individual and group approaches to access various communication options, educational options, amplification advocacy, and support in transitioning.

Early interventionist/provider (EI): a private or public service provider that works with families to educate them about language development of children with hearing loss and ways to facilitate communication development. Typically utilizing a family-centered approach, EIs conduct interventions to increase language skills that are modeled (via tele-practice or in the home) for the parents so they can use them in everyday life.

Early intervention service coordinator: designated at the Individualized Family Service Plan (IFSP), this person is responsible for implementation of all services in the IFSP through monitoring of services, frequent consultation with the parents through home visits, phone calls, and other meetings to provide collaboration and cooperation among all service providers involved in a child's IFSP.

Early Intervention team: includes a service coordinator, the parents, and the following specialists, as needed: a Speech Language Pathologist (SLP), an early interventionist (EI), an Auditory Verbal Therapist (AVT), a Physical Therapist (PT), and an Occupational Therapist (OT), etc.

Earmold: part of a hearing aid that sits in the ear canal, made of plastic, acrylic, or other soft material.

Ear, Nose, and Throat physician (ENT): medical and surgical specialist who diagnoses, manages, and treats disorders of the head and neck, including the ears, nose, and throat. Typically diagnoses middle ear issues related to hearing loss, consults and conducts cochlear implant surgery and other medical-related issues with people who are d/Dhh.

Educational assistant: an individual who assists the teacher with classroom responsibilities and/or is assigned one-on-one to assist a student with special needs with physical and/or educational activities. Also referred to as a teaching assistant or a paraprofessional, the educational background requirements depend on the district's guidelines and the individual.

Educational interpreter: an individual who provides sign language interpretation of auditory information in the school setting, educational interpreters are defined as a related service provider and member of the educational team and work in public and private school systems and are legally responsible for implementing the Individualized Education Program (IEP) for the students they serve.

Educational plan (EP): an outline of coursework that is required to complete a degree.

Emotional and behavioral challenges/ Emotional Behavioral Disorder (EBD): Children with emotional and behavioral challenges may present with an inability to build and/or maintain satisfactory interpersonal relationships with peers and/or teachers; an inability to learn that is not explained by intellectual, sensory, or health factors; consistent or chronic inappropriate behavior or feelings under typical conditions; pervasive unhappiness or depression; a tendency to develop physical symptoms or pains associated with

personal or school challenges. A student with emotional or behavioral challenges exhibits one or more of the above characteristics of sufficient duration, frequency, and intensity that it interferes significantly with educational performance so that the provision of special educational services becomes necessary.

English Language Learners (ELLs): individuals who come from non-English speaking homes and are learning English as their second or third language. Students in the school system may require specialized or modified instruction while they are acquiring English skills. Also referred to as limited English proficient (LEP), English Learners (ELs), and for students who are d/Dhh, Deaf Multilingual Learners (DML).

Etiology: the cause of a condition; doctors and audiologists use this term regarding deafness to describe causes (i.e., damage to the inner ear or cochlea, genetic, side effect of syndromes, etc.).

Eustachian tubes: canals in both ears that are between the middle ear and the pharynx that equalize pressure of the tympanic membrane (eardrum).

Evidence-based decisions: making educational decisions based on assessment (both formal and informal) and intervention data that utilize materials and strategies derived from research in the educational field.

Expressive language: language (English, ASL, or other) expressed by an individual either through-the-air (voice or sign) or written.

Family-centered early intervention: includes 10 guiding principles that focus on access, content, and processes in early intervention services for infants and toddlers who are d/Dhh and their families. The family and ways to support them in facilitating language development for their child is the primary focus and should be applied to all early intervention services.

Filipino Sign Language (FSL): the national sign language of the Philippines that contains its own grammar and is not based on the spoken Filipino language.

Fingerspelling: representation of the individual letters of the alphabet of a spoken language through various handshapes in sign language.

First language (L1): the language an infant learns from birth and typically the native language of the family.

Fluency: in the field of reading this term is used to describe the skill of reading text with accuracy, expression, and rate of speed. The National Reading Panel (2000) emphasized the important role fluency plays in reading comprehension, although not sufficient on its own for comprehension, it is a necessary component of the reading comprehension process.

Fluid build-up: an accumulation of fluid in the middle ear; can lead to infection and/or conductive hearing loss if not treated.

FM/DM (frequency modulation/ digital modulation) system: assistive listening systems that clarify and amplify the sound by wirelessly transmitting sound directly from the microphone receiver the speaker is wearing to the listener's FM/DM device. This decreases background noise, distance, and reverberation for the listener.

Formative assessment: periodic formal and informal assessment to monitor student learning and use data to guide and individualize instruction with the goal of pinpointing strengths and weaknesses to target instruction and increase academic skills (e.g., quiz, language sample, rubric).

Free and Appropriate Public Education (FAPE): a provision within the Individuals with Disabilities Education Act, FAPE ensures students with disabilities receive an education that is free (at no cost to their families), appropriate for their individual needs, and provided within the public education system.

Functional Behavior Analysis (FBA): an assessment-based system to identify the motivations, triggers, and causes behind a student's inappropriate behaviors in order to change them to more appropriate behaviors. The Individualized Education Program (IEP) team writes an FBA by conducting observations, interviews, and collecting performance data.

Gallaudet University: a federally-chartered private university established for deaf and hard of hearing students in

Washington, D.C., that utilizes a bilingual instructional and communication approach (i.e., ASL and English).

Gastric tube (G-tube): is a tube inserted through the abdomen to deliver nutrition directly to the stomach. Children who have chronic difficulty eating by mouth can receive the fluid or calories needed for growth through a G-tube.

Genetic trait: an observable phenotype within an individual, such as height or eye color, established by genotypes (part of an individual's DNA sequence) or environmental factors.

Gifted and talented (GT): demonstration of exceptional abilities, aptitudes (i.e., reasoning), or competence (i.e., performance in the top 10% of achievement) in one or more domains, such as math, language, sensorimotor skills (e.g., art); definitions vary by state in the United States; gifted and talented educational services are supported by the Every Student Succeeds Act.

Graphic organizer: a visual display that shows relationships among information, ideas, concepts, etc.

Hard of hearing: commonly refers to an individual with mild to moderate hearing levels who uses listening and spoken language, sign language, or a combination of both to communicate. Auditory access is usually acquired through use of hearing aids, a cochlear implant, FM/DM systems, soundfield systems, etc. Individuals self-define and self-label based on their lived experiences.

Hearing aid: a sound amplification device for individuals who are d/Dhh. Worn bilaterally or unilaterally, hearing aids come in a variety of styles either behind-the-ear (BTE) or in-the-ear (ITE) and can be analog or digital.

Hearing aid trial: to ensure proper fit and benefit, audiologists typically offer a free trial of hearing aids for about a month.

Hearing level/hearing loss: the decibel (i.e., intensity) level at which an individual can hear and comprehend sounds across multiple frequencies. Levels of hearing loss include mild, moderate, severe, and profound.

Hearing screening: initial hearing assessment that can be conducted with newborns (Auditory Brainstem Response [ABR]) or school-age (pure-tone audiometer) children. If the initial test is not passed, then a second follow-up screening should be conducted, and if failed, should be followed by an assessment with an audiologist.

Hertz (Hz): unit used to measure the frequency of sound; defined as one cycle of sound per second; represents the frequency of sounds across the X-axis of an audiogram.

High frequency: (1) speech sounds that fall between 2,000 and 8,000 Hertz (Hz), such as /s/, /f/, and /th/, and may be more difficult to hear than lower frequency sounds (e.g., /e/, /d/, etc.) for someone with hearing loss; (2) words seen frequently within printed text, such as the Dolch list of high frequency sight words.

Highly qualified: a designation introduced for educators by the No Child Left Behind Act (2000) that defines highly qualified teachers as those who have a bachelor's degree, state teacher certification/licensure, and evidence of knowledge in the content areas that they teach, which is decided upon at the state level.

Home language: primary language used in the home and community by a family; may differ from the primary language used at school, English.

Home signs: a non-linguistic communication/vocabulary system based on gestures used by individuals in a family to communicate with a d/Dhh or hearing person who is not proficient in a sign language.

Hypernasality: results from an increased airflow through the nose during speech. This abnormal resonance of sound indicates an abnormal coupling of the oral and nasal cavities, including impaired movement, coordination, or timing of the velopharyngeal valve, during speech. Hypernasality is associated with speech sounds that are phonated, not affecting voiceless consonants, making it most apparent on vowels.

Implicit bias: is the bias in judgment and/or behavior that results in attitudes and stereotypes toward an individual or group of people, which operate below conscious awareness. Implicit bias is in contrast to explicit bias, which reflects the attitudes or beliefs one holds at a conscious level.

Inclusive/inclusion: general and special education students learning beside each other in the most accessible environment possible with special education personnel supporting the general education teacher to meet the needs of each student's Individualized Education Program (IEP).

Individualized Education Program (IEP): mandated by the Individuals with Disabilities Improvement Act (IDEIA), this legal document is created by a multidisciplinary team (general and special education teachers, administrators, school counselors, educational assistants, school psychologists, parents, student, etc.) for students between 3 and 22 years of age who receive special education services. The document outlines a student's learning needs, placement(s), accommodations, and educational goals based on evidence-based decisions (assessment data, progress monitoring data, classwork, observations, interviews, etc.) of the team.

Individualized Education Program (IEP) team: consists of members who create the IEP and typically includes the parents, at least one of the student's general and special education teachers, a school administrator or district representative, a school psychologist, the student (at least by 14 years of age), and any other educational specialists (Occupational Therapist [OT], Speech Language Pathologist [SLP], Physical Therapist [PT], behavior specialist, etc.).

Individualized Family Service Plan (IFSP): mandated by the Individuals with Disabilities Improvement Act (IDEIA), this legal document is created by a multidisciplinary team (early interventionists, parents, Speech Language Pathologist [SLP], and other specialists) for children from birth to 3 years of age who qualify for early intervention special education services. The document outlines the amount and location of the family-centered early intervention services the child will receive.

Individuals with Disabilities Education Act (IDEA, 1990, 1997): a federal act in the United States that mandates all children with disabilities receive a free appropriate public education (FAPE) within a Least Restrictive Environment (LRE) that meets their individualized needs and provides equal accessibility to academic, social, behavioral, and post-secondary supports.

Individuals with Disabilities Education Improvement Act (IDEIA; 2004): reauthorization of the IDEA 1997.

Intellectual disability: a disability that significantly limits intellectual functioning and adaptive behaviour. An IQ score of 70 or below qualifies students to receive special education services under this disability category.

Interpreter: a certified person who translates one language into another via voice or sign language.

Intervention: an instructional strategy or combination of strategies to address a student's specific academic or behavioral needs.

In-the-ear digital hearing aid: are custom fit aids that are individually manufactured to fit the wearer's external auditory meatus (ear canal). Children are not commonly fit with ITE hearing aids as the rapid growth of the ear would result in a poor fit.

IQ: Intelligence quotient is the number used to rate a person's cognitive capabilities.

Itinerant TODHH: this teaching role includes traveling to multiple schools within the same district to provide weekly/monthly services to students who are d/Dhh. Services include co-teaching/assisting the teacher in the general education classroom in providing academic support or instruction and consulting with the general education teachers in the school to provide Individualized Education Program (IEP) services to an eligible student.

Japanese Sign Language (JSL): the official sign language of Japan and used within the Deaf community.

Joint reference: the act of two people referring to or looking at the same object/person.

Language sample analysis: an evaluation of a student's productive (expressive) language (spoken or signed) sample; many times the analysis is completed with a rubric, checklist, or formal assessment (e.g., Kendall Proficiency Levels for sign language).

Learning disability (LD): One category of disability as defined by the Individuals with Disabilities Education Improvement Act (IDEIA) characterized by a disorder in under-standing or using language, either spoken or written, or a disorder in completing math calculations.

Learning Support Specialist: an educa-tional specialist who assists teachers and service providers in the creation of an educational environment to differentiate learning to meet students' individual learning styles and needs.

Least Restrictive Environment (LRE): a provision within the Individuals with Disabilities Education Act, LRE ensures students with disabilities receive an education in an environment that is the least restrictive, which typically is defined as the maximum amount of time in a general education setting with their peers without disabilities in their local neighborhood school; however, for students who use sign language as their primary mode of communication, the LRE may be a school for the deaf that provides all instruction and communication in sign language.

Life skills curriculum: lessons that focus on acquiring functional skills that will lead to a productive adult life. Some of these skills include self-care, shopping, communication, cleanliness, meal preparation, and adaptive modifications.

Ling sounds: the Ling Six Sound Check assesses whether a child can hear the speech sounds needed to build listening and spoken language skills.

There are six sounds (*mm, oo, ah, ee, sh, s*) that should be repeated back to the examiner by the child in a quiet environment without visual cues.

Listening and spoken language (LSL): a communication approach (also referred to as oral/aural approach or auditory-verbal approach) that focuses on utilizing children's residual hearing, along with assistive listening devices, to gain audiological access to develop listening and spoken language skills.

Listening and Spoken Language Specialist (LSLS): professionals (teachers of the d/Deaf and hard of hearing, speech-language pathologists, audiologists, etc.) that have com-pleted certification training and examination and are typically desig-nated as a Certified Auditory-Verbal Therapist (LSLS Cert. AVT) or Certified Auditory-Verbal Educators (LSLS Cert. AVEd). These specialists work closely with families to provide support, assessment, and intervention to assist children in acquiring listen-ing and spoken language with a focus on listening skills.

Listening fatigue: a temporary condi-tion that can occur after prolonged listening (i.e., auditorally or visually); symptoms include tiredness, lack of attention, etc.

Listening Inventory for Education-Revised (LIFE-R): a behavioral assessment designed to verify the quality of the classroom listening environment from the standpoint of the individual student. The LIFE-R is an interactive, electronic version available to users at no cost (http://successforkidswithhearingloss.com/life-r/).

Lost to follow-up: When an infant who did not pass his/her newborn hearing screening fails to receive the next step of treatment, whether rescreening, comprehensive audiologic evaluation, or enrollment in early intervention, they are considered lost to follow-up.

Low frequency: speech sounds that fall between 250 and 1000 Hertz (Hz), such as /e/, /d/, and /m/, which may be easier to hear for someone with hearing loss than higher frequency sounds (e.g., /s/, /f/, and /th/).

MacArthur Communicative Development Inventory (CDI): a parent-report assessment instrument (i.e., checklist) that is used to document specific vocabulary and phrases that children are familiar with receptively (i.e., listening comprehension via spoken language) between 3 and 36 months of age; also can be used with children the language delays outside of this age range.

MacArthur Communicative Development Inventory for American Sign Language (ASL-CDI): a parent-report assessment instrument (i.e., checklist) that is used to document specific vocabulary and phrases that children are familiar with receptively (i.e., listening comprehension via signed language) between 3 and 36 months of age; also can be used with children the language delays outside of this age range.

Magnet program: a public school or program with specialized curricula that generally have an application process and admit students from various districts.

Mainstreamed: placement options for students with special needs that include inclusive environments in which students receive some academic periods in the general education classroom and some in a small group, resource classroom with a special education teacher.

Mandatory reporter: professionals who have frequent contact with vulnerable groups of people, such as children, and are legally required to report incidences or suspicion of abuse or neglect.

Manifestation determination: a provision within the Individuals with Individuals with Disabilities Education Improvement Act (IDEIA) that provides for an evaluation of whether or not a student's inappropriate behavior is directly related to his disability or improper implementation of his Individual Education Program (IEP); if the behavior is a direct result of the disability, then a Behavior Intervention Plan is created and implemented. If the behavior is not directly related to his disability or improper implementation of his IEP, then the student is held accountable to the school's general discipline plan, such as suspension.

Manifestation determination review: a meeting mandated by the Individuals with Disability Education Improvement Act (IDEIA) that must occur with 10 school days of the inappropriate behavior incident. The Individualized Education Program (IEP) team should provide documentation for the meeting (review of the IEP, observations reports, assessment data, incident notes, etc.).

Mapping: refers to the programming of the speech processor of a cochlear implant, in accordance to the needs of the user to maximize audibility. During the mapping process, an audiologist adjusts the amount of electrical stimulation, according to threshold (quietest) and comfort levels that each electrode delivers to the cochlea. These adjustments are based on the user's behavioral responses or on computer algorithms.

Medical home: As recommended by the American Academy of Pediatrics, a child's medical care should be delivered by a primary care physician who can manage and facilitate all aspects of care. The child's primary care physician establishes a relationship with the family to ensure care is easily accessible, family-centered, and culturally responsive. These characteristics encompass the medical home. For children who utilize hearing technology, the medical home can also refer to the audiological home, which includes the ENT/otolaryngologist, pediatric audiologists, or cochlear implant team, or related service providers. The medical home is distinguished from the educational team, though in well-coordinated service delivery, there will be overlap and collaboration among providers.

Medical model: a term used by sociologists to describe the viewpoint that deafness is an illness or disability that should be treated medically.

Mental imagery: a visual representation of things or events in someone's mind.

Mexican Sign Language (lengua de señas Mexicana; LSM): Mexico declared LSM a national language in 2005, and it is the language used by the national education system of the d/Deaf and within the Deaf community in urban regions of Mexico. A distinct grammar and discourse structure differentiates LSM from Spanish.

Microtia: a congenital (i.e., in-utero) deformity of the outer ear (pinna); the outer ear does not fully develop and is often smaller in size with a small or absent lobe.

Middle ear: the air-filled cavity of the ear from behind the eardrum, across the ossicles, the upper part of the eustation tube, and the round window of the cochlea where sound waves are amplified and sent to the inner ear.

Mild hearing loss: residual hearing thresholds between 20 and 40 decibels.

Mindfulness exercises: self-regulating practices that involve focusing on the moment and one's environment to reduce anxiety and stress.

Misarticulations: the distortion, omission, substitution, or addition of phonemes in speech. For example, one common misarticulation of a /k/ occurs when the speaker substitutes it for a /t/.

Miscue analysis: a method of reading assessment that identifies errors a student makes and strategies the student uses while reading aloud (in spoken or signed language).

Mixed hearing loss: a combination of conductive and sensorineural hearing loss and can range in severity from mild to profound. In a mixed hearing loss, damage occurs in both the outer or middle ear as well as in the inner ear or auditory nerve.

Mode of communication: the method/system/language by which a student communicates, including listening and spoken language, sign language (e.g., American Sign Language, Pidgin Sign, Signing Exact English, etc.), simultaneous spoken and signed language (i.e., Simultaneous Communication or Sim-Com), cued speech, etc.; a communicator may adjust his/her mode of communication to match specific communication partners via codeswitching.

Modeling, prompting, shaping: three methods by which an educator can assist a student in acquiring a skill or behavior; modeling refers to the educator explicitly showing the student how to do the skill or behavior; prompting refers to giving the student a cue to engage in the skill or behavior; and shaping refers to providing feedback on the student's attempt at the skill or behavior.

Moderate hearing loss: residual hearing thresholds between 55 and 70 decibels.

Moderate spastic cerebral palsy: the most common type of cerebral palsy in which individuals experience spastic, stiff, involuntary movement of the muscles.

Modification: a change in the content a student is taught or expected to learn; frequently found within a student's Individual Education Program (IEP).

Multidisciplinary team: a group of service providers from different disciplines whose experience, qualifications, and skills can contribute to improving outcomes through collaborative practice.

Mutual gaze: sharing eye contact with another person, a form of interpersonal communication.

National Technical Institute for the Deaf (NTID): a technological college for students who are deaf or hard of hearing, housed within the Rochester Institute of Technology (RIT), which offers multiple instructional approaches to maximize communication access.

Near-sightedness: also called myopia, this refractive error of the eye causes individuals to have difficulty seeing objects far away.

Neonatal Intensive Care Unit (NICU): an intensive care unit in a hospital that specializes in treating premature and ill infants.

Occupational Therapist (OT): a specialist trained in techniques that increase access and comfort in the educational environment so students with special needs can meet their Individualized

Education Program (IEP) goals and objectives. This may include accommodations and modifications for fine or gross motor skills, self-care, and assistance with social interaction.

Ophthalmologist: a doctor that specializes in the diagnosis and treatment of conditions of the eye.

OPTIONSchools: an international, non-profit organization that seeks to advance listening and spoken language education through the provision of information and support to program and school leaders. Member schools and programs seek to increase their effectiveness, efficiency, and ability to teach children to listen and talk. The coalition of schools advance listening and spoken language education by: promoting educational options, measuring outcomes, establishing and sharing best practices, and raising awareness through advocacy.

Orientation and Mobility Specialist (O&M): a certified educational professional with specialized training in instructing students with visual impairments to safely travel in their school and community environments.

Orofacial anomalies: structural or functional disorders of oral cavity or face. These often stem from genetic or congenital defects. Cleft lip and or cleft palates are common types of orofacial anomalies, which often arise from genetic or congenital defects.

Ossification of the cochlea: bone formation inside the cochlea.

Otitis media with effusion: A mucoid secretion accumulates in the middle ear and stops the ossicles from vibrating freely, therefore reducing hearing levels. Otitis media is typically referred to as an ear infection, but this type occurs slightly before or after an infection (one day to many weeks) and prolongs the amount of fluid in the ear and time of reduced hearing levels. If left untreated, it can result in a conductive hearing loss.

Otoacoustic emissions (OAE): a low-level sound evoked with an auditory stimulus to determine the function of the cochlea and outer hair cells to identify hearing levels and etiology of hearing issues.

Otolaryngologist: see *Ear Nose and Throat physician.*

Ototoxic medicine: medications that are known to cause hearing loss, tinnitus, or disequilibrium by damaging the cochlea or vestibular systems. Examples of ototoxic medications include certain *aminoglycoside* antibiotics (often the ones ending in "micin") and cancer chemotherapy drugs (e.g., cisplatin, carboplatin). The use of these ototoxic medications can result in sensorineural hearing loss, dizziness or vertigo, or both.

Pair and share: An instructional strategy in which the class is divided into multiple pairs of two students, who discuss a given topic then redeliver what they discussed to the whole group.

Paraprofessionals: see *Educational assistant.*

Parent advocate: a volunteer who understands students with disabilities and the Individual Education Program (IEP) process. The advocate typically has experience with various cases involving children and adolescents with special needs and can help parents during the IEP meeting to advocate for what they feel is the most appropriate Free and Appropriate Public Education (FAPE) in the Least Restrictive Environment (LRE).

Parent liaison: school professionals who work to establish communication with parents by helping them obtain information and support to ensure their child's academic and social success. *Parent* liaisons may facilitate parenting classes, connect parents with community resources, and support teachers in establishing effective collaboration with parents.

Part B program of the Individuals with Disabilities Education Improvement Act (IDEIA): includes the school age programs for children with disabilities 3–21 years of age and mandates the development of an Individualized Education Program (IEP).

Part C program of the Individuals with Disabilities Education Improvement Act (IDEIA): includes the early intervention program for children with disabilities birth to 2 years of age and mandates the development of an Individualized Family Service Plan (IFSP).

Partial insertion: this refers to partial insertion of the electrode array of a cochlear implant, often due to ossification of the cochlea, therefore affecting the number of channels and depth of insertion.

Peabody Picture Vocabulary Test, Fourth Edition: a receptive test of English vocabulary; the examiner states a vocabulary word and the examinee points to one of four pictures that matches the meaning of that word. This standardized assessment provides scores that estimate the verbal ability and scholastic aptitude of students in age equivalency.

Pediatric AzBio Sentence Lists: an assessment of 450 sentences recorded from a female speaker to evaluate the speech perception abilities of listeners.

Phonemes: the smallest units of a language (i.e., sounds in spoken language and parameters such as handshape, movement, and location in signed language) that are combined into words to make meaning.

Phonetic level inventories: the inventory and structure of the phonemes and combinations of phonemes within a spoken language. These inventories can be used to assess the segmental and nonsegmental aspects of speech at phonetic levels.

Phonological awareness: the ability to manipulate the sounds within words, including segmentation of words into syllables; identification of initial, medial, and final sounds; and elision (i.e., removing a sound and identifying the word that remains).

Physical Therapist (PT): a specialist trained to rehabilitate any physical limitations to increase functional mobility and increase accessibility in the educational environment so that students with special needs can meet their Individualized Education Program (IEP) goals and objectives.

Picture Exchange Communication System (PECS): an augmentative/ alternative communication program that involves six phases using positive reinforcement to encourage individuals to exchange/indicate pictures to make requests, conveys ideas, and communicate words and sentences with people in their environment.

Placement and Readiness Checklists (PARC) General Education Inclusion Readiness Checklist: a series of checklists that Individualized Education Program (IEP) teams can use to make decisions regarding placement for students who are d/Dhh.

Positive behavioral and intervention supports (PBIS): proactive school-wide approach to provide behavior supports for students through prevention rather than punishment. This interactive approach uses outcomes, data, practices, and systems as key elements in a collaborative network to acquire positive academic behaviors.

Post-activation habilitation services: those auditory habilitation services provided after an individual receives a cochlear implant.

Post-lingual deafness: hearing loss or deafness that occurs after acquisition of spoken language, usually after the age of three years; less common than prelingual deafness

Preferential seating: the student's seat in a room is placed in the optimal position to maximize benefit of his/her auditory or visual access; not always in the front row of a room.

Prelingual deafness: hearing loss or deafness that is present at birth or that occurs before the acquisition of spoken language, usually before the age of 3 years.

Preschool Language Scale (PLS-5): a developmental language assessment intended for children from birth through 7 years of age that assesses attention, interaction, school readiness, theory of mind, emergent literacy skills, and language tasks.

Pre-teaching vocabulary: the process of selecting words within instructional materials that are unknown to students (as determined by a pretest) and teaching them in advance of their appearance within instruction so that students are familiar with their meanings when they see them in connected text.

Profound hearing loss: residual hearing thresholds between 90 and 120 decibels.

Psychosocial criteria: a part of the cochlear implant candidacy evaluation involves psychosocial evaluation. For children, this process includes formal and informal assessment of developmental milestones, including the child's capacity to learn. Additionally, the team evaluates parent stressors and family support as part of the psycho-social criteria. A social worker can work with the family to navigate the services needed to maximize their child's outcomes. Family expectations are also discussed because gaining an understanding of the family's resources and challenges is essential.

Pull-out service delivery: the pull-out model involves removing a child from of his/her classroom setting for the provision of specialized instruction. The pull-out services could involve either one-on-one or small group service delivery.

Pure tone audiometry (PTA): is the primary test used to identify hearing thresholds as the basis for diagnosis and treatment. Through PTA, audiologists can determine the degree, type, and configuration of an individual's hearing loss.

Push-in service delivery: the push-in model involves providing specialized services within the child's mainstream or classroom environment. Push-in services, rather than pull-out, may result in more time for students to spend time with friends, fewer disruptions to class routines, and increased communication among specific team members.

Receptive language: language (English, ASL, or other) that is understood by an individual when expressed either through-the-air (voice or sign) or written.

Referred for follow-up: children who do not pass hearing screenings, either in infancy or childhood, are referred for follow-up with a trained audiologist.

Reinforcement audiometry: see *Visual reinforcement audiometry.*

Remediation: in the remediation approach, a therapist will work with a child one-on-one, in a small group, or within a classroom to help the student overcome difficulties involved with a specific disorder. In contrast, in early intervention and developmental synchronous models, practitioners aim to provide services and supports that will prevent delays and deficits from occurring.

Residual hearing: any functioning hearing for one who is d/Deaf or hard of hearing; that hearing is frequently amplified to maximize the individual's access to sound.

Resource: a small group classroom setting separate from the general education classroom where a special education teacher provides direct instruction that is specialized to meet the individual need of each student based on his or her Individualized Education Program (IEP) goals and objectives.

Response to Intervention (RTI): a multi-tiered approach that aims for early identification and support for students with special needs in the general education classroom by providing a universal screening through research-based teaching methods with progress monitoring (tier 1), small group targeted interventions (tier 2), and intensive interventions and comprehensive evaluation for eligibility for special education services (tier 3).

Response to Intervention (RTI) team: a team that typically consists of a school administrator (e.g., principal), RTI coordinator, general education teacher, special education teacher, literacy or reading specialist, school psychologist, speech-language pathologist (SLP), and possibly individual parents.

Retell: the process of telling a story that has been accessed via spoken or signed language or read by an individual student as a measure of story comprehension.

Reverse slope sensorineural hearing loss: a hearing loss in which the individual has limited access to low frequency sounds, such as the vowels of English, and has near-typical hearing access to the high frequency sounds of English, such as /s/, /f/, and /th/. This is the opposite of most people with sensorineural hearing levels, who tend to have access to low frequency sounds but not high frequency sounds.

Role shift: the process of identifying different speakers within a narrative by shifting the head and shoulders to indicate a change in character and attributing subsequent utterances to that character.

Routines Based Interview: a method of gathering data and assessment information to inform interventions.

The semi-structured interviews focus on developing a list of functional outcomes, assessing how the family functions within their daily routines, and empowering a positive relationship with the family.

Scaffold(ing): the process of developmentally sequencing lessons to build upon each other, thus providing background information for new knowledge gained and reducing the cognitive load of tasks.

School for the deaf: a private or public institution that educates students who are d/Deaf or hard of hearing, usually through sign language, including hearing and Deaf teachers and staff who are proficient in sign language. A day program buses students to a central school location, and a residential program has dormitories where students live during the school week and/or year. Classes are small groups and can be modified to meet the needs of diverse learners.

School psychologist: a certified professional who supports and works with educators to apply educational, developmental, clinical, and community psychology, along with applied behavior analysis (ABA) techniques, to evaluate and make recommendations that increase academic, social, and emotional outcomes for all students.

Second language (L2): the second language an individual learns is not their native language but is the language of a community in which they live or work. May be acquired synchronously or asynchronously with a first language (L1).

Section 504 of the Rehabilitation Act of 1973: the first U.S. federal civil rights law to offer protection to people with disabilities within agencies that receive federal funding.

Section 504 plan: a plan of the accommodations, modifications, and other services that will support a student with a disability; students who are d/Dhh typically qualify for a 504 Plan instead of an Individualized Education Program (IEP) if their hearing levels do not interfere with their academic achievement but they require accommodations to maintain their assistive listening equipment and/or an interpreter.

Self-advocacy: the set of skills that allow an individual to make his/her own decisions, obtain information to understand things that are of interest, identify those individuals who will provide support, be aware of personal rights and responsibilities, and solve general problems. The self advocacy skills of children who are d/Deaf or hard of hearing are a primary factor in determining success or failure across educational, community, social, and work settings.

Self-contained: see *Small group.*

Sensorineural hearing loss: the most common type of hearing loss, which is caused by damage to the cochlea or nerve pathways to the brain.

Severe hearing loss: residual hearing thresholds between 70 and 90 decibels.

Shared Reading Project: this project was developed by the Laurent Clerc National Deaf Education Center to support families when reading to their d/Dhh child using ASL. Strategies to enhance engagement and comprehension are guided by the 15 principles for reading to Deaf children based on Deaf adult reading techniques.

Sight words: most frequently used and repeated words in English print, with 50% of all texts made up of the same 100 high-frequency function words, including determiners (e.g., a, the, that), conjunctions (e.g., and, but), prepositions (e.g., of, to, in), pronouns (e.g., I, you), and auxiliary verbs (e.g., is, are).

Signal-to-noise ratio: the relationship between the signal (sound) and undesired sound (noise). The louder the signal the better it will be understood if there is background noise, by reducing background noise and increasing signal strength.

Signed English: a sign system, as opposed to a language, that combines English signs and syntax, rather than ASL syntax, to convey thoughts and ideas through-the-air. ASL vocabulary is used in English word order and function words (i.e., the, am, to) and word endings (-ed, -ing, -s) are often omitted.

Signed Spanish: a sign system, similar to Signed English, that uses Mexican Sign Language (lengua de señas Mexicana; LSM) vocabulary in Spanish word order.

Sign language: a visual system of communication that includes hand, body, head, shoulder, and facial movements to convey meaning. In the United States there is one natural sign language, ASL, and two sign systems, Signed English and Signing Exact English (SEE), which attempt to visually represent English structures.

Sign-supported speech: the combined use of spoken language and signed language, with an emphasis on the spoken mode over the signed mode.

Simultaneous cochlear implants: occur when both of a recipient's bilateral cochlear implants are placed during a single surgical procedure. This is in contrast to sequential bilateral cochlear implantation in which a recipient's implants are placed during two different surgical procedures, with a varying duration of time between each surgery.

Size-and-shape-specifiers (SASSes): a category of ASL handshapes that show the visual characteristics of figures and objects.

Small group: a setting separate from the general education classroom where a special education teacher provides direct instruction that is specialized to meet each student with special needs' Individualized Education Program (IEP) goals and objectives. Also referred to as self-contained.

Social identity: a person's concept of who they are based on their memberships within groups.

Softband bone-conduction: a bone-conduction hearing aid attached to a softband is used for infants and toddlers with conductive hearing loss. The soft band is an adjustable elastic band worn around the head so young children can wear their bone conduction devices before their skull growth and development is appropriate for a surgical abutment.

Soundfield systems: a speaker system that can be used in any school setting to increase the even distribution of speech sounds throughout the room so that all learners can hear the person using the microphone. Shown to increase attention for both d/Dhh and hearing students.

Speech articulation: see *Articulation.*

Speech banana/string bean: when indicated on an audiogram, identifies the common placement of specific phonemes according to frequency and intensity. For example, by looking at the speech banana one can see that the phoneme /d/ has energy at around 350 Hz and /f/ has energy at around 4000 Hz. When a child's aided thresholds are drawn onto the speech banana, one could identify which phonemes would be accessible to the listener and which would be missed.

Speech Discrimination (SD): the percentage of spoken words that one correctly identifies after listening to a series of words.

Speech Language Pathologist (SLP): professionals with clinical training in assessment and interventions to increase communication, speech, and language.

Speech perception: the process by which the sounds of language are heard, interpreted, and understood. The purpose of speech perception testing is to assess the child's ability to both perceive and discriminate speech information. There are several clinical uses of speech perception testing. First, a child's speech perception performance can help determine whether or not the child is benefiting from hearing devices. Additionally, speech perception measures allow a comparison of the differences between sensory devices and track performance over time. Finally, speech perception data in combination with speech and language outcomes allow practitioners to plan and monitor habilitation.

Speechreading: the visual clues of a speaker's lips, mouth, facial movements, gestures, body language, and posture, which supplement the listener's understanding. When visual clues are used along with residual hearing, a listener can make use of the speaker's verbal communication, intonation, and context to infer meaning and enhance comprehension.

Speech Reception Threshold (SRT): the intensity in decibels at which a person can understand 50% of speech sounds demonstrated by repeating words to the examiner; can also be used to crosscheck the validity of pure tone thresholds during an audiological assessment.

Standard deviation: represents the amount of variation from the mean/average; calculated by taking the square root of the variance (average squared differences of the mean); one standard deviation above and below the mean is considered low-average and high-average, respectively.

Standard score: calculated by subtracting the mean from a raw score and dividing by the standard deviation, this score allows educators to compare scores across assessments, even though they have varying raw scores. Also called z-score.

Study skills: typically a time set aside in which a teacher assists students with their various assignments from other classes.

Summative assessment: an assessment to evaluate a learner against a benchmark or the performance of other learners after they have acquired a specific set of information (e.g., teacher-made unit test, performance task, standardized assessment, etc.).

Teacher of the d/Deaf and hard of hearing (TODHH): a professional with specialized training in the psychosocial and academic development of children and students who are d/Dhh, who is qualified to conduct assessments and develop interventions to increase behavior, language and communication, and literacy skills. TODHH also may have specialized training in sign language, listening and spoken language, or a combination of both.

Teacher of students with Visual Impairments (TSVI): a professional with specialized training in the psychosocial and academic development of children and students who have visual impairments and who is qualified to conduct assessments and develop interventions to increase behavior, language, communication, and literacy skills. A TSVI also may have specialized training in braille and/or orientation and mobility.

Tele-practice: using telecommunications (videoconferencing tools) to deliver speech language pathologist (SLP), early intervention, or audiological consultation through synchronous or asynchronous services.

Through-the-air: a general term in the field of deaf education that includes communication via both spoken and signed languages, as both are transmitted to the receiver through the air via the hands and/or the mouth.

Torrance Tests of Creative Thinking: an assessment used within gifted identification in which students draw and title pictures or write about uses for objects.

Touch and feel books: a specific type of interactive book developed for toddler to preschool age that allows children to experience embedded textures.

Transition meeting: a transition meeting is required under the Individuals with Disabilities Education Improvement Act (IDEIA) for students who are receiving special education services when they transition from early intervention to preschool, preschool to kindergarten, and middle school to high school. Students typically participate in their transition meeting when they are 14 years of age, or earlier if deemed appropriate, to provide input on their transition from high school to post-secondary experiences.

Transition plan: the section of the Individualized Education Program (IEP) that provides a template for identifying, planning, and conducting activities that will assist a student with special needs to transition after leaving school. Long-range academic and career outcomes, an action plan, and expertise from agency professionals (e.g., vocational rehabilitation) are included in an Individualized Transition Plan (ITP).

Treacher Collins syndrome: a rare inherited condition in which the facial bones and tissues are underdeveloped, resulting in a smaller jaw and chin, presence of defects in the ear bones that result in hearing loss in about half of affected individuals, and in some cases, cleft palate and eye abnormalities that may affect vision.

Turn-taking: a conversational organizer that is used in discourse when people communicate one at a time by constructing contributions to the conversation, responding to other comments within the conversation, and transitioning to a new speaker. All these practices are accomplished with linguistic and non-linguistic cues and may need to be rehearsed and practiced with students who are d/Dhh who may not be aware of these cues.

Unaided and aided audiometric thresholds: Tests of hearing sensitivity can provide unaided and aided audiometric thresholds. An unaided audiometric threshold refers to softest sound audible to an individual at least 50% of the time. The aided threshold represents the softest sound audible to an individual using personal hearing device(s) at least 50% of the time. See also *Pure tone audiometry.*

Unilateral hearing loss/level: hearing loss in one ear.

Universal Design for Learning (UDL): a framework for designing school buildings, infrastructure, curriculum, personnel, and classroom environments to provide accessibility to the most diverse possible range of learners in a flexible, instructional environment. The core concept is to plan for all learners from the beginning so that materials/experiences do not have to be modified to meet learners' needs.

Universal Newborn Hearing Screening (UNHS): a systematic effort to reduce the age of identification of hearing loss by health organizations by identifying newborns with hearing loss through audiological assessment at birth; includes follow-up procedures for families with children who are identified as having hearing loss and are coordinated with early intervention agencies.

Uptake/language uptake: the active recognition, interaction, and response to communicative interactions

Usher syndrome: a syndrome that affects both hearing and vision losses, including mild to profound and/or progressive hearing loss, and retinitis pigmentosa, which causes night blindness, loss of peripheral vision, and progressive impairment; there are three types (Type 1, 2, and 3).

Visual Communication and Sign Language Checklist: a standardized checklist to document a child's sign language development from birth to age 5 years.

Visually impaired/vision loss: a reduction in vision, or condition of low vision that cannot be fully corrected with glasses, contact lenses, medicine, or surgery and can range from mild to severe.

Visual reinforcement audiometry (VRA): an assessment of hearing level thresholds in infants and toddlers ages 6 months to 3 years of age. Audiologists train examinees to look at lighted toys or videos on either side of them when they hear sounds through the earphones or soundfield speakers in a sound booth.

Visual schedules: those pictures, graphics, words, and visual aids that tell students what activities occur and in what sequence. Visual schedules can be general or specific, based on the needs of the learner. For example, visual schedules can outline the events of the month, week, or day. A common example includes a calendar or planner.

Vocational rehabilitation (VR): federally funded in the United States and administered by each state, these services provide supports, typically post-secondary or in the transition planning process, to individuals with disabilities to assist them in gaining employment. They can provide coordinating services to school personnel, work with the school team to develop a transition plan, assist parents in understanding the vocational rehabilitation process, and work with community members to ensure meaningful employment opportunities for their clients.

Voluntary mediation: the initial step of due process established by the Individuals with Disabilities Education Improvement Act (IDEIA), which encourages parties involved in an IEP-related complaint to voluntarily attempt to resolve the issue through a mediator instead of proceeding to the more costly and time-consuming court system.

Wechsler Intelligence Scale for Children (WISC-IV): an intelligence test for children 6–16 years of age that is individually administered and which generates a Full Scale IQ (IQ score).

Wide-band hearing aids: The wider the frequency response range of the hearing aid, the less gain will be required, thus wider bandwidth aids can provide improved speech intelligibility in quiet and in noise. The audiologist is able to make a wide range of sounds audible in an automatic way by using compression circuitry with no volume control.

References

American Speech-Language-Hearing Association. (2017). *Technical report cochlear implants: Working group on cochlear implants*. Retrieved from http://www.asha.org/policy/TR2004-00041/#sec1.5

Anderson, D., & Reilly, J. (2002). The MacArthur Communicative Development Inventory: Normative data for American Sign Language. *Journal of Deaf Studies and Deaf Education, 7*(2), 83–106.

Ayantoye, C. A., & Luckner, J. L. (2016). Successful students who are deaf or hard of hearing and culturally and/or linguistically diverse in inclusive settings. *American Annals of the Deaf, 160*(5), 453–466.

Borders, C. M., Bock, S. J., & Szymanski, C. (2015). Teacher ratings of evidence-based practices from the field of autism. *Journal of Deaf Studies and Deaf Education, 20*(1), 91–100.

Borders, C. M., Meinzen-Derr, J., Wiley, S., Bauer, A., & Embury, D. C. (2015). Students who are deaf with additional disabilities: Does educational label impact language services? *Deafness & Education International, 17*(4), 204–218. doi:10.1179/1557069X15Y.0000000006

Brown, A. S. (2005). The art and science of home visits. *ASHA Leader, 15*, 6–7.

Bruce, S. M., & Borders, C. (2015). Communication and language in learners who are deaf and hard of hearing with disabilities: Theories, research, and practice. *American Annals of the Deaf, 160*(4), 368–384. doi:10.1353/aad.2015.0035

Cannon, J. E., & Hubley, A. (2014). Content validation of the Comprehension of Written Grammar assessment for Deaf and hard of hearing students. *Journal of Psychoeducational Assessment, 32*(8), 768–774.

Cannon, J. E., & Luckner, J. (2016). Increasing cultural and linguistic diversity in Deaf education teacher preparation programs. *American Annals of the Deaf, 161*(1), 89–103.

CHARGE Syndrome Foundation. (2017). *Overview: CHARGE Syndrome Foundation*. Retrieved from https://www.chargesyndrome.org/

Collier, V. P. (1987/1988). *The effect of age on acquisition of a second language for school*. Retrieved from http://www.thomasandcollier.com/assets/1988_effect-of-age-on_acquisition-of_l2-for-school_collier-02aage.pdf

Cummins, J. (1979). Linguistic interdependence and the educational development of bilingual children. *Review of Educational Research, 49*(2), 222–251.

Cummins, J. (2000). *Language, power, and pedagogy: Bilingual children in the crossfire.* Clevedon, England: Multilingual Matters.

Davidson, K., Lillo-Martin, D., & Chen Pichler, D. (2013). Spoken English language development amongst native signing children with cochlear implants. *Journal of Deaf Studies and Deaf Education, 13,* 238–250. doi: 10.1093/deafed/ent045

Dunn, L. M., & Dunn, L. M. (2007). *Peabody Picture Vocabulary Test-4rd Ed. (PPVT-4).* San Antonio, TX: Pearson.

Dunn, L. M., Padilla, E. R., Lugo, D. E., & Dunn, L. M. (1986). *TVIP: Test de Vocabulario en Imágenes Peabody: Adaptaciòn Hispanoamericana* [Peabody Picture Vocabulary Test: Hispanic-American adaptation]. San Antonio, TX: Pearson.

Easterbrooks, S. R. (2010). *Comprehension of Written Grammar (CWG).* Unpublished assessment, Department of Educational Psychology and Special Education, Georgia State University, Atlanta, Georgia.

Easterbrooks, S. R., & Baker, S. (2002). *Language learning in children who are deaf and hard of hearing: Multiple pathways.* Boston, MA: Allyn & Bacon.

Enns, C. J., Zimmer, K., Boudreault, P., Rabu, S., & Broszeit, C. (2013). *American Sign Language: Receptive Skills Test.* Winnipeg, MB: Northern Signs Research, Inc.

Faurot, K., Dellinger, D., Eatough, A., & Parkhurst, S. (1999). *The identity of Mexican Sign Language as a language.* Retrieved from http://www.sil.org/system/files/reapdata/48/36/65/48366558185615738050142493565122778251/G009i_Identity_MFS.pdf

Fenson, L., Marchman, V. A., Thal, D. J., Dale, P. S., Reznick, J. S., & Bates, E. (2007). *MacArthur Bates Communicative Development Inventory.* Baltimore, MD: Brookes Publishing Company.

Gallaudet Research Institute. (2013). Regional and national summary report of data from the 2011–2012 Annual Survey of Deaf and Hard of Hearing Children and Youth. Washington, DC: GRI, Gallaudet University.

Gerth, M., & Huliska-Beith, L. (2006). *Ten little ladybugs.* Franklin, TN: Dalmatian Publishing Group.

Grosjean, F. (2008). *Studying bilinguals.* New York, NY: Oxford University Press.

Guardino, C., & Cannon, J. (2016). Deafness and diversity: Reflections and directions. *American Annals of the Deaf, 161*(1), 104–112.

Hands & Voices. (2012). *Downloadable documents.* (2012). Retrieved from http://www.handsandvoices.org/resources/docs.htm

Hands & Voices. (2014). *Transition to preschool.* Retrieved from http://www.handsandvoices.org/articles/early_intervention/V8-4_transition.htm

Howell, J. J., & Luckner, J. L. (2003). Helping one deaf student develop content literacy skills: An action research report. *Communication Disorders Quarterly, 25*(1), 23–27.

Individuals with Disabilities Education Improvement Act of 2004, 20 U. S. C. 33 § 1400 et seq. (2004). Reauthorization of the Individuals with Disabilities Education Act of 1990.

Jackson, R. L. W., Ammerman, S. B., & Trautwein, B. A. (2015). Deafness and diversity: Early intervention. *American Annals of the Deaf, 160*(4), 356–367.

Johns, J. (2017). *Basic Reading Inventory: Kindergarten through grade 12 and early literacy assessments* (12th ed.). New York, NY: Kendall Hunt.

Johnson, C. D. (2011). *PARC: Placement and Readiness Checklists for students who are deaf and hard of hearing.* Retrieved from http://www.handsandvoices.org/pdf/ PARC_2011_ReadinessChecklists.pdf

Joint Committee on Infant Hearing. (2007). Year 2007 Position Statement: Principles and guidelines for early hearing detection and intervention programs. *Pediatrics, 120*(4), 898–921.

Luckner, J., & Pierce, C. (2013). Response to intervention and students who are deaf and hard of hearing. *Deafness and Education International, 15*(4), 222–240.

McIntosh, K., MacKay, L. D., Andreou, T., Brown, J. A., Mathews, S., Gietz, C., & Bennett, J. L. (2011). Response to intervention in Canada: Definitions, the evidence base, and future directions. *Canadian Journal of School Psychology, 26*(1), 18–43. doi: 10.1177/0829573511400857

McWilliam, R. A., Casey, A. M., & Sims, J. (2009). The routines-based interview: A method for gathering information and assessing needs. *Infants & Young Children, 22*(3), 224–233.

Mitchiner, J., Nussbaum, D. B., & Scott, S. (2012, June). *The implications of bimodal bilingual approaches for children with cochlear implants* (Research Brief No. 6). Washington, DC: Visual Language and Visual Learning Science of Learning Center.

Muse, C., Harrison, J., Yoshinaga-Itano, C., Grimes, A., Brookhouser, P. E., Epstein, S., et al. (2013). Supplement to the JCIH 2007 Position Statement: Principles and guidelines for early intervention after confirmation that a child is deaf or hard of hearing. *Pediatrics, 131*(4), e1324–e1349.

Musselman, C., & Akamatsu, C. T. (1999). Interpersonal communication skills of deaf adolescents and their relationship to communication history. *Journal of Deaf Studies and Deaf Education, 4*(4), 305–320.

National Center for Children in Poverty. (2016). *United States: Demographics of low-income children.* Retrieved from http://www.nccp.org/profiles/US_profile_6.html

National Center for Children in Poverty. (2017). *United States: Measuring poverty.* Retrieved from http://www.nccp.org/topics/measuringpoverty.html

Office of the Assistant Secretary for Planning and Evaluation, U.S. Department of Human Services. (2017, January 31). *U.S. federal poverty guidelines used to determine financial eligibility for certain federal programs* (2017 HHS Poverty Guidelines). Retrieved from: https://aspe.hhs.gov/poverty-guidelines

Ohmori, S., Sugaya, A., Toida, N., Suzuki, E., Izutsu, M., Tsutsui, T., et al. (2015). Does the introduction of newborn hearing screening improve vocabulary development in hearing-impaired children? A population-based study in Japan. *International Journal of Pediatric Otorhinolaryngology, 79*(2), 196–201.

Ouellette, T., & Costello, C. (n.d.). *Without borders: Using tele-therapy to expand access. St. Joseph Institute for the Deaf.* Retrieved from http://infanthearing.org/meeting/ ehdi2010/ehdi_2010_presentations/Using%20Teletherapy%20to%20 Expand%20Access.pdf

Padden, C., & Ramsey, C. (1998). Reading ability in signing deaf children. *Topics in Language Disorders, 18*(4), 30–46.

Petitto, L. A., Berens, M. S., Kovelman, I., Dubins, M. H., Jasińska, K., & Shalinksy, M. (2012). The "Perceptual Wedge Hypothesis" as the basis for bilingual babies' phonetic processing advantage: New insights from fNIRS brain imaging. *Brain and Language, 121*(2), 142–155. doi: 10.1016/j.bandl.2011.05.003

Petitto, L. A., Katerelos, M., Levy, B., Gauna, K., Tétrault, K., & Ferraro, V. (2001). Bilingual signed and spoken language acquisition from birth: Implications for mechanisms underlying early bilingual language acquisition. *Journal of Child Language, 28*(2), 453–496.

Pizzo, L. (2016). d/Deaf and hard of hearing multilingual learners: The development of communication and language. *American Annals of the Deaf, 161*(1), 17–32.

Rose, D. H., & Gravel, J. W. (2010). Universal design for learning. In P. Peterson, E. Baker & B. McGraw (Eds.), *International encyclopedia of education* (pp. 119–124). Oxford, England: Elsevier.

Sandy, K. B. (2016). Early intervention: A multicultural perspective on d/Deaf and hard of hearing multilingual learners. *American Annals of the Deaf, 161*(1), 33.

Schick, B., Williams, K., & Kupermintz, H. (2006). Look who's being left behind: Educational interpreters and access to education for deaf and hard-of-hearing students. *Journal of Deaf Studies and Deaf Education, 11*(1), 3–20.

Schleper, D. (1995). Reading to deaf children: Learning from Deaf adults. *Perspectives in Education and Deafness, 13*(4), 4–8.

Semel, E. M., Wiig, E. H., & Secord, W. (2004). *CELF 4: Clinical Evaluation of Language Fundamentals-4 screening test.* San Antonio, TX: Pearson.

Shippen, M. E., Simpson, R. G., & Crites, S. A. (2003). A practical guide to functional behavioral assessment. *Teaching Exceptional Children, 35*(5), 36–44.

Signing Time Store. (2017). *Two little hands store.* Retrieved from http://store .signingtime.com/

Simms, L., Baker, S., & Clark, M. D. (2013). *Visual Communication and Sign Language Checklist.* Washington, DC: Gallaudet University. Retrieved from http://vl2 .gallaudet.edu/resources/vcsl/

Soukup, M., & Feinstein, S. (2007). Identification, assessment, and intervention strategies for deaf and hard of hearing students with learning disabilities. *American Annals of the Deaf, 152*(1), 56–62.

Spahr, A. J., Dorman, M. F., Litvak, L. M., Cook, S. J., Loiselle, L .M., Dejong, M. D., et al. (2014). Development and validation of the pediatric AzBio sentence lists. *Ear & Hearing, 35*(4), 418–422.

Stredler-Brown, A., Moeller, M. P., Gallegos, R., Corwin, J., & Pittman, P. (2004). *The art and science of home visits* (DVD). Boys Town, NE: Boys Town Press.

Swanwick, R., & Watson, L. (2007). Parents sharing books with young deaf children in spoken English and in BSL: The common and diverse features of different language settings. *Journal of Deaf Studies and Deaf Education, 12*(3), 385–405. doi:10.1093/deafed/enm004

The Center for Speech and Hearing. (n.d.). *Teletherapy.* Retrieved from http://centerhearingandspeech.org/teletherapy/

Torrance, E. P. (1972). Predictive validity of the Torrance Tests of Creative Thinking. *The Journal of Creative Behavior, 6,* 236–262. doi: 10.1002/j.2162-6057.1972.tb00936.x

U.S. Department of Education, Office of Special Education and Rehabilitative Services, Office of Special Education Programs. (2015). *37th Annual Report to Congress on the implementation of the Individuals with Disabilities Education Act, 2015,* Washington, DC. Retrieved from http://www2.ed.gov/about/reports/annual/osep/2015/parts-b-c/37th-arc-for-idea.pdf

Wagner, R. K., Torgeson, J. K., Rashotte, C. A., & Pearson, A. N. (2013). *CTOPP-2: Comprehensive Test of Phonological Processing.* Austin, TX: Pro-Ed.

Wechsler, D., Kaplan, E., Fein, D., Kramer, J., Morris, R., Delis, D., & Maelender, A. (2003). *Wechsler intelligence scale for children: Fourth edition (WISC-IV)* [Assessment instrument]. San Antonio, TX: Pearson.

Wolbers, K. (2008). Using balanced and interactive writing instruction to improve the higher order and lower order writing skills of deaf students. *Journal of Deaf Studies and Deaf Education, 13*(2), 258–277.

Zimmerman, I. L., Steiner, V. G., & Pond, R. E. (2011). *Preschool Language Scales (PLS-5)* (5th ed.). London, England: Pearson Education.

Index

Figures and tables are indicated by "f" and" "t" following the page numbers.